The Teacher's Guide to
MEDIA LITERACY

The Teacher's Guide to
MEDIA LITERACY

Critical Thinking in a Multimedia World

CYNDY SCHEIBE
FAITH ROGOW

CORWIN
A SAGE Company

KH

CORWIN
A SAGE Company

FOR INFORMATION:

Corwin

A SAGE Company

2455 Teller Road

Thousand Oaks, California 91320

(800) 233-9936

Fax: (800) 417-2466

www.corwin.com

SAGE Ltd.

1 Oliver's Yard

55 City Road

London EC1Y 1SP

United Kingdom

SAGE India Pvt. Ltd.

B 1/I 1 Mohan Cooperative Industrial Area

Mathura Road, New Delhi 110 044

India

SAGE Asia-Pacific Pte. Ltd.

33 Pekin Street #02-01

Far East Square

Singapore 048763

Acquisitions Editor: Carol Chambers Collins
Associate Editor: Megan Bedell
Editorial Assistant: Sarah Bartlett
Production Editor: Amy Schroller
Copy Editor: Paula L. Fleming
Typesetter: C&M Digitals (P) Ltd.
Proofreader: Dennis W. Webb
Indexer: Faith Rogow
Cover Designer: Michael Dubowe
Permissions Editor: Adele Hutchinson

Copyright © 2012 by Corwin

Printed in the United States of America

Library of Congress Cataloging-in-Publication Data

Scheibe, Cyndy.

The teacher's guide to media literacy : critical thinking in a multimedia world/Cyndy Scheibe, Faith Rogow.

p. cm.

Includes bibliographical references and index.

ISBN 978-1-4129-9758-4 (pbk.)

1. Media literacy—Study and teaching (Elementary)
2. Critical thinking—Study and teaching (Elementary)
I. Rogow, Faith, 1958- II. Title.

P96.M4S34 2012
371.33—dc23   2011039021

This book is printed on acid-free paper.

11 12 13 14 15 10 9 8 7 6 5 4 3 2 1

8/23/12

Contents

Partial List of Materials Available on the Companion Website
(www.TGML.info)
Color PowerPoint slides of all images in the book (in single file)
General Support Materials
    Glossary of Terms and Concepts
    The Fabric of Media Literacy: The Threads
    Key Questions to Ask When Producing Media Messages
    Media Literacy Organizations and Resources
    Links Between Media Literacy and Education Standards
    Stories of Student Engagement
Suggested Lessons and Activities
    Lesson Idea Grid
    Examples of Misleading Charts and Graphs
    PowerPoint and Lesson on Agenda Setting
    Examples of Counter-Ads
All Materials for Lesson Plans in Chapter 7

List of Figures and Tables, Reflection Boxes, and Voices From the Field

List of Figures and Tables

Reflection Boxes

Voices From the Field

Preface

It was a stunning finding: more than a third of the 112,000 respondents to the initial Knight Foundation *Future of the First Amendment* (Yalof & Dautrich, 2005) survey of high school students said the First Amendment goes too far in the rights it guarantees. These students didn't believe "that people should be allowed to express unpopular opinions or newspapers should be allowed to publish freely without government approval of stories" (p. 1). Such results indicate a profound lack of understanding of the role of media in a democracy. They suggest a preference for avoiding opinions that challenge one's worldview and an inclination to rely on others to serve as gatekeepers of information rather than a willingness to question others or learn how to discern credibility for oneself. This is a wakeup call: we as educators need to do a better job of teaching about media, free speech, and democracy. And media literacy education can help.

As long-term media literacy educators who bring to the task a combined thirty-five years of staff and curriculum development experience, we have drawn from the growing body of theory and practice from a range of countries, perspectives, and disciplines to develop an educational approach that specifically applies to the United States.[1] But what most distinguishes *The Teacher's Guide to Media Literacy* from these works is that while they focus on *how to teach media literacy*, we focus on *using media literacy to teach*.

As a result, we pay a lot of attention to how people learn. We look at how practices and theories familiar to educators—but often missing from media literacy texts—apply to media literacy education. In addition, this is the first book to be based specifically on the *Core Principles of Media Literacy Education in the United States* developed in 2007 by the National Association of Media Literacy Education (NAMLE). As two of that document's co-authors, we are able to link theory to practice with dozens of activity ideas and lesson plans based on our own experiences and those of the many teachers with whom we have worked.

Media literacy has been identified as one of the key 21st-century skills by an amazingly wide range of organizations from the Catholic Church, the United Nations, and the American Academy of Pediatrics to professional education organizations like National Council of Teachers of English (NCTE) and National Council for the Social Studies (NCSS). In *Curriculum 21: Essential Education for a Changing World* (Jacobs, 2010), ASCD includes media literacy as one of the key areas for transforming schools and education. Support for media literacy has also come from the Partnership for 21st Century Skills and other business groups, as well as other government agencies. Joining the groundswell in acknowledging that media literacy overlaps with other critical literacies necessary for successfully navigating today's world, a growing number of states specifically require aspects of media literacy education in assessments for graduation.

In classroom after classroom, media literacy has demonstrated a power to reach all kinds of students, even those who have been uninterested in school. It is much more than a response to changing technologies; it is a vital and effective way to create a culture of inquiry in US schools and meet today's most pressing educational needs. We offer these pages as a springboard for educators who are ready to jump into the media literacy pond. We think you will find, as we have, that the waters are invigorating.

Acknowledgments

This book has been several years in the making, and along the way we have been inspired and supported by more people than we can possibly name here, including many of the scholars whose work we cite, the teachers who have worked with Project Look Sharp, those we have learned from at conferences and workshops across the nation, and our own students.

We owe a deep debt of gratitude to the staff of Project Look Sharp, whose work is strongly reflected in this book, including teacher extraordinaire Chris Sperry, curriculum kit writer Sox Sperry, image expert Rebecca Rozek, and accomplished cat herder Sherrie Szeto. Sherrie, in particular, has been instrumental in the development of the companion website for the book.

We also appreciate tremendously those at Ithaca College who have strongly supported media literacy integration and the growth of Look Sharp's work both on and off campus, including Tanya Saunders, former dean of the Division of Interdisciplinary & International Studies, and Leslie Lewis, current dean of Humanities & Sciences. We thank, as well, Carol Collins and Corwin for their interest in our work and recognition of the importance of media literacy education.

Also, our appreciation to the dedicated colleagues who have served on NAMLE's board—we know how hard you work. We offer special thanks to former board members Frank Baker, Renee Hobbs, and Elizabeth Thoman, whose insights and energy have played a major role in growing media literacy education in the United States, and also to Elana Rosen, without whom the *Core Principles of Media Literacy Education* would never have been written.

On a personal level, Faith thanks current and former colleagues in the PBS system who, early on, served as a receptive audience and provided opportunities to hone training and curriculum development skills. And gratitude beyond words goes to Adele Brown, whose extraordinary friendship over the decades has sustained me—body, mind, and soul.

Cyndy thanks those colleagues who got her started in the challenging exploration of media effects and media literacy, especially her longtime mentor, John Condry. He would have enjoyed this book, and I continue to miss him every day. And to my beautiful and patient daughter, Ariana Carvell, my love and gratitude; you are the light of my life.

And finally, we thank each other. This has been an uncommon partnership—testament that, indeed, the whole is greater than the sum of its parts.

Cyndy Scheibe and Faith Rogow,
Ithaca, New York, 2011

PUBLISHER'S ACKNOWLEDGMENTS

Corwin gratefully acknowledges the contributions of the following reviewers:

Veronica Andes
Assistant Director of Curriculum, Instruction, and Staff Development
Wilson School District
West Lawn, PA

Frank Baker
Consultant/Media Educator
Media Literacy Clearinghouse
Columbia, SC

Deborah Mellion
Director of Literacy and Title I
Cranston Public Schools
Cranston, RI

Sandy Moore
English Teacher
Coupeville Middle and High School
Coupeville, WA

Cheryl Oakes
Collaborative Content Coach for Technology
Wells Elementary School
Wells, ME

Michelle Saylor
Director of Curriculum, Instruction, and Staff Development
Wilson School District
West Lawn, PA

About the Authors

 **Cyndy Scheibe** is the Executive Director and Founder of Project Look Sharp, one of the leading media literacy organizations serving K–12 and college educators in the United States and a pioneer of curriculum-driven media literacy education. She is also an Associate Professor in developmental psychology at Ithaca College, where she has taught courses in developmental psychology, media research, and media literacy for more than twenty-five years, and serves as the Director of the Center for Research on the Effects of Television Lab and Archive. A dynamic speaker and workshop leader, she was a founding board member of the National Association for Media Literacy Education and is author of several articles on media literacy education and practice. She is a contributing editor to many of the media literacy curriculum kits developed by Project Look Sharp and co-authored the Critical Thinking and Health kit series based on media literacy for elementary grades. She received her PhD in Human Development (1987) from Cornell University.

 **Faith Rogow** was the founding president of the National Association for Media Literacy Education (NAMLE), a founding advisor of Project Look Sharp, and a founding editorial board member of the *Journal for Media Literacy Education*. She has been a leading media literacy educator, theorist, and strategist for more than two decades with a special interest in early childhood, pedagogy, and diversity issues. Her work is notable for merging academic expertise with grassroots sensibilities. In 1996 she created Insighters Educational Consulting to "help people learn from media and one another." An award-winning speaker, master teacher, and training designer, she has taught thousands of educators, child care professionals, media professionals, and parents to understand and harness the power of media. She has created educational outreach materials for projects ranging from *Sesame Street* and *Sid the Science Kid* to hundreds of independent films, including those featured on PBS's *P.O.V.* She is the author of many articles about media literacy, as well as *Gone to Another Meeting: A History of the National Council of Jewish Women* (University of Alabama Press, 1993). She received her PhD in history (1988) from Binghamton University.

Introduction

It is an exciting time to be a teacher. For only the second time in human history, the very nature of what it means to be literate is shifting, and that shift is being played out in schools and libraries across the world.

The first shift, ignited by the invention of the printing press, was about *who* should be literate. The new capacity for mass production challenged the idea of literacy as the province of a select elite and revealed the power that the ability to read and write gave to those who possessed it. That revelation was so compelling that Church officials persecuted printers, fearing that their authority would be undermined if everyone could read (and interpret) the Bible for themselves, and in early America it was against the law to teach slaves to read. Eventually, such resistance gave way to the requirements of democracy, which made clear that if the power to govern was to transfer from monarchs to an educated electorate, then virtually everyone needed to be literate.

Today we are witnessing a second historical shift. Instead of raising questions about *who* should be literate, it requires us to ask, "*What does it mean* to be literate?" Like the first shift, the second has been prompted by changes in technology. Widespread availability of digital and interactive communication technologies provides access to nearly unlimited information and global audiences. This has irrevocably altered the very nature of education and the basic skills needed to function as an informed citizen, productive worker, effective parent, and lifelong learner. This book is about what it means to be literate in today's complicated media environment and how teachers can use media literacy education to engage students and prepare them to thrive in the ever-shifting terrain of the digital world.

In architecture, triangles make very strong structures. So it is with our approach to media literacy education, which rests on a three-sided foundation: it is literacy based, inquiry based, and curriculum driven. We advocate for this approach to media literacy education because we believe that it has unparalleled potential to meet the most pressing needs in our schools while also preparing students for their most essential roles in a democratic society.

EXPANDING TRADITIONAL LITERACY

Today, even "traditional" print sources, such as textbooks and newspapers, routinely mesh text, images, and sometimes sound. In this environment, literacy skills that are limited to decoding, analyzing, and writing in print aren't enough to earn a student the full benefits of being literate.

Neither is doing the same old things with high-tech innovations. Like influential educational philosopher Paulo Freire, we think of literacy as the broad set of skills and habits that enable one to engage thoughtfully with the community and the world (see, for example, Freire, 1973; Freire & Macedo, 1987). So media literacy isn't about automatically championing new technologies; rather, it is a way to help students who live in a technology-dependent world regain the power that traditional literacy once enabled.

The realities of participatory digital culture mean that every student needs to develop higher-order thinking skills. It isn't just a workforce preparation issue. Without the ability to think critically, evaluate and synthesize the information they access, solve problems both independently and collaboratively, and communicate their understanding effectively to others, students will quickly be overwhelmed. And without reflection, students have the power of new media technologies in their hands without the ethical grounding to use them well and wisely.

For us, this new reality is why the questions "What does it mean to be literate?" and "How can those literacy skills be developed?" form the core of media literacy pedagogy. The resulting approach is deeply grounded in critical thinking and established literacy practice; it expands conventional routines to accommodate a wider range of content and formats, but does not seek to replace traditional literacy or pit print against screens in a misguided and futile competition.

A literacy framework allows us to step outside a "media as the problem" paradigm without sacrificing the skeptical eye that we want students to bring to the media they encounter. It enables us to value students' existing knowledge, skills, and talents while challenging them to take responsibility for their own learning and develop evermore sophisticated "filters."

BEYOND ADVERTISING AND PROTECTION

Those who think of media literacy education as primarily about teaching students to analyze advertising or to protect themselves from the (presumed) harmful effects of playing video games, going online, or watching TV and movies will find something different here. To borrow from an iconic marketing phrase—this is not your father's media literacy.[1]

Some concerns about harmful media influences certainly have merit, but they are not a viable foundation for literacy-based media literacy education in schools. It does not make pedagogical sense to approach education from the perspective of protecting children from harmful content; educators don't teach children to read in order to protect them from bad books, and though we recall days of junior library cards and locked stacks that kept adult materials away from children, we have never encountered a teacher who taught lessons about "book safety." Those types of protectionist strategies cannot work to make students skilled readers of books, and they will not produce skilled readers of other media.

In fact, approaching media literacy education with the primary goal of inoculating children against harmful media content is incompatible with the constructivist pedagogies that are at the core of this book. As author James Baldwin put it, "The purpose of education, finally, is to create in a person the ability to look at the world for himself, to make his own decisions . . ." (1998, p. 678). Educators cannot tell students what to think about media and teach them to think for themselves at the same time. Moreover, doing so risks alienating students, turning them into cynics every time broad indictments of media contradict their own experience.

More recently, master teacher and author of *Never Work Harder Than Your Students & Other Principles of Great Teaching*, Robyn Jackson, noted,

> Constructivist theory argues that meaningful learning happens when students try to make sense out of the world by filtering new information through their own existing knowledge, concepts, rules, hypotheses, and associations from personal experiences. Our job is to help our students find their own voices and develop their own understanding of the subject matter. (2009, p. 174)

As constructivist educators, we heartily agree. Children are more engaged and more likely to remember what they have learned when they grapple with material and figure out things *for themselves* than when they are simply told what media mean or what the effects of particular media are.

Media literacy education embraces constructivist pedagogy because it provides the necessary foundation for authentic inquiry in a way that drill and practice, strictly scripted curricula, or didactic instruction cannot. The resulting teaching methods have a substantial track record of engaging all kinds of students, placing the acquisition of basic skills and knowledge—as well as higher-order thinking skills—firmly within their grasp.

A CURRICULUM-DRIVEN APPROACH

Ours is a broad vision, and we are fully aware of the practical concerns about how to implement media literacy education in classrooms already pressed for time and resources. That is why we take a curriculum-driven approach in which media literacy is integrated into existing core content.

Pioneered by Project Look Sharp, this approach asks teachers to identify places in their own curriculum where media literacy methods could improve instruction, student engagement, and/or student performance and then develop customized lessons that address those needs. Because these activities combine media literacy skills with core content, effective use of instructional time is maximized, and in many cases lessons take up no more class time than before media literacy was introduced.

The integration of media literacy into existing curricula does not negate the need for specialized media literacy electives. There will always be a place for classes or activities offering advanced or specialized training in media analysis and media production to interested students. But media literacy education cannot succeed if it is exclusively relegated to elective courses any more than traditional literacy would be effective if it was taught only as a curriculum enhancement.

MEDIA LITERACY AND EDUCATION STANDARDS

Curriculum-driven media literacy education is an especially promising strategy for schools seeking to address the requirements of state and national standards. In fact, a cursory look at some of the current standards makes it difficult to see how they could be achieved *without* integrating media literacy into standard coursework or without teachers who are trained in media literacy pedagogies.

Consider, for example, this "Anchor Standard" from the Common Core English Language Arts Standards (2010; http://corestandards.org): "Integrate and evaluate content presented in diverse media and formations, including visually and quantitatively, as well as in words" (Reading, K–5). This standard would be impossible to meet without expanding traditional literacy in exactly the ways that media literacy education suggests.

The National Council for the Social Studies recognized media literacy as being so core to its curriculum standards that in 2009 it adopted a detailed position statement acknowledging that

> we live in a multimedia age where the majority of information people receive comes less often from print sources and more typically from highly constructed visual images, complex sound arrangements, and multiple media formats. The multimedia age requires new skills for accessing, analyzing, evaluating, creating, and distributing messages within a digital, global, and democratic society. ("Rationale")

Like the 2007 ISTE *National Educational Technology Standards for Students (NETS)*, which recognizes that new media technologies bring more than a need to know how to click on the correct button or insert the proper command code, many standards recognize that basic literacy requires "critical thinking, problem solving, and decision making."[2] Even the Common Core State Standards Initiative's *Standards for Mathematical Practice* (2010b) feature problem solving and using evidence to "construct viable arguments and critique the reasoning of others" (Introduction, #3). And the "Overview" from the *National Science Standards* (CSMEE, 1996) couldn't be more clear when it says, "Inquiry is central to science learning" and goes on to explain that students should be able to ask questions, make careful observations, communicate ideas to others, "identify their assumptions, use critical and logical thinking, and consider alternative explanations" (p. 2).

It is no coincidence that as you read this book, you will see these same goals embedded in descriptions of media literacy. Although the specific phrase *media literacy* is infrequently used in state and national standards documents, the *skills* described in those documents—the interpretation and evaluation of a variety of documents through careful observation and close readings; the use of reason, logical inference, and evidence to assess the validity of arguments; the ability to collaborate effectively with diverse partners and clearly communicate one's ideas; and the ability to apply all of those to many types of media—are the bread and butter of media literacy education. For more on the links between media literacy and educational standards, see the companion website.

CORE PRINCIPLES OF MEDIA LITERACY EDUCATION

The grounding of media literacy in inquiry, literacy, and education is embodied in the *Core Principles of Media Literacy Education in the United States,* a foundational document developed by the National Association for Media Literacy Education[3] (NAMLE) in 2007 (see Appendix A). Reflecting the wealth of experience, knowledge, and wide range of disciplines of its many co-authors, the *Core Principles* reflect contributions from education, psychology, communications, media arts, feminist film theory, cultural studies, multicultural education, public health, commercial and independent media production, preK–16 teaching, and education settings outside of schools. The resulting synthesis, like media literacy education itself, is inherently interdisciplinary.

We draw on this rich intellectual heritage to consciously use media literacy education in the service of creating a culture of inquiry. We explore what educators can do to nurture lifelong learners who are curious, skeptical, respectful, and open-minded and who have the ability to share ideas in the context of the mediated environment in which they live. And because these attributes defy the constraints of "silos" so often constructed around subject areas or academic disciplines, they provide an opportunity for schools to use media literacy to strengthen their overall curriculum by fostering cooperation among all teachers, with media literacy providing the common thread linking one class or topic to another.

MEETING CURRENT AND FUTURE NEEDS OF EDUCATORS

Some veteran educators may decide to ignore media literacy, assuming that it is just another passing fad and that if they wait it out, it will eventually go away. But while the types of media that we expect students to analyze and create are certainly likely to change over the coming years, as long as media continue to play a significant role in society, there will be a significant, universal need for media literacy education.

The educational needs that media literacy can address are substantial. An inquiry-based approach to media literacy education is an excellent way for schools to

- integrate 21st-century skills,[4] including the abilities to think independently, work collaboratively, problem-solve, and reflect on one's own work.

- teach the higher-order critical thinking skills needed in today's workplaces and communities—and do so even in the context of mandatory rote testing.
- address the explosion of media technologies in an educational context that respects media use as part of students' culture outside school and bridges schoolwork with students' real-world experiences.
- address the convergence of media technologies by focusing on long-term skills and knowledge that apply across technologies and types of media messages.
- expand literacy instruction by transforming rather than adding to class time, an essential strategy for a curriculum already overburdened with objectives and material to cover.
- improve educational outcomes by engaging students on their cultural territory and addressing their interests, as well as accommodating a broad range of learning strengths, skill levels, and degrees of fluency with English.
- integrate the teaching of skills and content.

It is, of course, possible to teach critical thinking without using media literacy approaches, and some schools have excelled at that task for many years. However, students—especially young students—do not automatically translate skills from one area to another, so they won't necessarily think critically about *media* unless we specifically teach them how to do so. And by teaching students to analyze *all* types of media, including media that they create, we avoid unintentionally conveying the message that they only need to think critically about some media forms and content some of the time.

Many education texts talk about the need to excite students about learning. We also want to excite teachers about teaching. In recent years, too many calls for educational reform have resorted to teacher bashing, blaming those who provide instruction for the system's failures. We categorically reject that approach. Successful media literacy education requires highly competent and skilled teachers. We offer the strategies described in these pages with great respect for the job that teachers do and hope that our work inspires and supports the efforts of educators in the way that so many classroom teachers have inspired us.

HOW TO USE THIS BOOK

Like traditional print literacy, media literacy is a skill set that applies to every subject area and all forms of mass media. So, in contrast to what one might find in a communications course, this book does not divide chapters by type of media but instead focuses on literacy skills that apply across all media formats. The emphasis on teaching, rather than on media formats and impacts, is reflected in the organization of the book:

- Chapters 1–3 look at what we mean by media literacy education.
- Chapters 4–7 lay out the pedagogy and practice for achieving that vision.

- Chapters 8–9 examine how to determine whether or not media literacy approaches are effective, as well as the challenges and benefits of media literacy education.

Also, to meet the needs of media literacy's multiple audiences, we have integrated a variety of resources that are not typical of all textbooks:

Reflection Boxes

Because everyone interprets media through the lens of their own experience, it is impossible to arrive at a clear analysis of media documents without awareness of what each person brings to the task. In media literacy, the basic epistemological question, "How do I know what I know?" morphs into queries like "What are my (or the media document's) sources of information?""Why do I think those sources are reliable?" and "What do I learn about myself from my response to this message?"

For educators, self-reflection is vitally important not only because it is essential for critical inquiry but also because what you believe influences how and what you teach.[5] So we have incorporated reflection boxes at selected points in the text. These are intended for you, the reader. You might pause as you are reading to think about the questions we have posed, or you might reflect on them later, perhaps talking about them with your classmates or colleagues. It is possible to teach media literacy without taking time for self-reflection, but you will be much more effective if you engage in this important part of being a media literacy educator.

Voices From the Field

Occasionally we want to share stories from classrooms—both our own and others'. We share these stories in Voices From the Field boxes.

Definitions

One consequence of the fact that every person interprets media through the lens of her or his own experience is that sometimes we think we have shared meaning even when we don't. In other words, we assume that everyone understands particular words or symbols or messages the way that we understand them, even though this is not always true. For example, in this book we use the following definitions:

- *Document* describes any media example under examination. In our usage, a YouTube video is a document. So is a song, poster, web page, video game, magazine cover, letter to the editor, podcast, sitcom, phone app, blog entry, etc.
- *Text* refers to words contained in a media document (e.g., a typical web or newspaper page may include text, graphics, and images).
- *Print* refers to a hard copy of words on paper (as in "That book is still in print.").

Throughout the book, we take care to define other terms that may have multiple meanings or may be unfamiliar to most readers. There is also a glossary on the companion website.

Activities and Lesson Plans

There are many activity ideas scattered throughout the book, as well as examples of complete lesson plans in Chapter 7. To help you find those that are most relevant to your work, there is a comprehensive Lesson Idea Grid on the book's website. Some readers will be tempted to go straight to those activity ideas and skip the rest of the book. We urge you to resist that temptation and join us for a more substantial and rewarding intellectual journey.

Our hope is that by the time you finish reading this book, you'll not only know how *we* have taught media literacy, you'll also know how to integrate media literacy into *your own* unique teaching situations. So, when we describe activities, we have taken great care to provide more than step-by-step instructions. We also explain how the things that we suggest help students develop "skills of expression" and/or "habits of inquiry"—the essence of media literacy. We pay special attention to the methods used to conduct the activity, because in many cases, altering what the teacher does—even a little bit—can make the difference between encouraging or inhibiting critical inquiry. You will understand these annotations more readily and have a better idea of how to implement an activity effectively if you read the entire book rather than going directly to the lesson ideas.

In addition, because our approach is curriculum driven and based on integrating media literacy into existing core content, we invite teachers to adapt activities and lesson plans to meet their own needs. To develop effective adaptations, educators need to understand not only how to do the discrete steps of a lesson but also why specific components are included and how they reflect an inquiry-based approach to media literacy.

Companion Website

We have included all of the curriculum materials referenced in this book (lesson plans, video clips, PowerPoint slides, handouts, etc.) on a special password-protected website (http://TGML.info). Throughout the book, when a resource is referenced that is available on the website, you will see a cursor icon. We will also be adding to these materials over time, and we invite feedback and additional suggestions from readers.

References to NAMLE's Core Principles

Sometimes you will notice the letters CP followed by a number (e.g., CP1.1). These are references to specific items in the NAMLE *Core Principles of Media Literacy Education in the United States* document (in Appendix A). These references provide signposts to help educators link theory and practice. In addition to serving as a tool for those who want a deeper understanding of the Core Principles, they also draw attention to the foundations that underlie our approach to media literacy.

Endnotes

In contrast to a standard citation method, we use endnotes to expand on the main text. Sometimes you will find an extended discussion of an ongoing debate in the field of media literacy, including explanations of our take on issues that have been historically significant. This is intended primarily for people who are veterans in the field. It will help situate our work in the context of existing media literacy initiatives.

We also use endnotes to suggest additional resources and activity ideas. These extensions will help the reader pursue an interest in a particular topic that is germane to media literacy but is beyond the scope of this book's capacity to give it detailed attention. Rather than reinvent the wheel, we point readers to others who have already done high-quality, in-depth work on the topic.

CREATING A CULTURE OF INQUIRY

One of the most exciting things about media literacy education for both students and educators is that it applies not only to our school and work lives but also to our personal lives. When parents talk with us (as educators) about the media literacy lessons their children have been learning in school, they are often amazed at how excited and empowered their children are by the information and ideas they have acquired. Sometimes parents describe things that they themselves have learned about media from their children; others tell us that their families cannot watch television or movies the way they used to because their children are pointing out ways in which the messages have been constructed. This "trickle-up" effect is a powerful way to connect school and home environments, and it reinforces the importance of media literacy for people of all ages.

Finally, as you read this book, we invite you to think about the development of your own "culture of inquiry" and to get in the habit of asking your own questions of all media by starting with the media document you hold in your hands: this book.

1

What Do We Mean by *Media?*

Those of us who live in developed nations are surrounded by media. From the moment we wake up until we go to sleep, media are part of our environment. They are so integrated into our lives that most people—even media-literate people—don't pay conscious attention to the majority of media messages that they encounter. Since people can't think critically about things they don't notice, a natural first step in media literacy education is to increase students' awareness of the role media play in their lives. CP3.6

To explore this point, we need to be clear about what we mean by *media*. That term can have different meanings depending on the context (for example, in art it might refer to clay or paint). In the context of media literacy, it refers to *mass media.*

In leading professional development workshops with educators, we often start by asking people to name the different kinds of mass media they have used so far that day.[1] The initial list usually includes

- radio,
- television,
- newspapers,
- magazines,
- the Internet/computers, and
- movies.

When we ask the same question of college students, on the other hand, they are likely to begin their list with

- cell phones,
- the Internet, and
- iPods or MP3 players.

Depending on participants' ages and the amount of time devoted to brainstorming, people also often list

- video and computer games,
- other recorded music (e.g., on CDs or records),
- billboards and other kinds of advertising (including words or images on clothing, signs in stores or sports stadiums, and food packaging), and
- posters and flyers.

In an election year, the list might also include forms of political communication like buttons, bumper stickers, and robocalls.

What's missing from those lists? Books. Despite the fact that books have been a major form of mass media for more than two centuries and are probably the most common form of media currently used in schools, our workshop participants—even when they are library media specialists (!)—rarely think to include books on their media lists. It could be that people associate the word *media* only with electronic technologies,[2] or perhaps they think of media as "bad" or harmful, and they think of books as "good." Whatever the reason, in an inquiry-based approach to media literacy education, it is essential to include books alongside newer forms of media.

REFLECTION: *YOUR MEDIA ENVIRONMENT*

Take a minute to think about all the different kinds of media that you have used or been exposed to from the moment you woke up today until right now.

- How does your list compare to the one generated by the workshop participants we described?
- Did you include things like this book, the logo on your shoes or coffee cup, the background music in the grocery store, or media that other people used in your presence?
- Why does it matter if we are aware of the media in our lives or our environment? What are the potential consequences of being aware of some media messages but not others?

BOOKS AND OTHER COMMON CLASSROOM MEDIA

No matter what any individual may believe to be true about the relative value of different types of media (e.g., printed text versus images on screen or traditional versus new media), if teachers want critical inquiry to become routine—that is, if they want it to become students' "default mode"—then they cannot selectively ask students to apply critical thinking skills only to some media forms while exempting others.

The inclusion of books as a form of media not only challenges some educators' ideas about media, it also challenges long-standing initiatives that define the primary aim of media literacy as getting students to reduce or eliminate their media use (i.e., screen time).[3] If—as we contend—media literacy is a logical extension of traditional literacy CP2 and the definition of *media* encompasses books, then an educational strategy designed primarily around limiting media use doesn't make much sense. Who would argue that we should keep students away from books?[4]

Books are not the only form of media missing from most educators' initial media lists. Also overlooked are media commonly found in US classrooms, such as posters of scenes from around the world, school newsletters sent home to parents, and maps (which reflect different perspectives about the world and often contain distortions of the relative size of countries and continents).[5] Even money (especially paper currency) functions as media, since it typically contains words and images that have been carefully crafted to convey messages to a country's own citizens, as well as to those of other nations (see Figure 1.1).

DEFINING *MEDIA*

A teacher's definition of *media* is crucial because it shapes how one practices media literacy education. We define *mass media* as having these characteristics:

1. Media convey messages through visuals, language, and/or sound.

2. Media messages are mass-produced for a mass audience and are mediated by some form of technology.

3. Producers of media messages are not in the same physical space as the receiver(s) of those messages.

This definition certainly encompasses things like books, maps, and the other media listed above, but not every form of communication is so clear-cut. For example, paintings certainly convey messages and are often reproduced in media formats, but the original painting is not mass-produced. Personal conversations via phone or e-mail would not fit the criterion of mass production either, although spam e-mail and some types of prerecorded phone messages certainly would. Producing effective digital video or PowerPoint presentations is often included as part of media literacy education, even when the presentations are not intended for mass production and when the producers are personally present when they are shown and are able to interact directly with the receivers viewing them. And new communication forms, especially those using digital technologies, have spawned a host of content (such as text messaging, with its unique vocabulary and grammar) that blur distinctions among media formats.

Figure 1.1 African and US Money as "Media" *Left to right—top row: Madagascar, Somalia, Liberia; middle row: Central African Republic, Sierra Leone; bottom two rows: United States.*

What do these examples of currency from Africa and the United States tell us about each nation and what that country values? What do you notice about the kinds of people pictured? Who is included and who is left out? What are the people doing? What facets of the culture or nation are featured? What did the country want to "show off"? What symbols and language(s) does each nation use? What kinds of evidence do these examples provide about the nation's relationship to other countries? Have choices about what is depicted on the currency changed over time, and what led to or influenced those changes? (To answer this question for the United States, check out the online currency exhibit of the Federal Reserve Bank of San Francisco at http://frbsf.org/currency/index.html.)

REFLECTION: *GAMES AS MEDIA*

Over the years we have had ongoing debates about whether or not board games are media. What do you think? Is a game like Monopoly an example of media? How about if it is played on a computer instead of on a physical board? What about games like chess or checkers or games like poker played with a regular deck of cards? What games have you played that you would consider media?

We accept a degree of "fuzziness" in defining *media* because media literacy education is not about excluding or privileging some forms of media over others. CP2.2 Instead, it is about equipping students to successfully navigate their world and think for themselves. If something does not exactly fit the definition of *media* but analyzing or creating it enhances media literacy skills, then teachers should include it in the scope of their work. Both in practice and in definition, the focus is on media *messages*—the content of the medium—rather than the technology or "channel" through which that message is delivered.[6]

This is not to suggest that educators should treat all media formats the same. On the contrary, a basic component of media literacy education is to compare and contrast messages across different media formats (in terms of their language and structure, communication techniques, and strengths and weaknesses CP1.1) and to examine how changing technologies and modalities influence the messages we receive and create. CP2.2 But we are less interested in the printing press and paper than we are in the changing content of books or newspapers, and less interested in the television set and the computer than we are in the information or entertainment they deliver.

It also means that while we are very much interested in how different people may interpret the same message in different ways, CP1.2 we are not suggesting that all things from which people might make meaning automatically count as media. For example, some people make meaning from the alignment of stars or see images in clouds, but it is obvious that stars and clouds are not media.

A more down-to-earth example would be clothing. Throughout history, people have worn particular items or colors of clothing to communicate messages about aspects of their identity (e.g., socioeconomic status, religion, nationality, or tribal membership). However, for clothes to qualify as media, they must convey a message created by someone other than the person wearing them, as would be the case with, for example, a T-shirt emblazoned with a brand name or company logo. In the former instance, clothes are a direct communication by the person wearing them, just as if he or she were speaking. In the latter instance, the clothing serves as mediated communication between a company and the people who see the clothing.[7]

REFLECTION: *CLOTHING AS MEDIA*

What articles of your clothing would qualify as media? How do you feel about wearing clothes that help others communicate a message? In what ways might these kinds of clothing function as both media and as direct expressions of personal identity?

- A rock band T-shirt
- A pro sports team jersey or hat
- A designer purse

The focus on message rather than the technology of delivery is all the more important as forms of media converge. By the time today's preschoolers enter the workforce, it will be common for a single device to serve as computer, phone, game console, radio, television, music player, GPS, camera, and audio recorder not to mention as calculator, alarm clock, calendar, and dozens of other functions no one has even thought of yet. Debates about the relative merits of various media-delivery systems are obsolete for someone who can use a completely customized, pocket-sized, wireless tool to access songs and TV programs, get maps and directions, post comments on a class discussion board, exchange instant messages with a friend, take notes, check homework assignments, play games, gamble, shop, search the globe for information, order a pizza, arrange an impromptu political protest, receive real-time safety alerts, post photos of coveted new shoes to a personalized birthday wish list, or watch a favorite sports hero from a choice of angles. In an age of media convergence and rapid change, the approach that makes the most sense for media literacy educators is to provide students with reading, writing, analysis, and reflection skills that apply across all technologies, including versions that will come in the future.

THE NATURE OF MEDIA MESSAGES: KEY CONCEPTS

In addition to adopting an inclusive definition of *media*, media literacy education embraces a set of core ideas about the nature of media.[8] In the past three decades, every major organization involved with media literacy has articulated a set of Key Concepts to describe those core ideas. Though specific wording varies, there is broad agreement on these six main points:[9]

1. **All media messages are constructed.** By definition, media messages are representations, filtered through human decisions and the constraints and capabilities of media technologies.[10] This fundamental concept serves to focus attention not just on the message itself but also on who is behind it and the purposeful way in which it was made.

2. **Each medium has different characteristics, strengths, and a unique "language" of construction.** Every type of media has its own set of "grammatical" rules that makes it comprehensible to users. In printed text, the grammar is familiar: nouns, verbs, sentences, paragraphs, and the like. In visual texts, the components of language are things like camera angles, juxtaposition, and movement. The language of audio texts includes sound effects; voice-overs; and the musical grammar of notes, rests, and dynamics. The Internet has elements like URLs, banners, and hotlinks.

   These languages make some media more effective than others at accomplishing specific communication tasks. For example, it would be quite difficult to teach someone to hit a baseball by assigning her or him to read a chapter in a book. But a video demonstration that included a voice-over describing how to hold the bat and swing could get someone started in less than sixty seconds.

On the other hand, the book chapter would be the better choice if the goal was to help a student understand the logic underlying a complex idea or debate, because logical arguments—like most printed texts—tend to proceed in a linear way and a person holding a book can read at his or her own pace, pause to ponder, highlight important phrases, write notes in the margins, and easily reread paragraphs or sentences.

3. **Media messages are produced for particular purposes.** Notice that this concept uses the plural *purposes*. People often have more than one reason for creating media messages, and many messages are created by teams of people, each with particular goals.[11]

4. **All media messages contain embedded values and points of view.** In addition to the obvious, media messages reflect the experiences and assumptions of producers and audiences, as well as societal norms and media conventions. For example, while the overt content of a clothing ad is about selling the clothes (or a brand), the choice of a particular model—his body type, height, weight, hairstyle and hair color, skin color, and age—also conveys implicit ideas and cultural preoccupations about beauty.

5. **People use their individual skills, beliefs, and experiences to construct their own meanings from media messages.** Audiences are active participants[12] in the communication process, and because every person is different, there is no such thing as an automatic interpretation that is true for everyone.[13] There are often dominant readings (i.e., interpretations on which most people would agree), and there can be inaccurate interpretations that are unsupported by evidence in the document, but it is quite possible for two people to interpret the same media text differently without either of them being wrong.

   This point is especially important for media literacy educators. Teachers often find that differences in age alone make it likely that they will encounter students who will disagree with them about what a media text means. Other common variables affecting interpretations of media messages include race, ethnicity, culture, gender identity, socioeconomic class, geography (e.g., rural/urban or region), prior knowledge, and political affiliation.

6. **Media and media messages can influence beliefs, attitudes, values, behaviors, and the democratic process.** We include the word *can* here because media influence is significant but it is neither absolute nor automatic. Media messages can influence people, but they don't always. Sometimes people ignore them or dismiss sources that they find irrelevant or less than credible. Sometimes the messages reach so few people that they are inconsequential. And when the messages are influential, they might not be so in predictable ways for all individuals. Nevertheless, media literacy education is built on the assumption that media matter.

   These Key Concepts help to clarify what we mean by *media*, and as such they represent a fundamental part of the *Core Principles of Media Literacy Education in the United States* (see Appendix A).

2

What Is *Media* **Literacy?**

In Chapter 1 we defined what we mean by *media*, so it might seem that all we have to do now is add a definition of *literacy* and the meaning of the phrase *media literacy* would be clear. But over the years, *media literacy* has been used in multiple ways and has come to mean very different things to different people. It's like the many variations on simple yeast breads: even when the basic ingredients are the same, different bakers can produce vastly different breads.

DEFINING *MEDIA LITERACY:* A SET OF CAPABILITIES

Over several decades, continents, and academic disciplines, a definition has emerged that characterizes *media literacy* as a set of capabilities applied to media messages and experiences.[1] A frequently cited version in the United States is "the ability to access, analyze, evaluate, and produce communication in a variety of forms."[2] That definition has not always provided clear direction for teachers, however, and it leaves out capabilities that are crucial for successful navigation and communication in today's complicated media world. A more current definition, articulated by media literacy expert Renee Hobbs (2010b), includes capabilities such as comprehension, collaboration, reflection, and social action.

In general, people who exhibit skills and knowledge in the following areas have what we would call *media literacy*:[3]

- *Access*—Having physical access to up-to-date media technologies and high-quality content and knowing how to use the technologies effectively

- *Understanding*—Comprehending basic, explicit messages from media sources as a precursor to being able to ask analytical questions about those messages
- *Awareness*—Paying attention enough to notice the presence of media messages and their role in one's life
- *Analysis*—Decoding media messages in order to think critically and independently about them
- *Evaluation*—Making informed, reasoned judgments about the value or utility of media messages for specific purposes
- *Creation*—Making media messages for particular purposes and using multiple media formats
- *Reflection*—Contemplating how personal experiences and values influence reactions to and production of media messages and assessing the full range of potential effects of one's production choices on oneself and others
- *Participation*—Initiating or joining in collaborative activities that are enabled by interactive media technologies, such as wikis, social networks, and virtual worlds

In addition to these eight elements, there is a strong assumption that media-literate people will have not only the ability to do these things but also the desire to do them—and then to *act* on what they learn. Inherent to media literacy is the idea that what students learn in class they will translate into real-world action.

Because media literacy is defined as a skill set, it does not function as a traditional content area. As with all subjects, skills are attached to learning content, but media literacy is not a defined body of facts about media that students are expected to master. Like traditional literacy, media literacy provides students with the tools they need to explore content in a wide range of subject areas. That content may sometimes include facts about media, but what we are describing extends well beyond that narrow task.

Despite agreement on the elements of media literacy, disagreements persist about what these terms mean when put into practice. Start with *access*, for example. How would you translate that capability into action? Would your ideas include any of the following?

- A teacher makes sure that every student who passes through his doors knows how to use wikis to work collaboratively.
- Parents concerned with digital-divide issues team up with school staff and civic groups to ensure that every student has home access to a laptop and a high-speed Internet connection.
- A civic club commits to raising funds for the school library to purchase several sets of award-winning bilingual children's books and translations of literature required for high school English courses.
- A high school computer class decides to submit a formal request to the board of education to remove filtering software that is preventing students from using social networks for a class project.

These are only a few of the possible interpretations. So while the above definition of media literacy provides common ground, it does not necessarily produce narrow or uniform practice, nor should it. After all, we are looking at literacy, and like traditional reading and writing, media literacy should be integrated throughout an educational system, not just taught by a single teacher in a single way.

THE FABRIC OF MEDIA LITERACY

In practice, because people enter media literacy education from different paths and perspectives, and with different objectives in mind, media literacy is like the weave of a complex plaid fabric—many intersecting stripes of varying widths and colors sometimes overlap, overshadow, blend, or exist in complementary but parallel worlds. The various interests that lead to media literacy education range from media appreciation (in the tradition of art history or literary criticism) to consumer education[4] (an outgrowth of a "buyer beware" society in which consumers are expected to know enough to protect themselves) to cultural criticism (which examines the interplay between media and culture to explain how media shape society, especially around social issues such as racism, sexism, homophobia, violence, and materialism) to parenting[5] and religion.[6] Other threads include vocational education, civic engagement, educational media, and popular culture.[7] The last is championed by teachers who see media as a way to keep their classes relevant and connected to their students' lives and the world outside of school. From these varied interests, educators typically combine selected threads to create their own cloth.[8] Depending on implementation, it is possible to weave any of them into sound media literacy lessons.

CRITICAL AUTONOMY: IDEAL VERSUS REALITY

One of the things that unifies all these interests, at least on paper, is the belief that media literacy should lead to critical consciousness and critical autonomy. That is, students should be able to examine their culture and think independently about it. As the Ontario Ministry of Education (1989, p. 7) summarizes, "Ultimately, media literacy education must aim to produce students who have an understanding of the media that includes a knowledge of their strengths and weaknesses, biases and priorities, role and impact, and artistry and artifice," but "the ultimate aim of media literacy is not simply a better awareness and understanding [of media]; it is critical autonomy."[9]

The embrace of critical autonomy, however, has not erased other divisions that affect what people think of as media literacy. For example, there are ongoing debates about just how much or which media are appropriate to bring into the classroom. Other tensions involve deeply held beliefs about the nature of children and childhood, who should control the curriculum, and the role of schools in society.

Though a stated goal of critical autonomy would suggest the adoption of a constructivist pedagogy, this occurs inconsistently in practice.[10] It is not uncommon for an educator to use a didactic teaching style to present a radical critique of media. Yet, as Len Masterman (1985) warns in his seminal book, *Teaching the Media*, the objective of media literacy "should not be to produce in pupils the ability to reproduce faithfully ideas, critical insights or information supplied by the teacher" (p. 24). CP1.5

There is great value in the field's diversity, especially as educators work to discover the most promising practices in a media landscape that is in constant flux. Instruction also benefits from the passion and creativity that many media literacy educators bring to their task. At the same time, as Kathleen Tyner (1998) and many others have suggested, if the central goal of media literacy is to have students think for themselves, then "to tell students what to think about media, no matter how subtly, would be inherently counterproductive" (Tyner, p. 148). And doing so increases the chances that students, robbed of the opportunity to make meaning for themselves or become conscious of how they make meaning, will disengage. So, to return to our bread analogy, you can mold your bread dough into any shape you want as long as your ingredients are inquiry based.

CRITICAL THINKING

Critical thinking is central to inquiry-based media literacy. But what does that really mean? When we ask our students how many of them have been told they need to use critical thinking skills, almost everyone raises a hand; when we ask how many of them have ever had critical thinking defined for them, almost all put their hands down.

If students don't really know what critical thinking is, it isn't reasonable to expect them to know how to do it. So we want to be very clear about what we mean. Like media literacy, critical thinking involves a number of elements. In Anderson, Krathwohl, Airasian, & Cruikshank's (2001) revision of Bloom's (1956) taxonomy, for example, critical thinking reflects six hierarchical skills: remember (knowledge), understand (comprehension), apply, analyze, evaluate, and create (synthesis). The overlap with media literacy capabilities is clear, especially when considering "power words" they associate with analyze (*decode, inquire*) and apply (*action, participate*).[11]

Others use a framework that specifically emphasizes inquiry. Browne & Keeley (2010), for example, describe *critical thinking* as

1. an awareness of a set of interrelated critical questions;

2. the ability to ask and answer critical questions at appropriate times; and

3. the desire to actively use critical questions.

The National Council for Excellence in Critical Thinking adds that critical thinking is more than processes and skills; it is "a habit, based on intellectual commitment, of using those skills to guide behavior" (Scriven & Paul, 1987).[12]

Both of these sources distinguish between weak-sense critical thinking, which is often used to defend our existing beliefs, and strong-sense critical thinking, which includes being aware of our own biases and perspectives, examining them rather than being blinded by them, and altering them in light of new evidence or compelling arguments. For example, do you know people who never question the veracity of a favorite talk radio host because they think he or she always "tells it like it is"? How about someone who believes everything that a favorite professor or author says? Those practices would represent weak-sense critical thinking.

In contrast, strong-sense critical thinkers look deeply at the strengths and weaknesses of evidence and logic, no matter the source of the information. They can watch, read, or listen to perspectives with which they largely disagree and, rather than discounting the entire program or individual outright, can acknowledge that some statements may be accurate and some not. Weak-sense critical thinkers question only things that they are already predisposed to doubt. Strong-sense critical thinkers are able to question everything.

VOICES FROM THE FIELD: *QUESTIONING* THE LORAX

Strong-sense critical thinking is easy to talk about and hard to do. We witnessed the challenges firsthand at a workshop where environmental educators and activists were trying out potential lessons for Project Look Sharp's *Media Construction of the Environment Kit* series. One activity consisted of contrasting the messages about environmentalists, loggers, and industrialists in *The Lorax* by Dr. Seuss (1971) and a rebuttal booklet, Terri Birkett's (1995) *Truax*, published by the National Wood Flooring Manufacturers' Association. As shown in Figures 2.1 and 2.2, the images of the central characters were very different in the two books, and both books included many stated and implied claims about resource depletion and trees that were inaccurate.

We asked the attendees to do a critical analysis of both books—identifying questionable content and stereotypes in each. The groups who were critiquing *Truax* had no trouble picking out content that was stereotypical or just wrong, but the groups critiquing *The Lorax* had a much more difficult time. Their willingness to question the stereotyping in the negative portrayal of the industrialist or the accuracy of messages about deforestation was tempered by their feelings about the topic and belief in the overall message of the book.

One of the best ways for educators to help students develop strong-sense critical thinking skills is to make routine the habit of asking questions about everything. In this case, high school environmental science students might actually do the *Lorax/Truax* comparisons. But even elementary-level students who read *The Lorax* might be asked to look at what they learn about trees from the book and consider whether or not everything that the book says or implies about trees was true.

Figure 2.1 *The Lorax* pits an industrialist (the Once-ler, on the upper left) and his Thneed factories against the Lorax (at the top of the stairs), who speaks for the bears and the trees. How are the Once-ler and the Lorax portrayed? What do these visual images convey about industrialists? Environmentalists? Manufacturing? Nature? What other messages do you notice?

Source: Dr. Seuss (1971).

Figure 2.2 *Truax,* produced by the Wood Floor Manufacturing Association to "correct inaccuracies in *The Lorax,*" pits Truax the logger (on the left) against an environmentalist (Guardbark, on the right). How are Truax and Guardbark portrayed? What do you notice about the skin tones of each character? What do the visual images and words convey about loggers? Environmentalists? Manufacturing industries? Nature? What other messages do you notice?

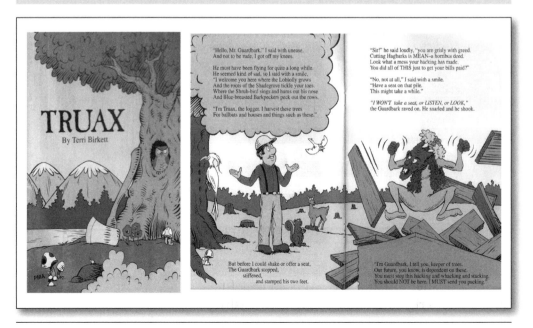

Source: Birkett (1994).

For media literacy education, we focus on five key components of critical thinking:[13]

1. **Curiosity and the desire to question**—Critical thinkers want to be in the game of wanting to know. They reject oversimplifications and seek all available evidence before drawing conclusions. When looking at media documents, they glory in "rich readings" rather than seeking a single, unassailable truth. CP6.3

2. **Ongoing engagement in the process of inquiry**—Critical thinkers acquire, analyze, and evaluate information in a continuous, lifelong process CP3.1 that allows them to draw conclusions that guide behavior or decisions (i.e., they apply what they learn). They question things with which they agree with the same rigor as things of which they are suspicious (thus demonstrating strong-sense critical thinking). CP1.3

3. **Inherent skepticism**—Critical thinkers are on the lookout for assumptions, motives, and evidence in stated claims. In contrast to cynics, who deal with the challenging task of living with media by taking an "I just won't believe anything," stance, skeptics approach media messages with confidence because they know what questions to ask and are well practiced in asking them. CP1.2, 4.2

4. **Valuing good reasoning**—Critical thinkers are able to distinguish between facts and opinions. They know what counts as credible evidence, seek and evaluate it, and use logic to draw their conclusions. CP1.4

5. **Flexibility and open-mindedness**—Critical thinkers are aware of and question their own assumptions CP6.1, 6.2 and are willing to change their opinions based on evidence. They accept a degree of ambiguity and uncertainty in the world and routinely consult diverse sources of information. CP5.1

Media literacy takes these elements of critical thinking and applies them to the analysis and creation of media messages. In so doing, it establishes these critical thinking skills as cornerstones for building other higher-order thinking skills like synthesis, evaluation, and problem solving and turns those into life-long habits.

INTERSECTING LITERACIES

Many educators will find familiar territory in media literacy because its goals overlap with the goals of other important literacies, each borrowing from the other. CP2.8 You might imagine a set of Venn diagrams with digital, information, technology or information and communication technologies (ICT) literacy, each sharing goals with media literacy. The overlap would include things like preparing students to use new technologies or access and evaluate information, but media literacy covers a wider range of media forms than other literacies, and it adds critical analysis to technical instruction.

Today we also have the concept of new media literacies, which assumes that students come to the table with basic media literacy skills and adds elements like collective learning and the use of alternative identities as a means to achieve full involvement in the participatory culture that interactive technologies have enabled. Media literacy and new media literacies share the goal of preparing students to negotiate the digital world, though the two diverge in terms of how much emphasis to place on basic media literacy skills as compared to newer skills like multitasking, play as a method of problem solving, and creating and using collective intelligence.[14]

Of course, this entire book is about the intersections between media literacy and traditional literacy. Other literacies—like visual literacy and critical literacy—are so central to our consideration of media literacy that they are dealt with in more detail later. And because we take a curriculum-driven approach to media literacy, there are always overlaps with content area literacies such as health, news, math, and science literacies. CP2.8

So what we're suggesting isn't a Snow White "mirror, mirror on the wall" scenario where educators need to declare a particular literacy as the "fairest one of all." Media literacy need not supplant work that teachers or librarians are currently doing; rather, it can enhance it.

WHY *LITERACY?*

As you explore the field, you may find yourself reading an article or book that refers to "media education," "media studies," "media ecology" or "21st-century skills" and think, "This sounds an awful lot like media literacy." Sometimes these variations represent substantive departures from media literacy; in other instances, the variations result simply from nuances in the way that terms are used in different countries or academic disciplines.

If you are a teacher, it probably is not worth spending a lot of time debating terminology. If it walks like a duck and quacks like a duck, it's a duck. In other words, if it uses inquiry-based practice to help you reach the goals of media literacy, then it is worth doing no matter what it is called.

We use the term media *literacy* because the concept of literacy is so core to our vision of how to implement media literacy education in schools. Media literacy is not merely adding media technology as a teaching tool or inserting a media analysis lesson or production project here and there. Rather, like traditional literacy, media literacy is an expansive approach to learning; we expect students to use media literacy skills throughout their day and throughout their lives. CP2.4

We are not alone in applying a literacy framework to media literacy.[15] The report from the National Leadership Conference on Media Literacy (Aufderheide, 1993), which was based significantly on earlier work in the United Kingdom, Australia, and Canada, begins with this paragraph:

Media literacy, the movement to *expand* [emphasis added] notions of literacy to include the powerful post-print media that dominate our

informational landscape, helps people understand, produce, and negotiate meanings in a culture made up of powerful images, words, and
sounds. (p. 1)

Media literacy has always been grounded in the reality that, because so
much important information is conveyed in images and sounds, to be literate
requires the ability to "read" and communicate with a wide range of visual and
auditory tools, as well as with print. As the National Leadership Conference
recognized, media literacy is not a repudiation of traditional print literacy but,
rather, an expansion of it.

In fact, given the many forms of media that integrate images and text (e.g.,
websites, newspapers, magazines, textbooks, etc.), one cannot be media literate
without being print literate. What media literacy adds to the discussion is the
recognition that print literacy is no longer enough. [CP2]

So, how do you become literate with respect to visuals and sound, as well as
printed text? Realistically, teachers can't master all of semiotics[16] and mass communications,[17] not to mention graphic and web design, video and film production, photography, music, and art history. Instead, media literacy borrows from
all these areas without duplicating everything that they cover.

VISUAL LITERACY

In every year of formal schooling, from preK through college, students are
required to spend a significant amount of time learning to read and analyze
printed words. The same is not true for learning how to read images, so media
literacy educators have historically spent considerable energy trying to fill the gap.
To do so, they have turned to semiotics, but they have had to wrestle with how to
apply the tenets of that discipline to both media literacy and to typical classrooms.

Semiotics studies all visual communication, including real-life interactions
that are not media. Some versions of semiotics posit absolute or universal
meanings for certain types of symbols, an approach that conflicts with media
literacy's notion that people interpret media through the lens of their own experience and do not always agree on meaning. So, semiotics analysis might identify a cigar as a phallic symbol, while media literacy would say that it is possible
for it to be used as a phallic symbol but it is also possible that "sometimes a
cigar is just a cigar."[18]

On the other hand, media literacy certainly shares with semiotics an interest
in careful and thoughtful observation. Moreover, semiotics offers vocabulary
that enables analytical conversations, and media literacy needs that vocabulary
to provide a common ground as students create and talk about media. So media
literacy borrows from semiotics but does not replace it or require a teacher to
master the entire discipline.

Reading Images

There has been some debate over whether or not the term *literacy* applies
to images.[19] In contrast to print, which appears to be a bunch of squiggles on

a page until one learns to decode its symbols, if we are born with sight, we comprehend a lot of visual information without anyone having to teach us anything. However, that is only part of the picture.

It is very clear that we actually learn how to interpret a great deal of visual information; that is, we learn how to "read" images and make meaning from them. Perhaps the best evidence for this is that many images do not hold a constant meaning across cultures.

For example, imagine a bridal gown. If you were raised in North America, the color of the image that came to mind was likely white. Why white? Because it symbolizes the purity or virginity of the bride. On the other hand, in many Asian cultures, white represents death—so it would be unthinkable to dress a bride in white. In those cultures, many traditional brides wear red as symbol of good fortune. Now imagine showing up at a North American wedding and encountering a bride wearing red. What would that mean?[20]

There is nothing natural or automatic about reading messages into the color of wedding attire. Somewhere along the line, we learned that a particular color in the context of a wedding dress has a particular meaning. In other words, we learned a visual language.

To better understand images as language, it is helpful to think of visual information as represented by the following mathematical equation:

$$\frac{\text{IMAGE} + \text{CONTEXT}}{\text{MESSAGE}}$$

We learn that particular images in particular contexts have specific meanings.

REFLECTION: *TEACHING ABOUT STEREOTYPES*

This equation can also help students think about stereotypes. We see a particular skin color (or hair type, eye shape, or even particular brands of clothing) in the context of people, and we have learned certain messages. What messages have you learned?

VOICES FROM THE FIELD: *VISUAL CUES FOR HATE*

Students in Faith's course about the history of the Holocaust found that the "image + context = message" equation helped them understand how Hitler managed to separate Jews (and other target groups) from the rest of the population. Most German Jews looked like everyone else. To convince the population that Jews were different and subhuman, the Nazis introduced a visual cue—the yellow star—and ran a propaganda campaign that associated negative characteristics with it. So in Nazi Germany, the image of a yellow star in the context of people conveyed a message designed to trigger hate.

For example, reconsider the color red. This time, instead of wedding gowns, assume that the context is traffic lights. We see red in the context of a traffic signal, and we have learned that the message is "stop."

Thankfully, the brain processes visual information very quickly, so we don't have to pause every time we approach an intersection and search our brains to remember that red means stop. Because we do not pause, we rarely think consciously about the visual language that we use to make meaning from what we see. Yet, we depend on the fact that this visual language exists in people's heads and that they use that language on a daily basis to make sense of the world. Just imagine the chaos that would ensue if we could not depend on the fact that everyone has learned that red in the context of traffic lights means "Stop!"

Images in isolation rarely provide enough information for such shared meaning to occur. It is the combination of an image with a particular context that creates meaning. Consider the image in Figure 2.3 and imagine that it is yellow.[21] What is it? Could it be something else?

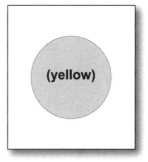

Figure 2.3

It might be a picture of an egg yolk, the backside of a smiley face, a rubber ball, the sun, or just a yellow dot. Without context, it is impossible to be certain. But if we add a few lines and two more colored dots—that is, if we add *context*—it is easier to draw a conclusion that would be shared by most of the people who viewed the image in Figure 2.4.

With this context added, most people would readily identify the original image as the yellow light in a traffic signal and would agree that it means "caution." That agreement, however, doesn't necessarily mean there is shared meaning.

For example, what happens when you replace the question "What does this mean?" with "When you see this, what do you do?" Some people will recall their defensive driving lessons and say that they slow down because the light is about to change to red. Many others will say that they speed up because the signal is about to change to red and they want to avoid waiting for the light to change back to green. Sometimes we assume shared meaning when other people may have very different interpretations. CP6.4

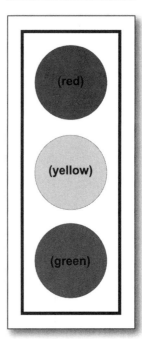

Figure 2.4

The traffic light is a simple example. To understand what happens when the visual information is more complex, we need to add another layer of processing. Many images have multiple meanings, so we learn to interpret selectively depending on the context. For example, color changes its meaning depending on where we see it. By moving a few lines and the positions of the dots, we can change the context of the traffic signal, where yellow indicates "caution," into the context of lollipops, where yellow usually means, "This is lemon flavored." (See Figure 2.5.)

Adding to the complexity, sometimes the color yellow doesn't give us any salient information at all. In lollipops, yellow may mean "lemon," but that isn't true for all candy. For example, yellow in the context of M&Ms tells you nothing about the flavor; no matter what the color of an M&M is, the flavor is still chocolate.

Figure 2.5 Lollipops

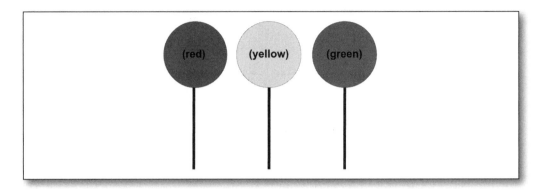

Going back to our earlier conversation and the colored dots in the traffic light (Figure 2.4), the red dot means "stop." In the context of the lollipops it might mean "cherry flavored." But surround it by a white rectangle and now you have the Japanese flag.

VOICES FROM THE FIELD: *WHAT COLOR IS THE SUN?*

When students in Cyndy's media literacy class identified the box with the red dot in the middle as the Japanese flag, she replied that they probably meant that the whole thing was the Japanese flag, but then she asked, "If so, what does the red dot itself mean?" They looked a little perplexed—and then a visiting teacher from Japan, Masahiro Kitazume, raised his hand and told everyone that it represents the sun. This led to a wonderful conversation about cultural differences in interpretation of color, especially since the students had earlier identified the yellow dot as the sun, which Masahiro thought was strange since he grew up believing that the sun was red!

Put the red circle in the center of concentric white and red circles, and it could be interpreted as bull's-eye. In today's American classrooms, many students will say "Target!" (referring to the retail chain), which is just one illustration of how powerfully our contexts are influenced by media messages and the extent to which mainstream popular media can create shared meaning in today's world.[22]

So, in addition to learning that specific images in specific contexts have particular meanings, our brains learn to sort out which images to pay attention to in various contexts. To begin to understand what that means for analyzing media, try answering this mathematics puzzle:

Which of these is numerically *most* different from the others? The difference has to be numerical (so the fact that thirty-one has a hyphen doesn't count, because that isn't a numerical difference).

1) one
2) thirteen
3) thirty-one

If you are like most people, you probably think the answer is "one," perhaps because it is a single digit (or has a value only in the ones column) in contrast to the double digits in "thirteen" and "thirty-one." But look again. Why can't "one" be the correct response?

Stumped? The answer can't be "one" because there are two "ones" ("1" and "one"). The best answer is 2. Not "thirteen," but the number 2 that appears to the left of it. It is the only even number in the example.

In twenty years of presenting this exercise to thousands of people, only twice has anyone said, "Two." So why do nearly all of us get it wrong? Because to our brains, this multiple-choice construct is so familiar that we are sure that we know exactly what to ignore and where to direct our attention. In our visual language, anything to the left of the parentheses is only for categorization purposes. So without being conscious of the fact that we are doing it, our brains eliminate half of the information presented. That is visual language at work. High-quality media literacy education makes students aware of their existing visual language and builds on that language to make it more sophisticated. CP6.2, 6.3

REFLECTION: *YOUR VISUAL LANGUAGE*

Consider, for a moment, what visual messages you pay attention to and what you ignore as you look at different types of media. For example, the authors grew up in an era when words moving across the bottom of a television screen were used only to signal an emergency like a weather warning. Today it is difficult for us to ignore that crawl and focus on the rest of the screen, even though we know that it is used for lots of nonemergency purposes like celebrity updates and program promotions.

What visual language do you use as you look at a newscast, a food or video game package, or a website homepage? What are you paying attention to (i.e., processing consciously), and what are you ignoring? What techniques do the makers of those media use to try to draw your attention to certain things and away from others?

Graphic Organizers

Some people also use the term *visual literacy* to refer to the use of graphic organizers, or the ability to create and interpret charts, graphs, diagrams, and the like. In education these skills and uses are most commonly encountered in science and math,[23] but they are also prevalent in news reporting, magazines, and websites. In these cases, the language is technical (e.g., ensuring that the x- and y-axes on a graph are properly labeled), and it is used to communicate an impression. So, for example, imagine that a graph representing a stock's performance is accurately labeled, but because of especially narrow spaces separating the months of the year from each other along the x-axis, the upward trajectory of the line makes it look like the value of the stock has significantly increased when, in fact, it has only risen a few cents. The data are accurate, but the impression they convey is misleading. Much of visual literacy isn't just a matter of knowing how to read the language but also a matter of attending to details and context of the presentation. For other examples of misleading charts and graphs, see this book's companion website.

MEDIA VOCABULARY

While visual literacy is a vital component of media literacy, it isn't enough. We want students to do more than improve their critical thinking and observational skills; we also want them to be able to talk about what they notice. That requires media vocabulary. Not only does a specialized vocabulary provide common ground for conversations when analyzing media or working collaboratively to create media messages, but human beings tend not to notice things for which they have no language. So the right vocabulary helps students notice things they might otherwise miss.

The specific terms that students and teachers need to know depend partly on which types of media they are using.[24]

- Conversations about still images include words like *foreground, lighting, camera angle, framing*, or *Photoshopping*.
- Conversations about video or film also include editing terms like *pace, fade*, and *jump cut*; words for specific camera motions such as *zoom* or *pan*; and terms that differentiate between types of shots like *establishing shot* or *close-up*.
- In a conversation about a video game, you might find yourself talking about *cheats, code, environment, animation*, or *skin*.
- Online networks, websites, and software applications add to the mix terms like *URL, wallpaper, banner*, and *pop-up*.

A special vocabulary can also assist in doing other types of media analysis, especially when analyzing advertising or other persuasive media content. Knowing specific terms can alert the viewer, listener, or reader to the presence of manipulative techniques that otherwise might go unrecognized. Some terms that we have found to be useful include[25]

- *Bandwagon*: The suggestion that everyone (or everyone who is popular) is doing something (or buying something), so you should too
- *Eye candy*: The use of appealing visual elements to attract the audience to the message and distract them from content that the maker of the message would rather go unnoticed
- *F.U.D. factor*: The practice of emphasizing fear, uncertainty, and/or doubt as a means of scaring the audience into buying a product or coming back to the same source for more information (Jackson & Jamieson, 2007)
- *Weasel words*: Vague phrases and "loophole" language that make claims sound better than they actually are (e.g., "as much as," "up to," "could be")
- Techniques used to win arguments, such as *red herring, ad hominem attack, straw person, glittering generality*, or *begging the question* (Browne & Keeley, 2010); see the glossary on the companion website for definitions of these terms.

Learning media vocabulary is not the objective of media literacy in the sense that a teacher would ask students to memorize lists of words to repeat back on a test. Instead, think of media vocabulary as a tool that enables media literacy. Introduce the vocabulary you need in the context of a specific lesson or project.

SUBLIMINAL MESSAGES AND MEDIA LITERACY

Despite being widely debunked, discussion of subliminals continues to surface in some media literacy circles, with media literacy positioned as an antidote that would enable people to spot the technique of subliminal messaging in much the same way that shining a black light on invisible ink would reveal hidden messages. The notion that media makers could insert images into our subconscious minds against our wills was first popularized by Vance Packard in his 1957 book *The Hidden Persuaders* and in a *Life* magazine report (Brean, 1958) of an experiment by James Vicary in which single frames inserted in a film exhorting moviegoers to drink Coca-Cola and eat popcorn supposedly increased concession sales. When challenged to repeat his movie frame study, Vicary admitted to having falsified data.

In his 1973 book *Subliminal Seduction*, Wilson Bryan Key revived the notion that ads were filled with subliminal messages (especially sexual ones). In 1974 the FCC took the step of banning subliminal messages in broadcast media despite little evidence that advertisers were actually using them and no evidence whatsoever that they worked. Since that time, *subliminal* has been used to refer to a range of purported ways to influence behaviors through the unconscious, including backward lyrics in rock music and self-help tapes designed for just about anything from losing weight to birth control.

Subliminal perception is a legitimate phenomenon; the term refers to processing that occurs below (*sub*) the threshold (*limin*) of conscious perception. Thus, a single frame of a film is subliminal because it occurs too fast to be consciously recognized, no matter how hard you try. However, the conditions under which subliminal messages influence human responses are very limited and typically happen only in highly controlled situations (see, for example, Bahrami, Lavie, & Rees, 2007; Strahan, Spencer, & Zanna, 2002). This is quite different from the typical claims made about "hidden" images or words in ice cubes and other ambiguous content in ads.

Advertisers certainly can and often do use airbrushing techniques to alter images in advertisements, but if you can "see" them once they are pointed out to you, then they weren't really subliminal to begin with. There probably are individuals (including bored employees) who have inserted messages into single frames in films or purposely airbrushed hidden messages into print ads as a joke, but that's far different from a wide-ranging conspiracy on the part of advertisers to unfairly influence us without our being able to protect ourselves against those techniques. Similarly, while someone could insert words into an audio track that are played backward or below the audio threshold, masked by music or white noise, scientific research shows that the claims about these techniques' influence on human attitudes and behaviors are solely due to a placebo effect (i.e., they work because we believe they will work).

Figure 2.6 Subtle ≠ Subliminal: What do you notice in this image?

International Coffee Ad (Viennese)

Source: General Foods International Coffee, *Better Homes and Gardens*, April 1993.

In fact, what many people label as "subliminal" is really just evidence of superficial processing of media messages. A media-literate person can apply the tools and techniques of media analysis—as well as general critical thinking skills—to notice things that a person who has not been trained to "read" images might miss. However, it has nothing to do with "hidden" messages. For example, take a quick look at the magazine ad shown in Figure 2.6.

Did you notice a dancing couple? (If not, look again at the steam). There is nothing subliminal about this image—it is subtle, but not below the threshold of your perception. Yet many people who read this book won't have noticed the couple in the steam before we pointed it out. Not noticing something doesn't make it subliminal. And just as an experienced reader notices more nuances in a novel than a beginner, the more media literate you are, the more visual details you are likely to notice. So if we increase your literacy by letting you in on some background information—that the campaign from which this ad was taken always included images in the steam—you will probably be able to recognize the "hidden" images in Figure 2.7 right away because you have the context and the tools for examination.

Figure 2.7 Now that you're more "literate," what do you see?

International Coffee Ad (Irish)

With students, you would want to do more than just point out things they might have missed. Using an inquiry-based method, you would want to open up the discussion by asking students to name other communication techniques they notice and encouraging them to think about the purposes of those features. So, for example, a good first step would be to notice that the first coffee ad uses a lot of warm brown tones (see color ad on companion website). But just noticing isn't enough. You would want to discuss why this would be advantageous to General Foods (which makes International Coffees). Why would this company want to convey a feeling rather than simply provide information about the product? Or you might want to help students become more literate by pointing out production issues. For example, it is difficult to photograph steam, so where steam is included in an ad, it is very likely to have been drawn in or computer enhanced.

Source: General Foods International Coffee, *Reform Judaism,* Fall 1995.

So media literacy is not about teaching people to "spot subliminals" but, rather, about teaching people to "read" and think critically about the techniques that media makers use to communicate and persuade. In other words, it is about making people more literate. CP6.3

3

What Is Media Literacy Education?

Media literacy education is about fashioning teaching methods that connect the dots between the vision of media literacy mapped out in the previous chapter and what actually happens in classrooms. Given the range of aspirations for media literacy, this is a significant challenge.

Many media literacy educators have defined their task primarily in terms of teaching about media, with a heavy emphasis on analyzing and critiquing media messages.[1] Certainly, the ability to deconstruct a range of media forms and content is absolutely central to media literacy education, but there's much more to it than that. To achieve media literacy's broader goals for students—developing a desire to question and enabling them to be open to changing their opinions in light of new information, to communicate effectively in a variety of media modalities, and to reflect and act on new understanding—we need to shift the focus from teaching about media to framing media literacy education as a rich and integrated process in which students and teachers learn from one another how to be literate in a media world. This framing helps avoid potential mismatches between media literacy goals and classroom practice.

Like traditional literacy—which teaches students to read and write so they can experience the pleasure of books and enables other types of learning and accomplishment—media literacy can enhance enjoyment of a wide range of media content, provide students (and their teachers) with a deeper understanding of themselves and their world, and instill the confidence to use that insight to act. This chapter explains how.

THE PURPOSE OF MEDIA LITERACY EDUCATION

As with all good curriculum design, we start media literacy education with specific outcomes in mind and then craft strategies that help students reach those goals. Our starting point has been summarized by the National Association for Media Literacy Education (NAMLE): "The purpose of media literacy education is to help individuals of all ages to develop the habits of inquiry and skills of expression that they need to be critical thinkers, effective communicators, and active citizens in today's world" (see Appendix A). In this statement, the goals are to create "critical thinkers," "effective communicators," and "active citizens,"[2] and the strategies to get there will fall into two categories: "habits of inquiry" and "skills of expression."

As we explore those strategies, seasoned educators will find things that are both familiar and new because in a literacy-based and curriculum-driven approach, media literacy education is grounded in existing educational practice. Two of the six Core Principles in NAMLE's *Core Principles of Media Literacy in the United States* (Appendix A) describe that model:

> **CP2. Media Literacy Education expands the concept of literacy (i.e., reading and writing) to include all forms of media.**

> **CP3. Media Literacy Education builds and reinforces skills for learners of all ages. Like print literacy, those skills necessitate integrated, interactive, and repeated practice.**

We will return to the curriculum-integration implications of these Core Principles at the end of this chapter, but we encourage you to keep them in mind as you think about how you might integrate "habits of inquiry" and "skills of expression" into your own teaching.

DEVELOPING HABITS OF INQUIRY

To some people, the phrase *habits of inquiry* might seem like a contradiction in terms. After all, habits are often actions we repeat so routinely that we do them unconsciously, without thinking, which would be the opposite of our goal. But if we can instill inquiry as a habit, then higher-order thinking skills will serve as a permanent filter through which students process the world.

Brain-based educators will recognize that what we are seeking is a meld of what psychologist Ellen Langer (1989) describes as "mindfulness" and taxon system memory. Mindfulness is about attending to nuance and modifying routines to account for changing contexts, circumstances, and new information. As Caine et al. (1999) note, "memories stored in taxon systems tend to be automatic and repeatable, even under pressure" (p. 173). Like a reader being able to recognize the letter *f*, these memories become so routine that they are unavoidable (i.e., once we know what an *f* is and what it symbolizes, our brains won't let us encounter that particular squiggle and not see it as a letter of the alphabet associated with a particular sound).

Mindfulness would suggest that we can be flexible in the use of such automatic memories. So a basketball player with an excellent three-point shot from the corner can modify her stroke to cope with an injury or shoot from a different part of the floor to get around a particular defense. But her ability to do so starts with establishing in taxon memory the mechanics of how to make a jump shot, and that requires practice. It is this essential role of repetition in creating automatic memory that explains why media literacy education cannot be delivered in a one-time or occasional lesson and expect to succeed in creating habits of inquiry. [CP3.2]

It is the "mindfulness" part of the equation that explains why inquiry is at the heart of everything that media literacy educators do. In fact, inquiry is so central to media literacy education that it is actually listed first among NAMLE's Core Principles:

CP1. Media Literacy Education requires active inquiry and critical thinking about the messages we receive and create.

And because inquiry is so important, media literacy educators spend a significant amount of time helping students learn to ask questions, not just when students are analyzing media that other people have made, but also—as Core Principle 1 notes—when they create media.[3] [CP2.1]

But just asking questions is not enough. As Elizabeth Thoman and Tessa Jolls (2005b) of the Center for Media Literacy have noted, "To become media literate is not to memorize facts or statistics about the media, but rather, to learn to raise the *right* [emphasis added] questions about what you are watching, reading, or listening to" (p. 190). In other words, it is important that students learn to ask *useful* questions. The axiom that the quality of the answers you get depends on the quality of the questions you ask is true.

NAMLE's Core Principles describe quality questions as "the specific types of questions that will allow students to gain a deeper or more sophisticated understanding of media messages." [CP1.2] The questions that media literacy educators pose in order to meet that goal have morphed over the years.

Historically, media literacy education emphasized analysis of film and television, and, accordingly, the questions tended to reflect theories from mass communications about audience and storytelling techniques. So, for example, in 1989 the British Film Institute posed a set of categories and what it called "signpost questions" (Bazalgette, 1989, p. 8):

- WHO is communicating with whom? (AGENCIES)
- WHAT type of text is it? (CATEGORIES)
- HOW is it produced? (TECHNOLOGIES)
- HOW do we know what it means? (LANGUAGES)
- WHO receives it and what sense do they make of it? (AUDIENCES)
- HOW does it present its subject? (REPRESENTATIONS)

These questions continue to serve as a core around which media literacy education is constructed, but in the same way that traditional literacy is no longer adequate for a media world, these questions could not address all the needs of an expanding array of educators. So various sets of questions have emerged over the years, each modified to meet specific needs.

For example, Canadian educators quickly added questions to help students consider societal consequences of media messages,[4] and several years ago Project Look Sharp was the first to add a specific question about credibility. The Center for Media Literacy's MediaLit Kit (Thoman & Jolls, 2005a), with which many US educators are familiar, limits its list to five questions in order to create a one-to-one correspondence with what it identifies as five key concepts about media.

USING THE NAMLE KEY QUESTIONS

To incorporate issues raised by new media technologies and link analysis to the broader goals of media literacy, in 2007 NAMLE developed an expanded set of questions. More than any other media literacy tool, this set of *Key Questions for Analyzing Media Messages* forms the foundation for building habits of inquiry about media messages.

The Key Questions grid (Table 3.1) is designed to provide both guidance and flexibility. Notice that it is divided into three columns:

1. The far left column uses foundational divisions from the field of mass communications. As you move to the right, you can see which types of questions flow from each division.

2. The center column divides those areas into ten categories of inquiry. These categories are not only physically in the center of the grid but are central to its approach. A media-literate person knows how to ask questions in each of the areas and does so routinely. We discuss each of these categories individually below.

3. The right-hand column suggests possible questions. [CP1.2] There are two very important things to understand about these questions:

   - They are opening prompts that are designed to lead into longer inquiries. For example, we don't ask, "Who made this?" just to have a name to memorize but because knowing who produced a message provides information that enhances students' understanding or increases their ability to engage in deeper inquiry.
   - You don't need to use the exact wording on the grid. In fact, the grid assumes that teachers and students will adapt wording to match the developmental needs of students and the specific content of the subject area or lesson. For example, instead of asking, "Why was this made?" a kindergarten teacher might teach her students to ask the more developmentally appropriate question "What does this want me to do?"

Question Categories

To determine when to ask different types of questions and how to follow up on them in class discussions, it is useful to consider what the topics of inquiry in the grid's center column reveal.

Table 3.1 Key Questions to Ask When Analyzing Media Messages

KEY QUESTIONS TO ASK WHEN ANALYZING MEDIA MESSAGES		
AUDIENCE & AUTHORSHIP	AUTHORSHIP	Who made this message?
	PURPOSE	Why was this made?
		Who is the target audience (and how do you know)?
	ECONOMICS	Who paid for this?
	IMPACT	Who might benefit from this message?
		Who might be harmed by it?
		Why might this message matter to me?
	RESPONSE	What kinds of actions might I take in response to this message?
MESSAGES & MEANINGS	CONTENT	What is this about (and what makes you think that)?
		What ideas, values, information, and/or points of view are overt? Implied?
		What is left out of this message that might be important to know?
	TECHNIQUES	What techniques are used?
		Why were those techniques used?
		How do they communicate the message?
	INTERPRETATIONS	How might different people understand this message differently?
		What is my interpretation of this and what do I learn about myself from my reaction or interpretation?
REPRESENTATIONS & REALITY	CONTEXT	When was this made?
		Where or how was it shared with the public?
	CREDIBILITY	Is this fact, opinion, or something else?
		How credible is this (and what makes you think that)?
		What are the sources of the information, ideas, or assertions?

Source: National Association for Media Literacy Education (NAMLE), *Core Principles of Media Literacy Education in the United States* (2007), http://www.namle.net/core-principles/.

Authorship CP1.1a

- Knowing who created a media message is often the first step in understanding purpose and determining credibility.

- There is frequently more than one answer to questions about Authorship. Naming the people (at least by job title) who produce things like newscasts, films, or games can help students learn about what it takes to create different types of media and serve as a reminder that members of the same team may have different (and even conflicting) purposes for making a particular media message.

- Authorship questions are also especially important in an online world where anonymity is common. Even when there is no way to determine exactly who created an online message, asking about Authorship can remind students of the array of possible answers. Rather than accepting anonymous postings at face value, they will at least wonder why a person or group might want to remain anonymous. An initial question about Authorship could lead to a deep discussion about when it is ethical or unethical to share media messages anonymously.

Purpose CP1.1c

- Questions about Purpose are often asked in conjunction with questions about Authorship. To encourage critical thinking, we want students to understand that human beings are complex and often act from multiple, even conflicting, motives. So the goal of the question isn't to find a single answer but to identify many possibilities and then use what students know about purpose to judge credibility and value. At the same time, strong-sense critical thinking would lead us to avoid using Purpose questions to deem material automatically as being without merit (e.g., "Is this is trying to sell me something? If so, I can dismiss everything it says without evaluating the specific claims it makes."). CP1.3, 4.12

- Considering the target audience for a message often helps to reveal a media maker's intentions. Furthermore, noticing the production choices that are made in order to appeal to particular audiences can help students become aware of cultural assumptions and stereotypes and, when appropriate, challenge them. For example, a student who concludes that girls are the target audience for a particular toy because the box is pink would be correct, but high-quality media literacy would extend the analysis to help students understand that the link between color and gender isn't natural and may limit their ability to make independent choices by pressuring them to conform to an imposed standard. So follow-up questions might probe whether it's true that only girls like pink, why in the United States pink is typically associated with girls and whether that is true in the rest of the world, and why marketers might repeat something that reinforces gender stereotypes. For more on how target audience questions can be used to explore stereotypes, see the "White Towel" lesson plan in Chapter 7.

Economics

- Economics questions identify funders and help students make reasoned arguments about whether or how sponsors' interests influence content.

- Deeper analysis requires students to look beyond individual media messages to media structures. [CP4.7] It would be impossible for students to understand the media culture that they live in without understanding the role that money plays in shaping the media they use. In the United States, it is especially important for students to understand that by legislative design, most media are privately owned, and as a result only a handful of corporations control nearly all mass media.[5] Corporations even own most of the sites on which independent, user-generated content is shared. For example, Facebook defines the parameters of your personal page (and can gather data about you and sell it to others), and YouTube can decide to respond to some complaints by removing content while ignoring others. Media analysis is rarely complete without considering the economic issues involved.

Impact

- Questions about benefits and harms are the essence of critical literacy. They implicitly acknowledge that media have power, and these questions provide a way to deepen the analysis so that students look at broad cultural or societal concerns, especially in terms of inequities and social injustice. [CP5]

- Questions about Impact can make the difference between reading, viewing, or hearing and analyzing. For example, it isn't enough to spot the use of a stereotype; it is also important to think about the consequences of the repetition of that stereotype, both on the targeted group and on the group that is deemed the "norm" or is privileged as a result of the stereotype. That's why it is important to ask about benefits or advantages as well as harms or disadvantages.

- Asking "Why might this matter to me?" integrates the Reflection aspect of media literacy into analysis and helps students connect the issues they study to their own lives, a prerequisite for opening up the possibility that they might act on what they learn. (See "Defining *Media Literacy*: A Set of Capabilities" in Chapter 2.)

- This is the category that provides an entrée into discussions of media effects. Entering such discussions in the context of interrelated questions helps educators avoid making blanket statements about media effects, thus giving the false impression that research conclusions are undisputable facts. It also encourages students to bring strong-sense critical thinking skills to media-effects claims by examining the validity of methods, the choice of issues, or the differences between news reporting on research and the research itself. [CP1.3]

Response

- This category of questions ties analysis to real-world action. Asking students what they might do in response to what they have learned requires an attentiveness to media that encourages a sense of responsibility and helps students see that they have opportunities to influence their world. That vision, and the actions that flow from it, can be an exceptionally important outlet for emotions raised by media analysis.

- As media analysis leads students to new insights, it can also challenge established beliefs and raise feelings of anger or frustration as students realize they have been mistaken or manipulated. Educators who ignore those feelings risk having anger morph into cynicism or having frustration overshadow students' sense that they have the power to act. By incorporating Response questions into media analysis, teachers open the door to agency and productive expression, which diffuse anger.

Content CP1.1d

- At the most fundamental level, Content questions are about the Understanding aspect of media literacy. Can students distinguish between different types of media (e.g., an organization's website that includes selected news stories versus a newspaper's website)? Do they understand the basic message(s) in what they see, hear, and read?

- Content questions also address the Awareness aspect of media literacy by revealing implied or covert messages. For example, nearly all third graders can tell you that a TV commercial is trying to sell something. But without practice in inquiry, they probably won't understand that the commercial may also convey value messages about things like beauty, materialism, or success. And they may not spot advertising that isn't in the form of a traditional commercial (e.g., recognizing that a Ronald McDonald balloon in the Macy's Thanksgiving Day parade is also an ad for McDonald's and that the entire parade is an ad for Macy's).

- This category also provides teachers with an opportunity to customize questions for particular subject areas. For example, "Where is this novel set, and how do you know?" is a Content question, as is a question like "What did the speaker mean when he said, 'Evolution is a theory'?"

- The Content category also includes questions about what is left out of messages that is important to know. Sometimes this is about spotting attempts to mislead (e.g., a major polluter circulates a video news release touting the company's new "green" certified headquarters without disclosing that it has been repeatedly fined for violating environmental protection laws).

- In other circumstances, Content questions address "agenda setting," that is, who has the power to control what gets reported (or omitted) and therefore has the power to select what is and isn't important enough to know about. By determining what people do and don't hear or talk about, agenda setters make some things seem normal while marginalizing other things.[6] For this purpose, the Content question is extended beyond "What is the message?" to ask "Why would they be conveying this particular message at this time?" or "Why *this* message and not some other message?" Follow-up questions might look at who is interviewed or labeled as an expert, which people get to speak for themselves, or what counts as knowledge. The discussion can delve even deeper with follow-up questions about whose voices or perspectives are presented and whose are rendered invisible, leading to questions about who gains and who suffers because of those choices. [CP4.5] For a noteworthy example of an initiative that uses questions about omissions to address agenda setting, see the Project Censored website (www.projectcensored.org), which provides an annual list of significant stories that mainstream news outlets underreported or didn't report at all. [CP4.1]

Techniques [CP1.1b]

- Technique identification is about learning the languages that different types of media use to communicate. Recognizing language choices helps students to become more effective decision makers as they communicate their own messages.

- Questions about Techniques are often tied to identification of target audience. Noticing how media change language or style for different target audiences can help students understand how to adapt their own language for various purposes (e.g., using one language for tweets and another for essays).

Interpretations [CP1.1e]

- This category acknowledges that audiences negotiate meaning. [CP6] Explicitly asking students to think about the fact that everyone interprets media through the lens of his or her own experience underscores the fact that interpretation is not automatic or entirely predictable.

- Interpretations questions can provide practice in perspective taking, generate appreciation for diversity, spark discussions where students learn to challenge one another in respectful ways, and expect (and provide) document-based evidence to support opinions. [CP4.4]

- To connect Interpretations with the Reflection aspect of media literacy, we also ask students what they learn about themselves from their reaction to media messages. This type of Interpretations question generates Awareness of how students' existing assumptions, visual cues, or belief systems influence the meaning they make. Such Awareness is vital for analysis because every person processes the world from an existing set of mental models and all learning is about adding to, altering, confirming, testing, or abandoning those models and replacing them with new ones. For example, at one of Faith's workshops, she asked teachers to analyze an illustration to determine the socioeconomic status of Arthur, the anthropomorphized aardvark from Marc Brown's children's books and TV series. One participant found herself explaining that the character couldn't be poor because he and his home were clean and orderly. As soon as she said it out loud she realized that the cues she was using to make judgments were faulty, based on unwarranted assumptions about the values held by those with limited financial resources. The insight about her existing mental model led her to alter that model and changed forever the way she viewed her students and their families.

Context

- Media messages don't appear in isolation; people don't just play one video game or listen to one song. By tying a media document to concurrent events and to other media, Context questions help students recognize patterns in media experiences and consider their cumulative and interrelated effects.

- We also ask about when or how something was shared with the public to provide context about media forms, structures, and ownership. CP4.7 Where did the message appear? Was it from an independent, corporate, or government source, and how might that have affected its content or form? Did it reach a lot of people or only a few?

- Historians always ask Context questions about when a document was created because the date can confirm its authenticity (e.g., the content matches a known sequence of events) and provide important insight about motives (e.g., What was going on at the time that made a publisher think people would be interested in this story?). In addition, because the meaning of terms and images can change over time (e.g., *gay* once meant "carefree") and figures and data can change over time (e.g., in 1968, if 100 million people had tuned in to a TV show, half the US population would have been watching the same show, while today that same number would be less than a third of the nation's population), knowing when something was created is essential for accurate interpretation. Another way to get at changes in context over time is to ask a follow-up question like "Why do you think this document was saved?" Asking questions about publication dates is an especially important discernment tool online, where things can circulate for a long time after they are completely out-of-date.

Credibility

- Credibility questions provide students with an opportunity to practice discerning opinion from fact. This can be especially important in an environment where popular news is increasingly a mashup of reporting, commentary, and entertainment and for online searches that are likely to result in a list including personal websites and blogs as well as educational and news sources.

- Credibility questions also provide a chance to explore nuance. For example, some sources can be credible on one topic without being credible on another. The hosts of a cooking show may be very credible on the characteristics that define a high-quality knife or pan, but that doesn't necessarily make them a good choice for advice on how to invest your savings. We want students to understand that information sources may be true or false, but they may also be some combination of the two.

- This category includes important questions about sources, including being aware of one's own sources ("Where did I get that idea?") and understanding that the sources we rely on have sources of their own. Source questions also provide an opportunity for teachers in different subject areas to help students learn the questions that are used to determine what is credible in particular fields. For example, a social studies teacher might ask, "Is this a primary or secondary source?" In science, the question might be about whether valid experimental methods were used to obtain results.

REFLECTION: *YOUR OWN KEY QUESTIONS*

These questions are designed to help people examine a wide range of media messages in many different contexts. Which questions seem most intriguing or useful to you? Which will be the easiest or hardest for you to integrate into your teaching? Are there other Key Questions that should be asked that aren't included on this list?

Notes on Using the Key Questions

In the next chapter, we explore specific ways to use these Key Questions to facilitate a media document decoding. In addition to the specific techniques you will find there, here are some general points to remember:

- **The way that questions are phrased matters.** As you adapt the grid's questions or create your own, the words you use are important because they shape the discussion. Whenever possible, wording should leave open the possibility that there is more than one answer. So, for example, instead of "Who made this and what was his or her purpose?" which suggests that there is just one author and just one purpose, we ask questions that can have multiple answers such as "Who made this?" and "Why was this made?"

- **Questions can be asked in any order.** Think of the grid in digital rather than linear terms and use the goal(s) of your lesson to determine an appropriate starting point. For example, Just Think, a pioneering US media-literacy project that focused on youth media production, always began its decodings with a Response question, asking "What feelings does this bring up for you?" before moving on to questions about Techniques and Purpose. Alternatively, in Chapter 4 we start a decoding with a question that ties directly to the curriculum rather than one of the questions from the media literacy grid (see Decoding Demonstration Example 1 from *Discovery of the Mississippi by de Soto* on page 75). Your choice of questions and sequence should reflect your own educational goals, the nature of the media document being analyzed or created, the age of the students, and the context in which the questions are being used.

- **You probably won't ask every type of question in every lesson.** So, for example, second graders might be very interested in exploring messages about money in their new "math" coloring books (a Content question) and discussing why their local bank might have donated the coloring books to their class (a Purpose question), but asking a Context question such as "When was this made?" probably won't be relevant to their exploration. That said, to become skilled critical thinkers in a multimedia world, students need to be able to ask questions from all of the categories, so teachers will want to provide opportunities to ask many different types of questions. When teachers integrate media literacy as a common practice throughout the school year, this is not difficult to accomplish.

- **Always follow up with a request for evidence.** [CP1.4] Until students internalize the process of inquiry and provide evidence without prompting, nearly every question should end with "What makes you say that?" or "What's your evidence for that in the document?" Not only does this get students in the habit of backing up their conclusions with evidence, but having to identify specific sources of proof (e.g., the document itself, their personal experience, research, another media source, or another person) helps them gain awareness about who or what they rely on most to shape their beliefs.

- **Leave room for students' own questions.** It is always an option to begin by asking, "What questions do you have about this media message?" and/or end by asking, "What else do you want to know?" This invites students into the process and lets them know that their questions have value. [CP4.8]

With so many types of questions to master, the task of inquiry can initially seem daunting. But when questions are integrated routinely into classwork, they eventually become second nature. Students who can use the categories are able to make meaning in new and more profound ways, extending the benefits of inquiry well beyond the walls of the classroom.

Why These Questions?

If our goal was simply to create proficient readers, viewers, or listeners, we could be satisfied with teaching students to spot production Techniques or use the language of semiotics to describe how a media message was constructed. And if media appreciation was a central goal, you might expect to see "What did you like?" as one of the Key Questions.[7] But media literacy education is much broader than media decoding and appreciation. Consider these Core Principles:

> **CP4. Media Literacy Education develops informed, reflective, and engaged participants essential for a democratic society.**

> **CP5. Media Literacy Education recognizes that media are a part of culture and function as agents of socialization.**

These statements acknowledge that if we want students to become critical thinkers and active citizens, we need to help them think beyond themselves and beyond the interpretation of any single media document to reflect on the social, economic, and political implications of media. It is the *combination* of questions in all the categories that provides students with a way to zoom out from a narrow focus on specific production techniques to see media documents in their broader cultural context and to envision possibilities for action. Like lookout posts in a well-built castle, media literacy questions should provide strategically placed windows from which to scan the culture in which we live, see its systems and structures, and respond accordingly.

So, for example, a Techniques question might help students see how a specific media document uses statistics to make a particular point. When inquiry also incorporates Authorship, Purpose, Impact, Credibility, and Content questions, students would ask the kind of questions that sociologist Joel Best (2008) recommends: How are these numbers socially constructed? Who produced them? What did they choose to count? How did they go about counting? Why did they go to the trouble? So media literacy education isn't just about what students notice in a media document but also about their ability to understand the document's significance in creating or supporting a particular worldview.

Likewise, media literacy education isn't about asking *if* there is a bias in a particular message because there is *always* bias in human communication. Simply being able to spot the existence of a bias is a dead end in terms of inquiry or discussion. Instead, as Core Principle 1.6 states, media literacy education teaches students to ask what the "substance, source, and significance of a bias might be." CP1.6

CRITICAL LITERACY

Critical literacy has provided important insights into this part of media literacy education. It uses the range and depth of media literacy questions to enable students to step back and see the constructed nature of media and how messages relate to equity or justice.

Students rarely develop critical literacy skills on their own because, as Jeff Share (2009) astutely observes, "the manner in which media cloak their role in reproducing hegemony as merely entertainment or information tends to hamper critical analysis of the inequalities of power in society and our relationships with media" (p. 14). So one of the very important things that media literacy questions can do is to give students the tools to pull back the curtain and see that media are not benign.

Once students can see the structures and patterns, they can exercise autonomy and opt to accept or reject agendas presented in media. As philosopher of education Douglas Kellner (1995) explains, critical literacy "gives individuals power over their culture . . . enabling people to create their own meanings, identities, and to shape and transform the material and social conditions of their culture and society" (p. xv). Viewed through this perspective, media literacy inquiry is not just about personal interpretation but also about recognizing the ways in which media can fortify a status quo that serves their own interests, often at the expense of competing interests.

Done well, such inquiry reveals to students a more accurate picture of the world than they would otherwise get from mainstream mass media. However, as educators we need to keep in mind that to achieve critical autonomy, students have to be free to come to conclusions that are not only independent of media influences but also independent of us.

We are not suggesting that teachers need to be "objective" (which is impossible) or that they should back away from partnering with students in the learning process by refusing to share their own views. Rather, skilled media literacy educators understand classroom dynamics; they know when it is appropriate to voice their own opinions and when doing so would inhibit critical inquiry. High school teacher Chris Sperry (2006a) describes it this way:

> If my students suspect that I am trying to teach them which media messages to believe and which to reject, I will break their trust. My behavior in the classroom must communicate that I value independence of thought backed by sincere and informed reflection. (p. 11)

Teachers who repeatedly give predetermined interpretations of media messages rob students of the opportunity to grapple with evidence and come to their own conclusions. Rather than mastering the skills needed to interpret for themselves, those students become accustomed to waiting for the teacher to do the work for them. Instead of developing the higher-order thinking skills that are at the heart of media literacy education, they come to see their job as memorizing what the "expert" says and repeating it back. Such students may test well, but they don't become autonomous, skilled thinkers. Drawing on the philosophies of Paulo Freire, Masterman (1985) explains: "If one of the major objectives of media education is the development of critical autonomy, then any pedagogy which makes students dependent upon the teacher will be counterproductive" (p. 28).

Because critical autonomy is an important outcome, there is reason to be cautious about fully embracing a critical literacy approach to media literacy education.[8] Advocates of critical literacy sometimes slip into a determinism that can actually steer students away from independent thought. Their division of the world into dualistic categories of oppressors and oppressed can lead students to see the world as less complex than it actually is.[9] In this dichotomous approach, media and the public are sometimes positioned in oppositional ways, with media designated as the only side with power.

However, as the final NAMLE Core Principle states:

CP6. Media Literacy Education affirms that people use their individual skills, beliefs, and experiences to construct their own meanings from media messages.

Australian media literacy scholar Barrie McMahon (2003) puts it this way: "Although the media are the agenda setters and offer preferred readings of their texts, they do not make the meanings for us. Ultimately we make our own meanings" (p. 3). Showing students that they have the power to act is one of the major components of media literacy education. Critical literacy can play a significant role in that process because, as UNESCO (2008) explains, it "teaches people to ask why things are the way they are and to take autonomous action to change them" (p. 1). But it must do so in a way that opens students to the possibility of pursuing social justice rather than by imposing critical literacy's social justice agenda.

When rigid ideology obscures complexity, it creates what Langer (1989) calls "category traps" that limit thinking to what will fit into the mind's preset notions of how the world works. Even when such ideological filters are built from ideas that we find appealing, they are still traps that inhibit critical thinking. In contrast, media literacy educators strive to instill in students an openness to new ways of thinking accompanied by rigorous use of evidence to test the validity of new ideas.

Despite its weaknesses, critical literacy makes important contributions to media literacy education. It can prevent self-reflection from turning into self-absorption or self-importance, and it can keep analysis focused on gaining insights about how one is positioned in relationship to the rest of the world. In addition, there are ways to embrace critical literacy's investigation of root causes, injustice, and inequity without being tripped up by its pitfalls.

For example, a health teacher might begin a billboard decoding with middle school students by asking, "What techniques does this use to encourage people to smoke?" If the discussion stops there, students—especially budding adolescents who often eagerly embrace oppositional positions and who already know that cigarette ads are intended to get people to buy cigarettes—may walk away thinking, "Everyone is just trying to fool us and make us do what they want, so I won't believe anything anymore." CP4.2

But consider the shifts that can occur if the discussion continues with questions like "Who benefits from people continuing to smoke?" and "Who benefits from people *not* smoking?" A class discussion about the fact that many people make money from cigarette sales—including less obvious beneficiaries like governments that rely on tobacco sales-tax revenue, ad agency employees, and the people who work at the local convenience store that sells cigarettes—can help students begin to think about the role that tobacco plays in their community, the economy, and their society rather than just about their own personal decisions to smoke or not.

And the discussion can dig even deeper with questions like "If it is harmful, why does the government allow it?" "If a product is dangerous, what responsibility do the people who make money from it have to disclose the dangers or pay for damages?" and "Where do values like the freedom to sell or use whatever products you want come into play?" Media literacy depends on these deeper questions to help students become critical thinkers and place them in the position of being able to make a positive contribution to their community as active citizens.

DEVELOPING SKILLS OF EXPRESSION

Key Questions are also featured in media literacy education's approach to skills of expression. As with reading, the writing side of media literacy education is an expansion of traditional literacy that remains focused on developing skills that will create "critical thinkers, effective communicators, and active citizens in today's world" (see Appendix A).

Creating Effective Communicators
for Today's World

In addition to students learning to communicate for many different purposes—persuasion, information, creative expression, etc.—media literacy education adds the dimension of learning to "write" using many different types of media. This doesn't mean just providing students with opportunities to create a video, website, podcast, multimedia presentation, or any of the dozens of other possibilities that media technologies make possible. And it isn't about providing students who have weak writing skills an "out" by allowing them to complete assignments using non-text-based communication, though that might be an appropriate way to provide differentiated instruction in some situations.

Rather, it is about equipping all students with the ability to communicate using text, image, and audio and enabling them to discern which types of communication—including nonmediated methods—are best for specific audiences, purposes, and circumstances. This includes not just selecting among various media but also understanding how and when to combine them (e.g., not just adding a graph or chart to a report but knowing when a graphic representation of data would be more compelling than words and knowing how to use the text to direct readers to graphic information).

The need to incorporate new communication technologies does not necessitate abandoning tried-and-true methods of teaching students to communicate. Many common writing strategies support media literacy goals. For example, freewriting and storytelling offer students opportunities for Creation with their own voice, portfolios or journaling support Reflection, and collaborative projects or peer review gives students a way to engage in Participation. Media literacy builds on, rather than replaces, these strategies.

The task of giving students access to multiple communication tools may seem daunting to some teachers, implying that they need to master every new technology in order to teach it to their students. In fact, as long as digital media continue to evolve at a rapid pace, asking teachers to know how to use every gadget or software program is obviously silly. So media literacy education suggests a different strategy. Teachers need to be open to the use of new technologies and keep up with advances enough to know (roughly) what is possible, including the strengths and weaknesses of available tools, CP1.1b how much time certain types of activities are likely to take, the potential for particular tools to improve (and not just change) instruction, and how they might assess student work created with various media technologies. The actual use of the technologies is likely to be determined by availability of equipment, space, and time and a willingness on the part of educators to relinquish some of their traditional classroom power to collaborate with students (who often discover new tools long before a teacher has an opportunity to introduce them in class).

By *collaboration*, we mean students and teachers exploring new technologies together, rather than teachers assuming that students have all the information and that educators need to do all the learning. In fact, while some students may know more about some technologies than their teachers, it is a myth that all students know how to use media technologies well,[10] especially for purposes beyond social networking and gaming. Even when students are using media with which teachers are not fluent, teachers will need to play the role of guide and be prepared to ask important questions.

Creating Critical Thinkers for Today's World

In media literacy education, inquiry is as much a part of the process of communicating as it is of analyzing media that others have made. Whether they are writing a traditional essay, making a poster advertising a school event, creating a Facebook page, or producing a complex multimedia presentation with video and sound, students should be asking themselves Key Questions about the Purpose, Audience, Impact, Credibility, and so forth. of the media they create. In this version of the Key Questions, the wording is designed to help students reflect on their own choices:

- *Content:* "What messages and impressions do I want to convey?"
- *Response:* "What kinds of actions do I want my audience to take in response to this message?"
- *Purpose and Context:* "Who is my target audience, and where or how will I share this with them?"

The complete grid for *Key Questions to Ask When Producing Media Messages* is available on the book's website.

There are several benefits to integrating such reflection into writing and production lessons, not the least of which is that doing so instills in students a sense of responsibility for the media they put out into the world. It also provides a hands-on opportunity to apply analysis skills, one of the strongest ways to help students remember what they learn. And it improves analysis skills by providing students an opportunity to encounter the various ways in which media are constructed. For example, a student assigned to create a thirty-second story for a TV or radio newscast quickly learns how editing choices influence message. Without inquiry, students may simply gain an appreciation for the amount of work that goes into producing a newscast. With inquiry, students also gain insight into how the topics about which the public is thinking and talking are shaped by those who control the selection and content of stories.

Creating Active Citizens for Today's World

In a curriculum-driven approach to media literacy education, writing and production activities provide fertile ground for teachers to encourage civic engagement. Assignments that embed choices help students find their own voice, even as they learn essential skills. Development of that voice is foundational for the development of critical autonomy and nurtures the creativity necessary for problem solving in a democracy. And when assignments involve choices about means of expression as well as content, they provide an outlet for creative expression that need not always be verbal or linear. Futurists like Daniel Pink (2005) see such creativity as important to twenty-first-century success, and scholars like Howard Gardner see it as important to developing students' full range of talents.

Some types of writing and production also naturally lend themselves to active citizenship. News writing and persuasion are easy to connect to current events and politics, but as Steven Goodman, founder of New York City's Educational Video Center, has observed, perhaps the most powerful tool for civic engagement is production of documentaries. As Goodman (2003) describes it, when the process is done with rigor, having to look at an issue, person, or community through the lens of a camera or the end of a microphone provides critical distance. And as student producers begin to distance themselves from their documentary subjects,

> the people they see and the problems they live with every day become visible to them as things outside their lives that can be held up to a critical light. They compare the story they have recorded to their own experiences and begin to question its truthfulness and form hypotheses of their own. (p. 42)

As they verify their conclusions through further research, students become participant-observers of their own community. And because they are researching topics that are literally close to home, they often become passionate about what they are doing, paving the way to civic engagement. The power of sharing the results of such projects, especially when the sharing reaches beyond classroom walls, can be transformative—for students and for communities.

In fact, the power of producing for an audience beyond teacher and classmates often improves student performance no matter what the project is. So media literacy education encourages teachers to design assignments that take advantage of media technologies that allow for public sharing of student work and that connect to real-world tasks. Doing so helps students and teachers accomplish the Participation and Action aspects of media literacy, providing opportunities for community engagement, collaborative online projects and conversations, and lessons on digital citizenship.

THE WAY WE TEACH

Whether or not students actually develop habits of inquiry and skills of expression to become critical thinkers, active citizens, and better communicators depends as much on *how* you teach as *what* you teach. [CP4.8] [11]

The simplest summary of how to teach media literacy is "Practice what you preach." If we want students to be strong-sense critical thinkers, for example, then we have to model analyzing all media messages, not just those expressing values that we hope students will reject. [CP1.3] If we expect students to be open-minded and respectful, then we have to be open to the parts of their culture that we may not share or approve of, including their media choices, and we need to learn how to challenge them in respectful ways. [CP2.5] And if we want them to develop critical thinking skills, we can't restrict their school experience to drill and practice or to teaching that rewards rote memorization to the exclusion of creativity and intellectual risk taking.

These types of teaching strategies in media literacy education are strongly reflective of Lev Vygotsky's social constructivist theory in which understanding emerges from dialogue between the teacher and students and learners are engaged in a continuous process of articulating their own views and perspectives in order to negotiate shared meaning (Pena-Pérez, 2000). In media literacy education, teachers scaffold media analysis by providing Key Questions and follow-up probes, then gradually back out of the process so that students can ask their own questions of media messages and reflect on their—and others'—interpretations of them.

For media literacy education to succeed, schools need to create the kind of sociocultural environment that Vygotsky discussed. However, they have not always been places that affirm in day-to-day practice the ideals set out by their mission statements or by teachers. Some have called the environment of schools the "hidden" or "shadow" curriculum, citing circumstances in which adults say that children and learning are a priority but the poor physical condition of a school building sends children the opposite message. Others, as education professor Pamela U. Brown (2005) has noted, lament students' materialism but choose to deal with revenue shortfalls by accepting commercial sponsorship of school buses, curriculum materials, and sports facilities. Media literacy education would teach students to recognize such contradictions if they appeared in media sources, all the more so when they encounter real-life hypocrisy. So, if media literacy educators expect to succeed, they need to understand that students are watching with a skeptical eye and model their ideals accordingly.

Supporting Independence

There are many ways in which teachers inadvertently make students dependent rather than independent. Even those who understand that the ultimate goal of media literacy education is not about teachers asking questions or even about students imitating the teacher's questions but, rather, about students learning to ask questions for themselves, can have trouble discerning when it is time to stop modeling (i.e., cut back on their own questions) and require students to take the lead and initiate the inquiry process themselves. Without the opportunity to practice free of a teacher's "training wheels," students aren't likely to ever develop their own habits of inquiry or skills of expression. Likewise, if teachers always choose the form of communication that students must use to complete assignments, students aren't likely to learn how to choose the best tool for the job.

Some educators also encourage dependency by teaching students to use media literacy questions to reveal one "right" meaning—the meaning favored by the teacher or by a cultural critic featured in a media literacy video or book. But sharing a critique of media without also sharing the skills that students need to critically analyze media for themselves is not sound media literacy education practice. [CP1.5] Media literacy will fail to create a culture of inquiry if it is about teaching students *what* to think rather than *how* to think. [CP1.3]

Another way that teachers encourage dependency is to reserve for themselves the role of "expert." Expertise models have proven to be exceptionally weak in the face of new technologies. As educators, we are accustomed to thinking that we need to learn all of the techniques and information first and then teach them to our students. While that may be true in some curricular areas (e.g., proper scientific lab techniques), when it comes to digital technologies, many students are already far ahead of their teachers—and by the time the teachers learn a technology, it will have changed. And that's okay—we can learn from our students, have them learn from each other, or just provide them with the individual option of applying technologies they are proficient in the assignments we give (and be prepared to marvel at the results). [CP3.4]

Creating a Culture of Inquiry

A variety of classroom practices flow from media literacy education's focus on inquiry, including attention to how a teacher's language affects the message. Phrasing can encourage or discourage inquiry. For example, a video teacher could describe "the right way to frame a shot" or could explain the possible outcomes of framing a shot in a particular way. The former leaves no room for creative interpretation; the latter requires a student to think more deeply about his or her goals and target audience.

Any sports coach knows that if you want an athlete to acquire skills, the athlete needs to be given a chance to practice those skills. Media literacy education is no different, except that the skills can sometimes challenge the status quo in ways that make educators uncomfortable. Teachers can't expect students to use reason if they reject students' well-reasoned, evidence-based opinions any time those opinions run counter to those held by the people in charge. [CP1.4] And it is unreasonable to expect students to act on what they learn or to become active citizens if they are consistently excluded from acting on their beliefs or participating in decision making at their school.

It is also unreasonable to teach students that when it comes to media analysis there can be multiple interpretations, but in all the other academic work there will only be one right answer (and instructors will expect you to pick it out correctly on a multiple-choice test). [CP6.3] School districts that attempt to improve test scores by emphasizing drill and practice or rote memorization at the expense of offering consistent opportunities for students to explore, discuss, ponder, or create are not likely to see students achieve the goals of media literacy education.

By engaging students in group work and project-based learning, by providing opportunities for students to find their own voices and express themselves clearly, and by valuing complexity, media literacy educators can create a climate of respect and teamwork that resonates throughout a school and throughout students' lives. [CP6.4]

Teachers Can't Do It Alone

Great media literacy teachers aren't hard to spot. They are the ones who remain flexible enough to change with the times, [CP2.6] challenge students to ask ever deeper questions, and provide meaningful activities that bridge schoolwork with life outside of class. But even great media literacy teachers can't do it alone.

As with other curricular endeavors, chances of success are dependent, in part, on institutional support. For example, though it is possible to do some media literacy education without computers, cameras, microphones, or Internet connections, effective media literacy education requires classrooms to be equipped with the tools to both analyze and produce media. [CP2.7]

In addition, if school districts are serious about treating media literacy as literacy, then they can't leave it up to one or two heroic "designated hitters." All teachers and support staff (especially library media and technology specialists) should be expected to include media literacy in what they do and should be given the necessary professional development and prep time needed to make that happen.

At a district level, leaders need to recognize that media literacy education can't be a "once and done" topic. Rather, it is an ever-evolving continuum of skills, knowledge, attitude, and actions. CP3.1 The competencies and knowledge involved require a sequenced curriculum over the span of multiple grade levels that is integrated into many types of lessons throughout the year. CP3.2 That takes comprehensive planning and cooperation, which will ultimately involve every stakeholder, and, of course, teachers who are willing to support one another's work.

Avoiding Common Missteps

As you step into the community of media literacy educators, you will find a variety of practices that may be worthwhile but that don't actually support an inquiry- or literacy-based approach to media literacy education. We mention some of them here to help you avoid getting sidetracked.

Media Literacy ≠ Media Reform

Some people see media literacy as a political movement. In our view, as *literacy*, media literacy education may have political consequences, but it is an educational discipline and not a political movement. It unabashedly promotes the tenets of democracy, but it does so without the kind of partisanship that could result in indoctrination rather than helping students to express their own values. CP2.9

Schools cannot reasonably be held accountable for media policy or media quality. What benchmarks would you use? It is not that we don't want to hold the people who make and regulate media accountable; it's just that we don't want to hold *schools* accountable for those who make or regulate media. CP2.10, 4.10, 4.12, 5.6

Of course, taking action is also an integral part of media literacy education, so if a political initiative originates with students, rather than at the direction of a teacher, that would be a sign of success. And one of the actions that media literacy education may inspire is to reform media. But media literacy education will fail in its central goals if it is designed with the explicit intention of reforming media.

Asking Too Few Questions

Sometimes it can be so exciting to watch students notice details that they had previously missed that teachers can forget to ask students to think about why those details matter. Suppose students walked into your class buzzing about the latest "reality" TV series. You help them ask Key Questions, and they discover that reality shows are actually edited—and sometimes explicitly staged—so they aren't as real as they might seem. Or they might find out that a music competition is actually created by a telecommunications company that makes money for every texted vote and that uses the show as research to predict artists' popularity so it can avoid investing in research and development. Those are all important things to know about how these types of media are made, and knowing them improves students' level of Awareness. However, they don't give students much useful information unless students are asked to think about why these particular arrangements might matter.[12] It isn't enough to ask students to look at the "what" without asking them to consider the "So what?" That's why media literacy education analysis does not stop with identification of production techniques.

Using the Wrong Launch Pad

Where you start influences the course you take, and starting from the premise that media are a problem is likely to land you in a place where you are either telling students what to do (rather than helping them find their own voice) or making decisions for students about what media to use or not use. The latter is censorship and, more important, sends students the message that you don't think they are capable of becoming responsible decision makers. Neither approach supports inquiry or literacy or helps students build skills. CP3.7, CP4.11

When your focus is on media as a problem, it is also easy to slip into didactic teaching. Reacting with nonverbal signals (e.g., the sounds of disgust that we call "danger clucks" or rolling one's eyes) to media examples you show or lecturing students about harmful media effects (presumed or actual) is far less effective than teaching students to evaluate research claims or to think through Impact questions for themselves. Adolescents in particular will resist lessons that they perceive as attacking youth culture (or any other part of their identity, including religion, language of origin or ethnicity, and political allegiance) rather than as genuine attempts to help them learn to think independently and critically.

Teaching students to be critical of media is not the same as teaching them to think critically. Rather than convincing students that what you say about media is correct, lecturing about media effects can be heard by students as scolding, which will lead them to shut you out. Or if what you say contradicts their personal experience, they might hear it as a rejection of their culture. Either way, you have failed to get students to hear your message, and you have undermined inquiry in the process. As educator Kevin Maness (2004) observes, "teaching *against* media is not the same as teaching *about* media" (p. 46). That's why media literacy education does not start from a premise that media are inconsequential or that media are a problem. CP5.5 Rather, it acknowledges that media are a part of life and asks students to reflect and think critically about what actions they might take to ensure that the role of media in their lives is a healthy one. CP3.6, 3.5

Making Assumptions About Your Students' Media Use

In a very general sense, statistics about how much time children and adolescents spend using media provide educators with a snapshot that can help them better understand the lives of their students. But be very cautious about relying on such statistics, because

- They can change very quickly and so may easily be out-of-date.
- News reports about media use are often presented with misleading headlines or overgeneralized conclusions; it is always best to identify original research data.[13]

- National media trends may not reflect the habits of your specific students; it would be more informative to ask your students about what media they use and how they use them. Even better, assigning students to investigate and report on their peers' media use provides excellent opportunities to exercise math, research, recording, writing, speaking, listening, and even ethical decision-making skills.

On the occasions when reports about media-use statistics fit into a curriculum-based lesson, you would certainly want to apply media literacy analysis skills to the headlines and the research. Who developed this number and why? Using what research methods? Were those methods valid? Does the number make sense?[14]

FEATURED EXAMPLE

Inquiry-Based Online Safety Education

The need for schools to address cyberbullying and other online safety issues provides an interesting opportunity to explore why the way in which one teaches is as important as what one teaches. Because they concern media, Internet safety initiatives are often included under the banner of media literacy education, but more often than not they use protectionist rather than inquiry-based approaches. This does not have to be the case. We suggest that if the goal is to have students implement safety strategies when adults aren't around, then online safety education should be taught in constructivist ways that emphasize critical inquiry.

The Concerns

There are valid reasons for a certain degree of anxiety around online safety, and schools have a responsibility to help students deal with the negative possibilities of using the Internet or wireless communication devices. Typical concerns fall into three areas:

1. Students may encounter or participate in creating material that can have negative consequences (e.g., revealing salacious images or private information that could be used by predators, marketers, prospective employers, or admissions officers or encountering websites or posts that incite hate, encourage dangerous health practices, attempt to defraud, or reveal developmentally inappropriate content).

2. Students may engage in or become the target of cyberbullying.

3. Students may download malicious material (malware), which can compromise network security and/or damage their own and others' computer systems.

Ineffective Practices

Sometimes fear that students will be harmed clouds the judgment of parents and educational leaders, leading them to throw sound educational practice out the window. Even people who

(Continued)

(Continued)

normally champion higher-order thinking skills sometimes accept the following counterproductive methods for teaching online safety:

- **Ban the technology or use content filters.** This strategy is counter to media literacy education because, while it may keep students safe at school, it won't make them literate. CP2.7 It provides no opportunities for critical thinking, skill development, or the demonstration of responsible behavior. It decreases the chances that students will use online resources effectively because it robs them of an opportunity to receive guidance about safety and ethics from knowledgeable adults who have their best interests at heart. And keeping media technologies or content out of the classroom doesn't keep them out of students' lives; it is a bury-your-head-in-the-sand approach to a very real challenge.

- **Scare students (or their families) with stories of online predators and other dangers.** Fear literally creates a physiological reaction that inhibits learning, so it doesn't make much sense to use scare tactics as an educational strategy for any reason (Fried, 2007). Doing so is a particular problem in media literacy education because the approach fails to assess the accuracy of the danger claims. In fact, a strong-sense critical thinker would quickly discover that the threat from online predators has been greatly exaggerated (see *Frontline's* "Growing Up Online," Dretzin Goodman & Maggio, 2008). Students are much more likely to be put at risk by their own online behaviors or by people they know.

- **Issue a list of dos and don'ts.** Even when the lecture is entertaining or the session is reviewing a thoughtful school online policy, talking at students instead of with them is still didactic instruction and is not likely to accomplish media literacy goals. Consider, for example, these excerpts from "Teaching Online Safety to Students" provided by the American Federation of Teachers (n.d.):

  o Instruct students that they should never, under any circumstances, give out any personal information, including their name, address, or phone number[,] in any type of chat room or on any social networking site. . . .

  o Emphasize that students should never meet someone that they have met online without the permission of their parents. . . .

  o Make sure that students know that people online may not be who they say they are. There is no way of knowing if somebody who claims to be an 11-year-old boy actually is one.

  o Explain to students the benefits of making their social networking sites private.

  o Be sure that students know that their "screen name" should not include personal information. Do not use birthdays, hometowns, etc.

  o Tell students that once they post information online, they cannot take it back. Even if they delete their information, it still exists on older versions of the site on other computers.

  o Caution students that if they want to post photos of themselves on social networking sites, they should limit access to their site to "friends only" and make sure the photos are appropriate and will not cause embarrassment to themselves or others. Every photo they post can easily become "public property," so students need to act accordingly. . . .

  Putting aside the fact that these instructions are primarily strategies for preventing contact with potential predators—the least common danger that children face on the Internet—there is a lot of important information here. But teachers are "telling," "explaining," and "cautioning" rather than "engaging," "exploring," or "asking." That negates what could be an opportunity for dialogue and makes it easy for students to dismiss the topic as just one more set of facts to memorize and repeat back rather than view it as anything they feel compelled to act on.

Inquiry-Based Media Literacy Strategies

As respected educators Carol Ann Tomlinson and Jay McTighe (2006) remind us, "Learning happens *within* students, not *to* them" (p. 22). This is especially true when we want students to internalize (i.e., in Piaget's terms, accommodate rather than assimilate) the learning in ways that change their behavior. Consider, for example, how the following alternative strategies for working with older students to foster engagement, dialogue, and reflection in ways that didactic instruction around online safety issues cannot.

- **Engage students in policy making.** People are more likely to take ownership of rules when they have had a say in crafting them. And if we are serious about the goal of graduating active citizens, then we need to offer students opportunities to function as active citizens in their school community. There are many ways to involve students in policy making. Here are a few strategies that might be used with students in Grades 5 and up:

  o **Project-based learning**—Ask students to design a "license" (like a driver's license) to go online. What would people need to know or be able to demonstrate in order to earn their online license? What actions might lead to revocation of that license?

  o **Partner with students**—Ask, "What would you need to do to keep yourself safe online?" "How would you teach online safety to younger students or siblings?" or "Which communication techniques would work best to convey messages to your peers about online safety and why?"

  In each of these scenarios, the teacher could ensure that all necessary content is covered by asking follow-up questions that keep the discussion or activity going, such as "We haven't talked about _____ yet. How would your policy address that?" or "Has anyone else had or heard of an online experience they want to address? How about the time last year when. . . ."

- **Use the Key Questions for analysis.** Because media literacy questions are designed to help students think deeply about the intentions and consequences of media messages, they provide excellent prompts for dialogue about online safety issues.

- **Use the Key Questions for production.** These can structure one-on-one or small-group conversations with students who have engaged in cyberbullying or sent inappropriate photos:

  o **Purpose**—Why am I making this?

  o **Response**—What kinds of actions do I expect people to take in response to this message? What are the likely or possible responses?

  o **Interpretations**—What do I learn about myself from my role in creating this message? Am I representing my best self?

  o **Impact**—What's my responsibility to my audience? Who might benefit? Who might be harmed, and in what ways?

- **Ask students what they already know.** What do they know about specific online safety issues? Where do they see or hear messages about online safety? What have they heard and

(Continued)

(Continued)

what were their sources of information? What evidence do they use to assess whether or not those sources of information are reliable?

- **Use a discussion of "target audience" to encourage students to get in the habit of thinking about how recipients of their messages might react.** Underscore the idea that one's intended audience may not be the actual audience. There is no way for an online author to retain absolute control over who will have access to texts, posts, photographs, survey responses, contact information entered into sweepstakes forms, and the like. Probe more deeply by asking a question like "How would you feel if the information (or photo) that you shared ends up somewhere you didn't intend?" Students can be invited to imagine specific audiences (e.g., parents, former friends, someone trying to sell you something, someone trying to con you, college admissions officer, or prospective employer).

- **Use Content questions about values to discuss what makes something "appropriate" or "inappropriate" and who gets to decide.** Or use an Impact question to help students think about why privacy (or the lack thereof online) might matter to them.

- **Use Credibility questions to spark a discussion about online predators.** Are the statistics true? How could you find out? Who collects the statistics and for what purposes? What would you count as credible evidence? What if your own experience or the experiences of your classmates contradict the statistics? Whom would you believe and why?

- **A Content question about what information is left out of reports might lead to a deep examination of which children are most vulnerable to online dangers.** Content questions could also probe what supports might be available to those kids and why our community and family structures haven't provided such supports. Such discussions can always end with a Response question about what actions students might want to take in light of the new information they have.

- **Include online safety as part of a broader initiative to develop digital citizenship skills.** In a comprehensive media literacy curriculum, students would be encouraged to see themselves as digital citizens with skills, rights, and responsibilities. They would learn how to be civically engaged by learning skills like how to add to a wiki, comment on a blog, use a social network, or collaborate on a project using an online document-sharing program. In this context, netiquette and safety rules would be tools that allow for participation rather than restrictions to prevent expression or exposure.

Each of these suggestions would need to be modified to ensure that they were developmentally appropriate, with more explicit and nonnegotiable rules laid down for young children and gradually more open and challenging discourse provided as children mature. But no matter what students' age, it is possible to use inquiry-based media literacy education to engage them in lessons about online safety.[15]

WHAT MAKES A CURRICULUM-DRIVEN APPROACH DIFFERENT?

In the *Media Literacy Resource Guide* published in 1989, Canadian educators were among the first to recognize that "teachers can teach the key concepts of media literacy in some form to *all students at any level*" (Ontario Ministry of

Education, p. 3). But, typical of the time period, the remainder of the document reflects a vision of media literacy education as being about "media and their influences," so after 6 pages of suggestions for various subject areas, the guide shifts to 143 pages of activities divided into sections by type of media (television, film, music recordings, etc.), with each section focused on teaching about the medium.

Our inquiry- and literacy-based approach leads us to a different way of looking at the challenge. To us, *curriculum-driven* means starting from what teachers already need to teach. Rather than asking educators to squish media literacy goals into an already bursting-at-the-seams curriculum, we encourage teachers to begin with their own teaching strengths, styles, and goals and then use what they know about media literacy to figure out how to do what they already do more effectively. This gives teachers a "twofer"—allowing them to teach core content and at the same time to build students' media literacy skills, as exemplified by the suggestions in this chapter's Featured Example for how media literacy might be used to provide mandated instruction on cyberbullying or online privacy.

Media literacy education is not the best way to teach everything, and we are not recommending that it replace what is already working well. But media literacy education can provide a way for veteran teachers to rejuvenate stale lessons. It can also be an effective way to reach students with diverse learning needs (differentiated instruction) and to engage students who have been otherwise uninterested. And nothing ignites more passion in teachers than students who are engaged in what they are learning.

Integrating media literacy takes a bit of practice, so even though its inquiry-based approach can be applied to numerous situations, it is okay to start with one or two discrete lessons. The more comfortable you become with its inquiry process, the harder it will be to design instruction that doesn't integrate media literacy. To facilitate the process of creating your own curriculum-driven media literacy lessons, we offer the checklist in Appendix B.

4

When Are Questions the Answer?

Teaching Students How to Analyze Media Messages

One of the most rewarding experiences for a teacher is to see students' "Aha!" moments, those transformative times when a new insight is realized or a new skill is mastered that influences future learning forever. The "deep reading" that media literacy education brings to documents often provides such moments.

In the approach to analysis laid out in this chapter, teachers act as facilitators and models for students' decoding work so that students acquire and improve their own capacity for inquiry. Mastering this method is a defining skill for inquiry-based media literacy educators.

THE FUSION OF DECODING, COMPREHENSION, AND ANALYSIS

The process of analyzing media documents is typically called "decoding" for meaning, "deconstructing" a message (reflecting the concept that all media messages are constructed), or "reading" a visual message that may include images, text, or both.

The use of the term *decoding* is slightly different in media literacy than in traditional print literacy. In traditional literacy, *decoding* generally refers to letter recognition and the ability to sound out letter combinations and syllables. It is a prerequisite to reading for meaning and is often taught to beginners separately from comprehension (understanding the words that a reader sounds out) and analysis (questioning the texts that one comprehends). In contrast, media literacy education inextricably combines them, expecting that students will learn all three skills simultaneously.

COLLECTIVE READING OF MEDIA MESSAGES

While media decoding can be done individually by the student as part of a written exercise, a "collective reading" by the whole class is generally more effective. In this collaborative effort, a facilitator (the teacher or a designated student) guides the analysis and discussion through the use of questions. The goal is not for everyone to reach consensus about what something means but, rather, to deepen everyone's insight. This group activity is a powerful way to develop a range of critical thinking skills while also teaching core content. [CP6.6]

As is true of other kinds of group work, "when teachers get the circumstances right, something remarkable happens: Students educate one another and end up knowing more than they would have working alone" (Frey, Fisher, & Everlove, 2009, p. 1). This is in part because the process exposes students to analysis and discussion with more highly skilled peers and adults, facilitating the students' learning and cognitive growth in what Vygotsky called the "zone of proximal development" (Moll, 1990). The teacher initially provides scaffolding through the use of questions and follow-up probes for evidence.

The collective process is beneficial for teachers as well. Leading a class through a document decoding provides the opportunity to assess students' comprehension, correct statements that are factually inaccurate, add additional information about the topic as needed, invite alternative points of view, and address issues that arise when students express different interpretations of the same message.

SKILL BUILDING

Decoding documents helps students develop a wide range of skills applicable to many core subject areas, especially science, social studies, health, and English/ language arts (ELA). It teaches students to

- distinguish fact from opinion,
- analyze point of view and identify biases,
- draw inferences, and
- make and defend conclusions using document-based evidence.

In addition, by providing practice in articulating one's point of view and listening to the interpretations of others, collective decoding develops skills of expression and creates opportunities to address learning standards for speaking and listening.

This process of deep reading, including hearing the opinions of classmates, challenges students to go beyond their initial (and sometimes superficial) responses or interpretations. And because students are expected to justify their conclusions with specific, document-based evidence, discussions tend to be respectful, even as students compare diverse opinions. Media analysis that uses a constructivist approach also encourages the development of moral reasoning as students clarify their own and others' interpretations and discuss ethical issues. [CP6.1,6.2]

ENCOURAGING MULTIPLE READINGS

In some approaches to media analysis, the instructor guides students to a particular interpretation or understanding of the messages. This approach is commonplace in critical studies, semiotics, and protectionist forms of media literacy but, in general, is not the most effective way to help students develop their own analytical skills.

REFLECTION: *PRODUCTIVE QUESTIONS*

Recently, a team of researchers* divided the questions that teachers typically asked of students into two categories:

Reproductive, i.e., those that "prompt students to imitate, recall, or apply knowledge and information taught by the teacher, through a mimicked process"; and

Productive, i.e., those that "provide students the opportunity to create, analyze, or evaluate." (p. 40)

The researchers found that in actual classroom practice, reproductive (comprehension) questions outnumbered productive (analysis) questions three to one. Of questions posed by novice teachers, only 15 percent were productive.

- Why do you think the researchers chose the terms *productive* and *reproductive*?
- How does your teaching approach compare to these research results?
- How might you use inquiry-based media literacy decodings to increase the number of productive questions you ask?

*Tienken, Goldberg, and DiRocco (2009).

Occasionally a question, especially one designed to determine what knowledge students bring to the table, has only one right answer (e.g., "Who painted this?" or "When was this website last updated?"). Such comprehension questions can be useful and are often included in a media literacy decoding, but they are never the endgame. Rather, media literacy educators encourage students to go beyond asking *what* they notice about the content of a document to ask *why* particular content is included or excluded.

A major goal of this approach is to help students to recognize that people construct their own meanings from media messages, so not everyone will interpret the message the same way. [CP6] Depending upon each reader's skills, beliefs, and background, he or she may have very different interpretations of a particular message. That means that the more different your students are from you (the teacher), the more likely it is that they may read the document differently than you do.

For many teachers, the biggest difference between themselves and their students will be age, but there are also likely to be differences in beliefs, attitudes, and life experiences. Research has confirmed the effect of such differences on media interpretation. For example, the interpretations of song lyrics by adults are often quite different from those of young music listeners (Condry, 1989). In one study using Madonna's song "Like a Virgin," Greenfield and her colleagues (1987) found that for children whose primary knowledge about the meaning of *virgin* was the Virgin Mary, the song had religious rather than sexual connotations.

In addition, even in a class where the students are all roughly the same age, there may be significant differences among the students themselves that are difficult to address (or even acknowledge) in respectful ways during class discussions. Because the collective reading experience is based on the recognition that everyone interprets messages through their own lenses, it provides the opportunity to explore these differences. In the process, the classroom becomes a place where divergent thinking is welcomed and respect for one another's opinions is the norm.

The acknowledgment that people interpret media through the lens of their own experiences and the resulting approach to analysis that affirms diverse readings challenge the "one right answer" approach so often used in education today. Some educators will see this as an obstacle, especially because, at first glance, the media-decoding approach we are describing may mistakenly seem like "anything goes"; it may seem to endorse the notion that all answers are equally fine or work much like a Rorschach (inkblot) test. But the questions and probes used in an inquiry-based decoding process take students beyond simplistic or superficial interpretations of media messages, even when those interpretations may be different from the teacher's. If the focus is kept on how well students back up their interpretations with document-based evidence, then document decoding imparts the inquiry and critical evaluation skills that will help students in other activities, including test taking.

That said, there may be times when the teacher (or any educator leading a decoding) will want to share her or his own interpretations or conclusions about a media message. For example, in US history classes, teachers may want to convey their own experiences related to more recent historical events (e.g., the Vietnam or Gulf Wars) and compare their personal experiences to what is described in the textbook or other sources.

In such cases, teachers should be aware that the classroom power dynamic, which establishes an inherently unequal relationship between teacher and student, can make students reluctant to share any perspective that contradicts the teacher's position, seriously eroding the benefits of the collective decoding process. Or students may succumb to the habit of accepting the teacher's interpretation as the correct one. Once they do that, they stop thinking for themselves. For these reasons, it is probably better for teachers to wait until later in the discussion to share their opinions and interpretations and, when they do share personal points of view, to make sure to explain exactly how they reached their conclusions.

FINDING MEDIA DOCUMENTS

An effective media decoding starts with the media document itself. Here are some guidelines.

1. **Start with a "rich" media document.** It should be appropriate for your students and relate to your curriculum goals. Begin by identifying both your curriculum goals (related to your core content) and media literacy goals. Think through how you will know if your goals have been reached through the decoding lesson (i.e., how students will demonstrate what they have learned). Then find media examples that relate to your goals and that allow for multiple questions to facilitate analysis.

   You may be able to get support in finding appropriate documents from your library media specialist. In his keynote addresses and workshop presentations, longtime media literacy educator Chris Sperry also encourages educators to "keep their Velcro buds active" by being alert to rich media examples they come across in their daily lives or that already exist in their school or classroom (e.g., books, instructional videos, posters, and newsletters). Often the deepest insights will occur with media that your students already use regularly but haven't thought much about, and students themselves can be encouraged to bring in examples from the media that they find intriguing, inspirational, confusing, misleading, or just plain wrong.

2. **Decode different types of media throughout the school year.** In this way, students learn to apply their decoding skills to a wide variety of media formats and modes of communication.[1] In preparing different lessons, consider using documents that are

   - contemporary and historic;
   - high and low tech;
   - mainstream and alternative;
   - commercial and independent;
   - professionally created and user generated; and
   - representative of different media genres (e.g., documentary and dramatic film; TV news, news analysis, docudrama, and reality TV; hip-hop, country, folk, and classical music) and media forms (e.g., audio, text, and visual).

3. **Address copyright issues appropriately.** Do you have explicit copyright permission to use this media document in your classroom? If not, can you apply fair use (e.g., by critiquing the document with your students)?

   Your media choices will, by necessity, be governed by the policies existing in your school district or building. However, legal precedents have not kept up with the rapid changes in media technologies, and existing school policy may not be up-to-date.

   We recommend following guidelines from a growing group of educators who believe that classroom critique of mass-media messages is essential to the development of core literacy skills in our media-saturated democracy and that the fair-use clause of the copyright law is designed to allow for just this kind of educational practice. This position has been summarized in Renee Hobbs's book *Copyright Clarity: How Fair Use Supports Digital Learning* (2010a).[2]

4. **Prepare the necessary background information and probing questions to teach about content and source.** Identify the background information students will need (if any) in order to decode the documents effectively. This might include things like vocabulary, historical or curriculum context, details about where a media document is from (e.g., whether information about a nation's government is from the Central Intelligence Agency's *World Factbook* at www.ciaworldfactbook.usor from the nation's own official website) or how influential a media example might have been (e.g., a song that was number one on the charts compared to one that never charted or an article printed in a mass-circulation magazine like *Life* compared to an article in an obscure newsletter). Then decide whether you will provide that information in class before the decoding or if it would make more sense for students to come prepared after having read about it.

   Craft evidence-based questions that ask students to apply the core content to their analysis and that reflect on issues of media construction and sources. What you choose to ask will be shaped by what you want to teach. For example, imagine analyzing the website for an Earth Day observance. A civics teacher might ask students to hunt for constitutional issues related to the organization's call for action (e.g., state versus federal jurisdiction, freedom to assemble, etc.), while a science teacher might have students examine the veracity of scientific claims underpinning the case for federal regulations. By tying document decoding to core content, teachers can address both skill development and content knowledge through the media literacy–decoding process.

5. **Less is more.** It is much more effective to do a "deep reading" of a few media documents than a superficial analysis and discussion of many media examples. Therefore, you will likely want to show short excerpts from videos (or films) rather than entire productions, since a few minutes of video content is very rich in audio and visual information. In some cases—especially when developing analysis skills in young children—it may make sense to show the same video clip several times, with a "deeper" analysis or different questions asked during each screening.

LEADING A DECODING

Leading an effective inquiry-based media decoding requires a bit of finesse. Psychologist M. L. J. Abercrombie (1960) recognized the challenge when she wrote, "How to tell students what to look for without telling them what to see is the dilemma of teaching" (p. 83).

In order to teach students what to look for, teachers should begin by clearly establishing educational goals that can be addressed through the document-decoding process. These may well include vocabulary and other core content that is taught during or prior to the decoding. Depending on the nature of the media document, teachers may want to familiarize students with certain terms that capture specific content or techniques that often appear in media messages (like *eye candy* or *weasel words*). However, the process should also be flexible enough to allow for the communication of factual information while allowing enough time to explore the unplanned—but often very rich and fruitful—directions in which the conversation may go during the decoding discussion.

In addition to the adoption of a flexible approach, the key to effectively leading a decoding of a media document lies in the use of questions. Try to put 80 to 90 percent of what you say in the form of questions, using the following guidelines:

1. **Set up the decoding by giving the context for analysis.** Provide the necessary background information and instructions *before* you start the decoding. For video clips, it is especially important to give students a heads-up about what to look for or a sense of what the follow-up discussion will focus on. Audiovisual messages are usually very rich in imagery, sound, and narrative, and people bring their own experiences and interests to the task. Therefore, without a specific focus for viewing, students may only pay attention to things that interest them rather than the content that is relevant to the discussion (e.g., a socially active middle schooler might focus attention on how cute a program's host is instead of on the science topic that the host is addressing, or a new immigrant might search for familiar landmarks in the news story on her country of origin rather than the facts shared by the reporter).

2. **Always start the decoding with a question.** Because they imply the expectation of an answer, questions ignite the brain in a way that statements do not. So questions always play an important role in engaging students. For a media literacy decoding, the questions might be general openings for comments, such as these:

   - What messages do you see (did you hear)?
   - What did you feel while you were watching (reading or listening to) this?
   - Does anyone have a comment or question to start off the discussion?

   This more general type of prompt works especially well with students who are already experienced media decoders.

When leading a decoding with students who are beginners, it may be more effective to start with a general-comprehension or background question about the document itself:

- What do you think this is from (and what makes you say that)?
- When was this made (or first distributed to the public), and what clues are you using to find your answer?
- Whom do you think this website is made for? Why?

If possible, use a specific question that relates back to your curriculum goal:[3]

- What do you notice about how this relates to (the book we just read, our study of Africa, etc.)?
- How does this challenge or confirm what we already learned about (electricity, the Civil War, etc.)?
- What are your impressions about (China, lemmings, Native Americans, etc.) from what you see (just saw, just heard)?

Or you can begin with one of the *Key Questions for Analyzing Media Messages*:

- Who is the target audience for this, and how do you know?
- Is this fact, opinion, or something else?
- Who might benefit from this message? Who might be harmed?

Or even questions that combine curriculum and media literacy questions:

- What techniques does the media maker use to convey messages about (math, freedom of speech, women, honor, etc.)?

Opening questions are important because they head the decoding in a particular direction and because they set a tone. Students aren't likely to engage for very long in a task that makes them feel inadequate, so teachers increase the chances that students will want to participate by phrasing the opening question as one that everyone in the room can answer (e.g., What do you notice about [insert curriculum tie here]?). An open-ended query invites students into the process by tapping into what they already know, rather than reminding them of what they don't know.

3. **Follow up on a student's answer with evidence probes.** You may want to clarify whether you are looking for general evidence (including from the person's prior experience) or specific evidence seen/heard in the document itself.

   - Where do you see that?
   - What makes you say that?
   - What's your evidence in the document?
   - How do you know?

4. **Continue to probe when appropriate, especially to get at key content points and perspectives.**

- **Expansions**—Tell me more about that. What do you mean by ___?
- **Interpretations**—What words might you use to describe him? How does this make you feel?
- **Clarifications**—So you're saying ___? Do you mean ___?
- **Restatements**—[Restate in slightly different words or while pointing to the relevant element of the image.]
- **Affirmations**—Yes! Interesting. No one's ever said that before!

5. **Open the discussion up to other participants:**

- Anyone else?
- What else do you notice? Anything else? [May be repeated multiple times.]
- Does anyone else have a different interpretation?
- I'm going to go around and have each of you say one word that describes ___ [a person or thing in the media document].
- Call on people by name (not to embarrass but to invite a student who might be reticent into the conversation): Maria, what do you think?

6. **Tailor your questions to fit the document and your own goals and needs.** You don't need to ask all of the Key Questions, even when doing a "deep reading" of a media document. Work toward increasingly sophisticated questions that draw from the students' broad knowledge about the topic, their personal values, and their ability to weigh conflicting sets of ideas. You might do this by progressing through questions from simplest to most sophisticated, for example:

- **Comprehension**—What is going on?
- **Analysis of the message itself**—Why was this message made? What techniques does it use?
- **Interpretations (analysis of people's responses)**—What are the potential effects of this message? Who benefits or is harmed?
- **Taking action**—What could you do to respond?

No matter what questions you start with, remember that the goal is to get students to think carefully about their answers and to back up their comments with evidence from the document itself. Keep the questions as open-ended as possible to allow for many different interpretations, even ones that you would not have predicted.

7. **Pay attention to how you ask the questions.** Be careful to model a respectful process of inquiry and listening. Use physical cues, including culturally appropriate gestures, to draw students in. Use positive affect and nonjudgmental responses as much as possible to create a welcoming atmosphere where students will feel comfortable expressing their opinions, even when other students (or you) may disagree. Always keep in mind the role you play as a model for your students. Also consider how you might configure desks or chairs in ways that facilitate discussion (e.g., in a circle so everyone can see everyone else and so that everyone's attention isn't just focused on you).

REFLECTION: *NOTICINGS*

When we lead decodings in staff development trainings, we typically designate a couple of people to do "noticings" about the way we lead the decoding (the kinds of questions we ask, etc.). The "noticers" often mention our body language, gestures, facial expressions, and tone of voice (especially when we respond to people's comments), as well as how we phrase questions and the number of questions we ask, as important elements that encourage participation and reinforce the process of collaborative inquiry. Think of a time when you have led students in a media literacy activity or imagine yourself leading a document decoding. What do you think a noticer would observe about the things that you do?

CAUTIONS

All educators make choices about how to approach course content and what examples to use. In doing document decoding, it's important to recognize the power behind your choice of documents. It is easy to fall into the trap of analyzing only media documents of which you are critical (e.g., manipulative advertising or political messages by someone you would not vote for). It is equally important to analyze media documents that you approve of (e.g., student-produced videos, media literacy videos critiquing media, political messages by someone you support), as well as documents that are not controversial or partisan (e.g., a poster of the water cycle or an animation of a simple machine).

As one can imagine, leading rich discussions of this nature can have pitfalls that may be difficult to avoid, especially when you are first starting out. Here are some things to keep in mind:

1. **As mentioned above, don't tell the students what to see or what the "right" answer is.** Continue to use questions to draw them to the points you want to make or to the right answer if there is one. For example, ask, "Where do you see physics at work in this scene?" and perhaps follow this with "In what ways does it illustrate or contradict the physics principle we learned yesterday?" instead of "Who can explain why this special effect couldn't possibly happen in real life?"

2. **Help students to analyze and evaluate media messages free from your judgments.** Craft questions that do not unintentionally bias student judgments up front. For example, ask, "What are the messages about Native Americans?" rather than "How is this depiction racist?" or "What values did the program promote?" rather than "How did the program romanticize family life?"

3. **Recognize how your own biases may show up in your body language, facial expressions, language, and framing.** If you only smile, nod, or provide affirmation for certain types of interpretations and not for others, students will catch on to your point of view even when you are careful not to express it verbally.

   Also, avoid making what we call "danger clucks"—gasps, throat clearing, or other noises and body language that convey to the students that you think this message is dangerous, outrageous, or wrong (even if that's what you think). Using danger clucks shuts down the conversation instead of opening it up and may even cause students to rebel against your interpretation (especially if you are seen as critical of "their" media).

4. **Don't set your students up to feel stupid or set traps to trick them.** There may be times when you want to surprise them by asking a question to which you know students are likely to give an incorrect or incomplete answer in order to make an important point. In that case, use "we" language:

   - We've learned to focus on ___, and we tend not to notice ___.
   - Why wouldn't we be likely to have thought of that?

   Or acknowledge your own tendencies:

   - That's what I would have said, too.
   - When I first read this, that's what I thought.

5. **Listen for resistance or for one-sided comments that are stated as truth.** For example, a student might dismiss a comment by saying, "You are reading into this." Probe accordingly:

   - Is there only one way to interpret that?
   - How might other people respond differently?

6. **Do no harm.** Be aware of the power of media messages and their potential to have unintended consequences. One typical example we have encountered is teachers who want to raise students' consciousness about the possible link between eating disorders and media depictions of models who are impossibly thin. To illustrate the health risks, they create a bulletin board or activity full of images of extremely thin models. While their intentions are good and they invite students to think critically about the images, what many girls see and remember is lots of extremely thin women who are popular, beautiful, and successful. They may even see boys admiring the photos. Rather than rejecting the image, they may be *more* likely to diet or engage in destructive eating behaviors as they attempt to look like the women in the pictures.[4]

   Lessons about stereotypes or prejudice should be approached with sensitivity because by showing examples of negative stereotypes, you are repeating them, which may reinforce rather than undermine their power. Such images may also evoke pain, embarrassment, sadness, or anger in students who have been the targets of bias-based harassment.

REFLECTION: *HARMFUL OR HELPFUL?*

To provide some historical context for his class's reading of *Anne Frank: The Diary of a Young Girl* (1952), an eighth-grade teacher decided to create handouts of anti-Semitic media from different parts of the world, including a short excerpt from Hitler's *Mein Kampf* (1933), several anti-Semitic cartoons from Belgium, and the transcript of a Father Coughlin radio program from the United States. The teacher clearly identified the media as anti-Semitic and led students in a decoding of each document. The students had previously been completely unaware of these sources and were especially surprised by the example from the United States.

In your view, what were the potential benefits of this lesson? What harm might it have caused? On balance, was introducing students to anti-Semitic media a good idea? Why or why not? What teaching strategies might tip the balance in favor of benefit over harm?

Because of this, you may want to contrast negative or potentially harmful messages with positive media representations (decoding both). Cue into and follow up with students who have particularly emotional responses and listen well to the meaning making of all of your students.

Also, be prepared to respond to the occasional student who, when looking at media stereotypes, will say something in support of the stereotype. This may range from an innocent—if ignorant—use of an offensive word to intentional use of hate speech. To protect students who may feel threatened by such comments and to establish the kind of safe space for classroom discussion that is a prerequisite for successful decoding, a teacher should never let such comments pass without a response.

It is beyond the scope of this book to provide detailed strategies for how to confront bias effectively.[5] What any given teacher does often depends on the specific students involved and the teacher's relationship with those students. However, by providing a way to engage students in further analysis, media literacy education offers a way to diffuse the situation or even turn a negative event into a positive learning experience.

Asking students to talk about who benefits and who is harmed by the repetition of negative stereotypes, or examining the connotations and power of words and why someone would choose to use one word rather than another, can provide a means to address the situation directly without attacking or embarrassing any individual student or getting into a one-on-one argument with the student who made the offending remark. Continuation of the collective-analysis process provides students with an opportunity to express support for those who might be victimized by prejudice, and it allows you an opportunity to demonstrate why the speaker's view isn't backed by valid evidence.

FEATURED EXAMPLE

Annotated Examples of Media Document Decoding

To illustrate the process of decoding using the guidelines and cautions we have described, here are two examples of document decoding. The first example would be appropriate for students in upper elementary grades and above, although the wording and nature of the questions and probes would vary depending on the grade level and content area of the class during which the decoding occurs. The second example is appropriate for preK and early elementary settings. These are not scripts to follow but rather examples of how a classroom conversation might go.

We started by selecting two sets of rich media documents for analysis. In addition to laying out how the conversation might occur as the teacher leads a collaborative decoding with an entire class, we have also included (in the right-hand column) some annotation on the media literacy techniques used and overall pedagogy, as well as examples to contrast how other approaches would differ from a media literacy approach to decoding.

Example #1: *Discovery of the Mississippi by de Soto* and *The Last Supper*

The first set of documents focuses on two paintings that represent first contact between Europeans and Native Americans during the sixteenth and seventeenth centuries: (1) a famous illustration of the arrival of Spanish explorer Hernando de Soto and his troops at the Mississippi River in 1541 (painted in 1855 by William H. Powell, a well-known nineteenth-century American painter) entitled *Discovery of the Mississippi by de Soto* and (2) an illustration of the arrival of Spanish Conquistadors at a pueblo in the early 1600s (painted in 1991 by Jonathan Warm Day, a renowned Taos Pueblo artist) entitled *The Last Supper*. Our illustration of a decoding of these paintings is done in the context of a high school US history lesson on westward expansion, although these documents could also be useful to decode in classes on European explorers, American history, Native Americans, stereotyping, visual sociology, or art history (from upper elementary school through college).

Learning Objectives	
History Objectives:	**Media Literacy Objectives:**
• Identify conflicting cultural perspectives in historical representations. • Learn about events and vocabulary related to westward expansion and European exploration of continental North America in the fifteenth and sixteenth centuries. • Discuss and reflect on aspects of first contact between European explorers and Native peoples and how those events influenced later beliefs and events. • Recognize how historical events and impressions are conveyed over time.	• Practice decoding visual messages, including the "grammar" of production techniques used in paintings (e.g., framing, lines, color, angles, lighting). • Apply *Key Questions for Analyzing Media Messages,* including questions of Authorship, Sponsorship, Purpose, Audience, point of view, and Credibility. • Reflect on who benefits and who might be harmed by the way in which historical stories are told and by whose stories are not told or not represented in traditional historical texts.
Vocabulary	
de Soto, first contact, westward expansion, manifest destiny, colonialism, tipi, peace pipe, totem pole, cultural perspective, pueblo, William Powell, Jonathan Warm Day, rotunda of the US Capitol building, DaVinci's *Last Supper*	

(Continued)

(Continued)

Figure 4.1 *Discovery of the Mississippi by de Soto* (cropped)

Artist: William H. Powell, 1853.

Source: http://www.aoc.gov/cc/art/rotunda/discovery_mississippi.cfm.

Decoding Demonstration Example 1	Notes
T = teacher; **S** = student **T**: We're going to continue learning about westward expansion across what eventually became the Midwestern United States. Today we consider how European colonialism provided a foundation for American expansion from the coasts into the country's interior. This painting depicts the European "discovery" of the Mississippi River by an explorer named Hernando de Soto. *[Project PowerPoint image of the painting.]*	To highlight the role of questions in the process of leading of this decoding, we've put all of the teacher's **questions in boldface.**
It is entitled *Discovery of the Mississippi by de Soto.* **Which one do you think is de Soto?** *[Lots of raised hands and chorus of voices and some laughter; the teacher calls on a student who has her hand raised.]* **S1:** The one on the horse. **T: What makes you think that he's de Soto?** **S1:** Because he looks like he's the most important one. **T: What makes you say he looks important?**	After a brief introduction, the teacher starts the decoding with a Content question that will probably lead to agreement and that the teacher can then build on to encourage a "deep reading" of this document. The teacher responds to student statements with probe **questions** that guide the discussion to focus on how de Soto was portrayed.

Decoding Demonstration Example 1	Notes
S1: Because he's the only one on a white horse.	
T: Is he the only one on a horse?	
S1: No, but he's the only one on a *white* horse.	
T: Why does the white horse make a difference?	
S1: Because white is supposed to be good and important; the good guys are always wearing white, and the bad guys wear black.	
T: Does anyone else agree with that? *[nods]* **Anyone disagree? Can anybody give me another example where that was true?**	*When a student makes a value statement or expresses an opinion, the teacher may want to check in with the rest of the class to see how much agreement there is. Teachers may want to have a set mode for assessing agreement, like using a "silent clap" (where students wave raised hands if they agree). Laughter, sighs, or groans can reflect spontaneous reactions by the class that are important to note. The teacher may want to ask the whole class, "So why did you laugh?" or "What were the groans about?"*
S2: The Lone Ranger? Cowboy movies?	
T: Why don't you all think about that and see how many examples you can find, maybe check around online or ask your friends and parents, and we'll talk about that more tomorrow. In the meantime, back to the painting.	*While this discussion of good guys and bad guys has led in an interesting direction, which the teacher may want to explore further, it also takes the discussion away from the core content information related to westward expansion. In this case, the teacher uses the opportunity to encourage students to make inquiries of their own outside of school—but in doing this, it's important for the teacher to check in with the students the next day to see if they found out anything and to spend some time discussing what they found.*
Danita said that de Soto looked important. **Anything else that makes him look important? Anyone?**	
S3: He's all by himself; he looks bigger than everyone else.	
T: What in this document, this painting, makes him look like he's by himself or bigger than everyone else?	
S3: All the white space around his head, and he's up on the horse, which makes him higher than everybody else.	
T: Anything else? *[looking around to the other students]*	
S4: Everybody else is in little groups, bunched up together, but he's not near anybody else, and there's all that space on the ground in front of him.	

(Continued)

(Continued)

Decoding Demonstration Example 1	Notes
T: **Anything else that makes him look important?** **S5:** Everybody else is looking at him. **T:** **Who is looking at him?** *[As students call out different people or groups of people, the teacher points to all of those in the painting who are looking at de Soto.]* **What about his horse?** *[laughter]* Yes, even his horse is looking at him! **Is there anyone who isn't looking at de Soto?** **S6:** The guy on the left with the white beard. **T:** **Where is he looking?** **S6:** Up, to God? **T:** **So who do you think this man might be?** **S6:** Some kind of religious person, a priest? **T:** Sure. **And where is de Soto looking?** *[asking the whole class]* **S2:** He's looking straight ahead. **T:** Sure—he's off looking westward. He's ready to move on through to the next cool place to discover. *[laughter]* Let's go back to the painting again, and let's go around the room and I'd like each person to give one word that you think describes de Soto and how he's portrayed in this painting. You can pass if you want. Let's start at the end of the third row with Sam. **S7:** Rich. **S8:** A leader. **S9:** Arrogant. **S10:** Powerful. **S11:** That's what I was going to say. I pass. **S12:** Like he doesn't care about others. **S13:** Dangerous. **T:** Okay, let's come back to "arrogant." Yuki, **what made you say he's arrogant?** **S9:** Because of his posture. **T:** **What about his posture?** **S9:** Because he's sitting up really straight, holding the reins, like he's really confident and isn't afraid of anybody. **T:** **Any other reason why he might not be afraid of anyone?** **S14:** Because he's in charge, everyone has to do what he wants.	*The teacher might cue students to some other pieces of evidence in the painting by pointing out elements of color and lighting, the lines of the tipis that direct attention toward de Soto, etc.—but ideally evoking responses from the students through questions (e.g., **What do you notice about the lighting?**) rather than simply telling.* *In a semiotics approach, the teacher would take more of a lead in identifying symbolism and signs in the painting (e.g., noting that the white beard—like the horse—represents goodness and godliness).* *Asides and comments made during a decoding that evoke laughter can be important in generating a relaxed atmosphere and shared understanding and cue the teacher into students' interpretations and meaning making.* *As each of the students responds, the teacher should give some kind of affirmation through a nod or brief comment. At any point, the teacher could stop and probe more deeply to explore a particular interpretation. Alternatively, the teacher could wait until several responses are given before coming back to a response worth probing further because it has the best chance of taking the conversation in a direction that will allow for the unpacking of core content information.* *In general, the teacher should avoid correcting student interpretations unless important factual information is misstated, stereotypical, or racist or if otherwise harmful comments go unchecked by other students.*

Decoding Demonstration Example 1	Notes
S15: And he's taller than anyone else, because he's on the horse—so he could just trample over anyone who gets in his way. **T:** This painting represents first contact between European explorers and Native peoples. De Soto and his men **were from Spain, and these events took place in 1541. What might the title of the painting,** *Discovery of the Mississippi by de Soto,* **say about the point of view that this painting portrays of this historical event?** **S19:** It ignores the Indians and says that the Spanish were the first people to find this river, or at least the only ones that mattered. **S11:** It only reflects the European point of view. **T: How do you think the Native people living here felt about de Soto's arrival, and what evidence is there in the document?** **S8:** They were afraid. Look at the way the women were cowering down on the ground in front of him. They're afraid of the cannons and afraid that the white men might hurt them. **T: Anyone want to add to that, or have a different viewpoint?** **S14:** I think the Native American men aren't afraid. They're standing up, and the one guy looks like he's the leader of the Native American tribe. **T: This one?** *[pointing]* **What makes him look like a leader?** **S14:** The thing on his head, and his posture. He's standing straight and looking directly at de Soto. And the other guy looks like he's bowing, and maybe he has a peace pipe in his hand? *Discussion continues; students raise different interpretations, argue with each other, while the teacher probes, pushing them to give evidence in the document to back up their interpretations.* *Other elements in the painting that might be explored:* • *The suggestion of movement (to the right) through the scene, conveyed by the pointing figure, open space in front of de Soto, position of horse's hooves, etc.* • *The differences in clothing/nakedness of the two groups* • *The weapons (cannon, etc.) held by the Europeans, compared to the piled weapons of the Native Americans* • *The totem pole that has apparently been knocked down (shown at the bottom of the painting)* • *The body language of the Native American men*	*This might be a point where the teacher would want to convey information about the time period and which European countries were represented by different explorers, possibly tying it back to Columbus's "discovery" of America in 1492.* *The titles of paintings and other illustrations are important indications of the painter's purpose and framing, influencing its meaning. They often add a rich component to class discussions.* *In a critical-studies approach, the teacher would be more likely to take the lead in pointing out the power issues in this painting. Questions would be more likely to follow from the interpretation already given by the teacher (e.g.,* **How has the artist conveyed the fear that the Native Americans feel over having their land invaded by the Europeans?***).*

(Continued)

(Continued)

Figure 4.2   *The Last Supper*

Artist: Jonathan Warm Day (Taos Pueblo), 1991.

Source: Thomas, Ballantine, & Ballantine (1993).

Decoding Demonstration Example 1	*Notes*
T: *[Show next PowerPoint image of second painting.]* Here is another painting representing first contact between European explorers and Native peoples. **From whose perspective is this painting constructed?** **S5:** The Native Americans'. **T: And what's your evidence of that in the painting?** **S5:** It's inside their home, looking out the door at the Europeans. **T: Anything else that conveys that this is from a Native American perspective?** **S8:** The style of painting—it seems like something that was painted by a Native American. **T: What makes you say that?** **S8:** The colors are more natural, browns and white and black, and the style is simpler with less detail.	*The teacher could choose to go back and forth between the two paintings comparing and contrasting the point of view, style of painting, portrayal of the Europeans vs. the Native Americans in terms of clothing, color, religious symbols, and weapons, etc.* *Students might reply by giving "evidence" from their own personal experience (e.g., We have a painting like this one that we got in New Mexico); the teacher can acknowledge their contribution while still steering them to give evidence* **from the document** *to back up their conclusions.*

Decoding Demonstration Example 1	Notes
T: **What are the messages here about first contact?** **S1:** That the white people or Europeans were scary. **T:** **And where do you see that in the painting?** **S1:** They're only shown in black silhouettes, and there's all that red that might represent blood or something like that. **T:** **And how do the Native Americans feel in this painting?** **S7:** I think they feel safe. **T:** **What makes you say they feel safe?** **S7:** Because they are up in the air, and they could pull the ladder up so the soldiers couldn't get them. **T:** That's a really interesting response—no one has ever said that before. **Does anyone have a different interpretation about how the Native people in this painting might be feeling, with evidence to back it up?** **S4:** I think they're afraid. The bowl is knocked over, so they must have just noticed the other men who had arrived, and the mother is comforting the little girl, who is probably afraid. **T:** **Anyone want to add to that, or have a different viewpoint?** *[Discussion continues. Students raise different interpretations, and the teacher probes, pushing them to give evidence from the document to back up their interpretations.]* **T:** These paintings are both examples of media messages that are conveying historical information. **Remember the** *Key Questions for Analyzing Media Messages* **that we've been using this year? Anyone remember what the first questions are?** **S10:** Who made this and what was their purpose? **T:** That's right. In the case of a painting, we'd want to know who painted it and when, and one of the clues to get at the painter's purpose might be to look at the title of the painting. In the case of this painting, the painter was a Taos Pueblo artist named Jonathan Warm Day. He painted this in 1991, and the title is *The Last Supper*. **What do you think he meant by giving it that title, and what does it tell you about his purpose?**	*Sometimes a decoding question or probe will lead to a totally unexpected answer (like, "They feel safe," when a much more likely response would be "They feel afraid.") While the teacher might express surprise—or say something like "No one has ever said that before!"—it's very important to keep bringing the students back to finding evidence in the document to support their conclusions, rather than saying or implying that an interpretation is wrong.* *As the decoding continues, the teacher will need to make choices about how much to continue with the probing and deconstruction and how much information needs to be conveyed directly in order to further the conversation. The choices about when and how deeply to probe should be driven by the goals of this particular decoding activity.*

(Continued)

(Continued)

Decoding Demonstration Example 1	Notes
S1: That this is the end of a peaceful existence for the Indians, that the white man is going to take over from now on. **S12:** I think he was trying to make a point about how hard it has been on Native Americans since their land and way of life was destroyed by the Europeans ever since they first began exploring America. *[Discussion may continue.]* **T:** **Which of these two paintings is more likely to appear in a US history textbook, do you think?** **S6:** de Soto's. *[The ensuing discussion should be guided to focus on why de Soto's painting is more likely to appear in US history textbooks, who makes those kinds of decisions, what perspectives of American history are typically included and which are left out, and the implications of who benefits from—and who might be harmed by— these facts.]* **T:** Another one of the Key Questions has to do with sponsorship and who paid for the message. **In the case of paintings, what would that mean?** **S8:** Who commissioned it? **T:** That's right. In the case of *The Last Supper*, no one commissioned it initially. The artist just painted it because he wanted to, although it was later bought by a Taos museum and has appeared in magazines and books. In the case of *de Soto's Discovery of the Mississippi*, who do you think might have commissioned it? **S15:** De Soto? **T:** That's a good guess, although he was long dead by the time this was painted in 1855 by William Powell, a famous American artist. In fact, the painting of *Discovery of the Mississippi by de Soto* was commissioned by the US Congress to commemorate that event, and it hangs in the rotunda of the US Capitol Building in Washington, D.C. *[Show next PowerPoint image.]*	*Here the teacher might want to ask if the students know where the more familiar version of the title* The Last Supper *comes from, explaining that it was the title of a famous painting by Leonardo daVinci of the meal that Jesus had with his disciples just before he was arrested. That painting also played a key role in the popular book and film* The Da Vinci Code *by Dan Brown.* *At this point, the teacher may steer the conversation more toward facts about the events related to westward expansion, encouraging students to make connections between what they are noticing in the paintings and information they have read about in their textbook or discussed earlier in class.* *A critical-studies approach is likely to focus this discussion on the power implications resulting from what gets included, or not included, in US history texts. This may also be the case in a media literacy decoding, but the conclusions will be evoked from the students through inquiry, rather than the teacher providing an interpretation.*

Figure 4.3 *Discovery of the Mississippi by de Soto* (rotunda of US Capitol)

Source: Photograph by Cyndy Scheibe.

Decoding Demonstration Example 1	Notes
T: Here's a picture of it hanging there. **What do you notice about it?** **S8:** It's huge! **T:** That's right. In fact, it's 12 feet high and 18 feet wide. **Notice anything else?** *[Teacher may want or need to show the original slide again, reminding students that this was the painting they started with.]* **S13:** Wait, there's more in the painting than we saw before! You can see the river, and there's a cross too. *[Students call out other comments.]* **T:** Yes! **Did you think it was strange that a painting titled *Discovery of the Mississippi by de Soto* didn't have any part of the Mississippi River in it?** And yet the image we've been looking at appeared in several US history textbooks. *[Show next PowerPoint image.]*	

(Continued)

(Continued)

Figure 4.4 *Discovery of the Mississippi by de Soto* (full painting)

Artist: William H. Powell, 1853.

Source: http://www.aoc.gov/cc/art/rotunda/discovery_mississippi.cfm.

Decoding Demonstration Example 1	Notes
T: This is the actual, full painting. **Why do you think it might have been edited or cropped in order to appear in an American history textbook?** Lots of answers can be explored in the ensuing discussion, including these: • To make the image smaller so it could fit more easily on a page in a textbook without being so small the details couldn't be seen • To crop out the religious cross that is prominent in the lower corner • To focus more on de Soto **T:** Any of those could be the case. **Is this an accurate representation of what happened during this event? How did the artist know what happened?** *[Discussion will follow, focused on the concept that paintings are just constructions of events, not facts.]* **T: So what do these paintings suggest about westward expansion in the United States?**	*In exploring this question, it's important not to let the conversation drift into "conspiracy" theories but to focus more on the implications resulting from this kind of editing, especially as a reflection of the Key Questions such as "What's left out of this message that might be important to know?" and the questions related to Credibility, Accuracy, and Purpose.*

Decoding Demonstration Example 1	Notes
S15: That it was seen as a good thing by white settlers, getting them more land and stuff, but a scary and dangerous thing by the Native Americans who already lived on the land.	
S16: That the settlers who went west were heroes, like the early explorers from Europe.	
T: **Do you think there are any other paintings that appear in your textbook that might reflect the same types of biases?**	
Ss: [nods]	
T: Tonight when you are doing your reading for tomorrow's class, I'd like you to take a few minutes to leaf through your textbook and reflect on the paintings and photographs included as illustrations. **What biases and limitations do you see that might give us a particular perspective on US history?** As you look through the textbook, you might also consider what facts and what stories are included and what facts and stories might be missing. **How does this reflect the point of view of the author(s) of this textbook? How might it influence our understanding of history?**	*The teacher might choose to expand on this decoding using one of the extensions described below, including dividing the class into smaller groups to investigate different issues that have come up during the discussion, with each group reporting its findings back to the whole class.*

Follow-up to the de Soto Decoding

Remember that this example is meant to serve as an illustration of how a collective decoding of paintings like this might proceed. It also shows how a teacher might handle student responses in order to allow for flexibility while still making sure to meet the goals and objectives of the lesson. It is not a script.

The student responses included here have been drawn from similar responses in more than thirty decodings that we have led for these particular documents. However, it is important to note that each time we have led a decoding, something new comes up that we didn't expect or haven't experienced before. You might expect, for example, that Native American students would interpret this differently than others because it touches their lives differently, and you will want to take this into account when choosing documents and developing analysis questions. The same might be true when working with students from other countries or cultures. Cyndy experienced one such encounter with a visiting graduate student from Vietnam:

> Shortly after Nhung Nguyen moved here from Vietnam, I showed her the de Soto slide as an example of the work we do, asking her, "Which one do you think is de Soto?" In all the decodings we had ever done, no one had ever said anything other than the guy in the center on the white horse—and that's what I firmly expected her to say. I was flabbergasted when she studied the painting seriously for a minute, and then pointed to the man with dark hair on a horse behind de Soto. When I asked her why she thought it was him, she said he looked to be the happiest and the most active person in the

(Continued)

(Continued)

painting. When I told her that wasn't it (expecting that surely now she would pick the man on the white horse), she studied the painting again and this time picked the Native American man with the headdress standing erect behind the Native American women. When I probed her to explain why she picked him, she said he looked calm, firm, and consistent. She was quite surprised when I told her the right answer—in part, because a white horse doesn't have the same meaning in Vietnam (it's not associated with leadership or bravery—it's more associated with romance), because a leader would not be out in front of his troops but, rather, would be protected by them, and because she felt the other men that she identified were more representative of leadership in their postures and facial expressions.

This example serves to reinforce the value of teaching through the use of open-ended questions. If Cyndy had just shown Nhung that painting and pointed out de Soto, telling her about his role in US history, we would never have known about those cultural differences in symbols and interpretations, and Nhung wouldn't have been able to join in the conversation about the painting. This exchange also provides a great example of how inquiry-based practice creates opportunities for sophisticated dialogue without falling into the trap of thinking that the teacher has to accept every interpretation as correct. After all, Nhung's evidence-based answer was wrong, and it would have been irresponsible and disrespectful not to explain to her why she was wrong. But because questions opened—rather than shut down—the discussion, those involved were able to learn something about both their own and each other's cultures.

Inquiry-based collective decoding, then, opens up opportunities for cultural differences (as well as individual differences) in interpretations to emerge This not only helps students become sophisticated thinkers, but it also makes people from all backgrounds feel welcome and appreciated, an especially important outcome in a nation where many teachers do not come from the same communities or cultures as their students. For another example of cross-cultural readings of media documents and messages, see the discussion of visual literacy in Chapter 2.

Extensions to the de Soto Decoding

- Have students investigate what other paintings appear in the rotunda of the US Capitol in Washington, D.C. Discuss with them what kinds of choices were made, who made them, and what they might indicate about the biases and perspectives of those in charge. Have them reflect on how they feel about those choices and who might benefit from—and who might be harmed by—those choices.

- Ask a Response question to prompt a discussion of what students might do given their discussions. Might they write to their members of Congress to express their feelings and concerns? Tell their parents and friends? Explore other possibilities of paintings that they might consider better representations of US history during this time period? Contact textbook publishers or those who adopt textbooks about their policy on depictions of first contact?

- While it might be assumed that the Native Americans depicted in *The Last Supper* are Taos Pueblo Indians (since that is the heritage of the artist Jonathan Warm Day), it's not clear what tribe of Native Americans is being depicted in William Powell's *Discovery of the Mississippi by de Soto* or how accurate Powell's rendering is of their culture. Students might investigate this issue, exploring the sources Powell used to reconstruct the event and historical information on which Native American tribes lived in the area where the event occurred. Why might Powell have relied on well-known Native American cultural artifacts (e.g., tipis, headdresses, peace pipe, totem pole) in his painting of this event?

Example #2: *Misleading Nutritional Messages in Cereal Commercials*

The second set of documents focuses on misleading nutritional messages in TV commercials and would be appropriate for an early elementary school class on health, nutrition, and/or consumer education (ages 5–7). Like older students, young children can engage in inquiry and analysis using the same inquiry-based process illustrated in the previous example; the process needs to be modified to use simpler language, include slightly reworded questions (see also Appendix B), and pay more attention to vocabulary and definitions. The decoding is based on a series of lessons in Project Look Sharp's elementary *Critical Thinking and Health* kits.

Young children learn best with concrete examples, so if possible, the teacher should have lots of examples of real or plastic foods and empty boxes of popular children's cereals to illustrate points about nutrition. These allow children to engage in hands-on activities like placing different foods into different food groups. Also, young children have some important cognitive limitations that need to be kept in mind, such as a limited ability to generalize concepts to new situations. Therefore, they need lots of practice applying the vocabulary and concepts to many different examples and need to have the same information "refreshed" and repeated over time.

Learning Objectives	
Nutrition Objectives	*Media Literacy Objectives*
<ul><li>Identify components of a healthy breakfast.</li><li>Learn about how sugar makes people feel and why it is not healthy to eat a lot of sugar.</li><li>Learn about cereals that are low in sugar.</li><li>Identify foods that belong to different food groups (fruit, dairy, grains, fats, sugars).[6]</li></ul>	<ul><li>Recognize and name some tricks used by advertisers in cereal commercials and packaging.</li><li>Understand the concept of *target audience* and identify the target audience for cereal commercials aimed at children.</li><li>Recognize the "complete breakfast shot" shown in cereal commercials.</li><li>Identify clues that might indicate that a cereal has a lot of sugar in it.</li><li>Practice listening and observation skills.</li></ul>
Vocabulary	
target audience, tricks, clues, fruit, dairy, grains, cereal, ingredient, complete breakfast shot, sugar, evidence	

(Continued)

(Continued)

Decoding Demonstration Example 2	Notes
T = teacher; **S** = student *Prior to the decoding, the teacher should lead a hands-on activity where students learn about different food groups (especially grains, fruits, and dairy) as well as fats and sugar, using real or plastic examples of different foods eaten for breakfast.* **T:** We're going to talk about a common food that is often eaten for breakfast called "cereal." **How many of you sometimes eat cereal for breakfast? How many of you had cereal for breakfast today?** *[Students raise hands, call out comments.]* **T:** There are a lot of different brands of cereal, and the companies that make them really want you to buy their cereals, so they sometimes try to convince you by showing you commercials to make their cereals look really good and fun. Let's watch one of those commercials. It was shown during an episode of the TV show *Spongebob Squarepants.* *[Show TV commercial for Honeycomb.]*	*To highlight the role of questions in the process of leading this decoding, we've put all of the* **teacher's questions in boldface.** *It is important that throughout the lesson that the teacher not stress too strongly that eating heavily sugared cereals is bad or wrong (since the children may have parents who buy and eat that type of cereal). Instead emphasize the importance of knowing what one is eating, the pitfalls in eating a lot of heavily sugared foods for breakfast, and the ability to make healthy choices.* *The teacher tells students that the commercial aired during* Spongebob Squarepants *in order to provide an important context that students will later use as a clue to determine the target audience for the commercial.* *This commercial combines live footage with cartoon images and includes special sound and visual effects, giant cartoon pieces of cereal, an exciting chase scene, and a humorous ending. The storyline involves a thief who steals a woman's purse and her box of Honeycomb cereal. She cries out for help ("Stop him! He's got my purse!"). A boy who is sitting nearby sees the thief running with the cereal box and hops onto his skateboard to rescue it. He turns into a cartoon Honeycomb creature, chases the thief through the crowd and street with lots of humorous mishaps, and finally knocks him down. A "complete breakfast shot" shows a huge bowl of cereal with a glass of juice, pitcher of milk, plate of toast, and plate of melon and kiwi fruit. A voiceover says, "Honeycomb cereal is part of this good breakfast." At the end the boy is happily eating the cereal (with the box but none of the other foods visible); the woman arrives and asks "My purse?" He looks at the camera and shrugs while he continues eating.*

Decoding Demonstration Example 2	Notes
T: So what product was that commercial selling? **Ss:** Honeycomb cereal! **T:** That's right! **And what did the people who made this commercial want you to do?** **S1:** Eat Honeycomb! **S2:** Buy their cereal! **S3:** Ask your mom to buy it for you so you can eat it! **S4:** Think Honeycomb is really cool! **T: Who was the target audience for this commercial?** That means, **whom do you think this commercial was made for?** **S1:** Moms? **T: What makes you think that the target audience might be moms? What is your evidence?** **S1:** Because they showed a mom who got her purse stolen, and they want your mom to buy it for you. **T:** Yes, that could be it. **Does anybody have a different answer for who you think this commercial was made for?** **S5:** Kids! **T: What makes you think that the target audience might be kids?** **S5:** Because kids watch *Spongebob*. And there was that boy and that funny cartoon guy in the commercial. **T:** Yes, lots of times when you see a commercial that is shown during a cartoon program or there are children or cartoons in the commercial, then those are clues that the commercial is probably made for kids. **Did anyone see any tricks that the advertiser used to make Honeycomb cereal look really great?** **S3:** That boy turned into that funny guy who rode the skateboard! **S6:** My cousin has a skateboard. He is really good! One time when we were at the park he went up (vrooooom) and spun around and then you know what? I tried to do that but I fell down, and then I skinned my knee and my mom got mad and said I couldn't do it anymore.	*With young students, the initial goal is not necessarily to get the exact right answer (i.e., "kids") but to help them think about target audience and to understand that advertisers sometimes target them with commercials like these. Gentle probing can be used to generate more answers, including the correct one. As children are shown more commercials to decode, the teacher can be more direct about what the correct answer is.* *Also, notice that rather than presenting students with a list of vocabulary to learn and memorize, the teacher includes the words as a natural part of her sentences and repeats important vocabulary like* target audience *and* clues.

(Continued)

(Continued)

Decoding Demonstration Example 2	Notes
T: The skateboard in the commercial reminded you of your cousin and his skateboard? **S6**: Yeah. **T:** Do you think he has fun riding it? **S6:** Yeah. He rides a lot. He's really good.	*Young children sometimes make comments that seem to come out of nowhere. Because those comments can completely sidetrack a lesson, often it is simply best to acknowledge them and move on. Here, the teacher used the child's free association to lead the class to a relevant point that advanced the decoding.*
T: So sometimes commercials show activities that remind us of fun things in our real lives. That's another good "trick" to remember. **Any other tricks that anyone saw?** **S4:** They showed the piano exploding, and the guy had piano keys in his teeth! *[All the children laugh.]* **T:** Yes. **Did anybody notice any other tricks used in the commercial?**	*The focus in this lesson is more on the nutritional messages than the tricks used to sell, so the teacher won't spend too much time delving into the details of advertising techniques. However, to develop higher-order thinking skills, it is always important to teach students to spot common tricks and special effects for themselves. This empowers them to draw their own conclusions and extend the learning from this lesson into their everyday lives.*
S8: There were really big pieces of cereal floating in his dreams, and he was eating the cereal at the end, and it looked really good. **T:** Did they show any other food besides the cereal in the commercial?	*At this point, children might call out more tricks they saw or heard, and the teacher can quickly confirm or expand on them. But since the point of the lesson is the misleading nutritional messages, the teacher should try to steer the conversation as quickly as possible to that.*
S6: He probably had milk on it when he was eating it. **T:** Yes, he probably did—**but did they show any other things to eat or drink besides that?** [Students shake their heads.] **T:** Okay, let's watch it again and practice our observation skills to see if they show any other things to eat or drink besides the cereal. *[Show TV commercial for Honeycomb again, this time pausing on the "complete breakfast shot."]* **T:** So what did they *say* about the cereal? **S4:** That Honeycomb is good for you! **S6:** That it's part of this good breakfast!	*Notice that the teacher doesn't fault the students for missing some important information. Instead, she invites students to practice their observation skills. Working these types of phrases into the dialogue helps students gain awareness of their own learning processes while letting them know that it is worthwhile to pay close attention to media documents. It also lets the teacher avoid conveying a sense of superiority (in kids' terms, the taunt "I know something you don't know.") where the students' job is to guess what the teacher wants to hear rather than to decode the document for themselves using evidence that they see and hear.* *Showing media documents more than once provides viewers with an opportunity to pick up things they might have missed the first time*

Decoding Demonstration Example 2	Notes
T: So was (S4) right? Does saying that it's "part of a good breakfast" mean that Honeycomb is good for you? What do you think? *[Some shaking of heads, some nodding—confusion]* **T:** It's a little confusing. Let's think like detectives and investigate which parts of this breakfast are good for us. **What else are they showing as part of a good breakfast?** [Students call out the foods—toast, milk, orange juice.] **T:** [POINTING TO THE MELON AND KIWI] **What is this?** **S7:** I think it's maybe kiwi? I love kiwi!	*around. This is especially important with video or other media in which images change and when working with young children.*

Figure 4.5 Example of a "Complete Breakfast Shot"

Source: Photograph by Rebecca Rozek.

T: That's right. Kiwi is something you don't see very often on television. *[pointing]* There's also a type of melon called cantaloupe. **What food group do you think kiwi and cantaloupe belong in?** **Ss:** Fruit! **T:** **Do you see anything else that is fruit?** **S4:** Orange juice!	*Depending on the children's answers, the teacher may need to repeat and reinforce what makes something a fruit (e.g., something that is grown outside on trees or bushes or plants, that has a lot of vitamins in it).* *It might be helpful during this part of the decoding to have a poster of the USDA's "My Plate" graphic from www.choosemyplate.gov or*

(Continued)

(Continued)

Decoding Demonstration Example 2	*Notes*
T: Yes, remember sometimes fruit can be squeezed to make juice. **What other food groups do you see?**	*a list of food groups nearby for reference, pointing to the appropriate food group when it comes up.*
S9: Milk!	
T: And what food group does milk belong to—does anyone remember?	*Notice how the teacher uses questions to make sure that the class covers many different food groups, asking if students see anything else when she knows they have missed something important, asking what other food groups they see, or asking about a particular food in the picture that hasn't yet been named. Leading an inquiry-based discussion requires using lots of questions, but it doesn't mean losing control of the content of a lesson. With older students who are developmentally able to engage in more sophisticated analysis, teachers would want to be somewhat more open-ended and less directive with their questions.*
S11: Dairy?	
T: Yes, that's right! Milk and cheese and yogurt all go in the dairy group. **What about the toast?**	
S8: Breads and cereals!	
T: Yes, and we call that the grains group. Remember it's more healthy to eat whole grains than white or refined grains because when they make those, they take out a lot of the fiber that is good for you. **Do you think this toast looks like whole grains or like white, refined grains?**	
Ss: *[mixed answers]* White?	
T: Yes! You can tell that it looks like white bread that's been toasted, so it's refined—and that's not as healthy as whole-grain bread. **And do you think they put anything on the toast?**	*Depending on the class and the time available, the teacher may decide not to go into the "whole grains versus refined grains" issue; young children are not likely to understand it fully, but it is always good to begin introducing ideas that you can build on in later grades.*
S4: Is that a big glob of butter?	
T: It looks like it, doesn't it? **What kind of food is butter?**	
S4: Umm . . . fat?	
T: Butter is certainly high in fat, and you might think it would belong to the dairy group because it's similar to milk and cheese. But you only need to eat a little bit of fat every day and it has lots of calories. So let's review: *[referring to the complete breakfast shot that is still in pause on the screen]* **What is in the picture that is in the fruit group?**	
S7: Kiwi!	
Ss: Orange juice. Melon. Cantaloupe.	*With young children, it is important to repeat key information both within and as a follow-up to the decoding.*
T: And how about dairy?	
Ss: Milk!	
T: What about grains?	
Ss: Toast—but white toast, not healthy toast!	
T: That's right. So far we have listed things that are part of a balanced breakfast. We have grains and fruit and dairy and a little fat. In commercials, we have a	

Decoding Demonstration Example 2	Notes
name for the part of the commercial that includes all those things. It is called a "complete breakfast shot," and it is in almost every cereal commercial you will see. **What other food do you see in the complete breakfast shot that we haven't talked about yet?**	Notice how the teacher integrates the definition of a key term by saying, **"We have a name for that."**
Ss: The cereal! *Honeycomb!*	
T: And what food group does the Honeycomb belong in?	
S4: *[Some may say cereal or grains; some may be unsure.]*	In the real classroom, students won't always have answers to your questions. Rather than supplying an answer, a teacher using an inquiry-based decoding method will help students determine how they can find the answer. Older students should be asked to provide their own suggestions for this (**"How could we find that out?"**), but with very young students it is usually more appropriate to go to an "expert source" for the information, which is what the teacher does here.
T: It's kind of hard to figure out cereals, because they're often shown in the grains group, but sometimes they have other ingredients added to them. Let's watch a video about cereal commercials and what it means when they say "part of a good" or "part of a complete breakfast."	
[Show video clip "Candy for Breakfast?" from Buy Me That 3!*]*	Buy Me That 3!: A Kid's Guide to Food Advertising *(1992) is one of a three-part series that was produced by Consumer Reports and shown on HBO in the early 1990s. The goal of the series was to teach children to be smart consumers about advertising. This clip features the host, Jim Fife, about to eat a bowl of cereal, surrounded by many boxes of popular cereal brands. There is a montage of "complete breakfast shots" from different commercials, and afterward he asks, "Part of a complete breakfast—what does that really mean? You might think you need to have one of these cereals to have a nutritious breakfast, but do you? The truth is the juice, milk, and toast will give you a nutritious breakfast without the bowl of cereal." He then goes on to talk about how much sugar is in these cereals, demonstrating that in a single box of Golden Crisp there are sixty-seven teaspoons of sugar, making it more like "breakfast candy." If you were to do this lesson without the clip, it would be important to re-create that demonstration.*
T: So what was he talking about?	
S5: That there's a lot of sugar in cereals. That cereal is just like candy.	
T: Yes—many cereals have so much sugar added to them that it is sort of like eating candy. **What cereals did you see in the video?**	
Ss: Apple Jacks. Smacks. Golden Crisp.	
T: So those are all cereals with sugar as a main ingredient. **Do you think all cereals have a lot of sugar in them?**	
Ss: *[Answers will vary.]*	
T: Actually some cereals have only a little bit of sugar in them. **Does anyone know a cereal that doesn't have very much sugar in it?**	
S3: Cheerios?	

(Continued)

(Continued)

Decoding Demonstration Example 2	Notes
T: Yes, Cheerios has only a little bit of sugar in it. Also Kix, and most oatmeal. And some cereals, like Rice Krispies, have more, but still not as much as they showed in the video. **So what do you think about Honeycomb? Do you think it might have a lot of sugar?**	*The teacher might want to name cereals that are made locally or "no-name" brands or organic cereals, depending on the audience. Showing a visual example (e.g., flattened cereal boxes, plastic food manipulatives) of what you want children to eat will help them remember what kind of package to look for next time they are in the cereal aisle.*
S1: Yes!	
T: **What makes you think it might have a lot of sugar in it?**	
S1: Because it's got honey in it, and honey is sugar.	
T: Yes, honey is a type of sugar that is made by bees. There are a lot of different names for sugar. And one of the clues to help us figure out if there is a lot of sugar in a particular cereal is seeing if one of those words is the name of the cereal. **Can anybody think of any other words that might be a clue that there is a lot of sugar in the cereal?**	
Ss: Sweet? Frosted Flakes? Honey?	
T: **And is there anything that you might see on the box that might be a clue that there's a lot of sugar in it?** *[Show different empty sugared-cereal boxes or pictures of cereal boxes in ads.]*	*For young children, it is especially important to integrate concrete, hands-on activities with viewing and decoding the video. In this scenario, we recommend that the teacher use lots of flattened empty cereal boxes to show during this discussion, especially ones that have names with words like* frosted, honey, *or* golden; *images of frosted or sparkling pieces of cereal; cereal that is chocolate flavored or has marshmallows in it; and cereals with cartoon characters on the box. It's also important to have boxes of cereals that are low in sugar like Cheerios and Kix. Having extra boxes on hand also provides the teacher with a chance to give students immediate practice using their new skills:* **Okay, what clues do you see on this box that would let you know what ingredients were in this cereal? Do you see any evidence that sugar would be a main ingredient?** *Students can also do that activity in pairs or small groups, and as each pair finds a clue, the teacher could hold up the box to see if everyone agrees.*
S9: Sugar on the cereal? Sparkles?	
T: Yes! **What if there are marshmallows in the cereal?**	
S10: Sugar! Marshmallows are made of sugar, right?	
T: That's right. **What if the cereal is chocolate flavored? Does chocolate have sugar in it?**	
Ss: Yes!	
T: So if we see or hear words like *frosted* or *honey* or *chocolate*, or the cereal has marshmallows as one of its ingredients or there are sparkles on the box, it probably has a lot of sugar. And the same thing is true if the cereal is brightly colored—that's also evidence that it probably has a lot of sugar in it. And another clue is if there is a cartoon character on the box—a lot of times, those cereals have a lot of sugar too. **Besides these clues, is there any other way you could find out how much sugar is in a cereal? Could you ask somebody?**	
S2: You could ask your mom or dad.	

Decoding Demonstration Example 2	Notes
T: That's right, you could ask an adult, and they could read the side of the package. *[Show side panel of a cereal box.]* See, right here it tells you how much sugar is in one bowl of cereal. So you could ask an adult to look and see how much sugar is in a cereal. Now let's watch one more commercial, and see if you can spot the "complete breakfast shot" where they show the cereal with other foods and listen for what they say. [Show TV commercial for Lucky Charms.] **T:** So what did they say about the cereal? **Ss:** It's yummy! It's got marshmallows! **S11:** Lucky Charms is a delicious part of a good breakfast! **T:** And what other foods did they show as part of a good breakfast? **Ss:** A glass of milk, an orange, a muffin. **T:** And what food groups did you see? *[Probe and confirm so they understand that there is dairy, fruit, and grains.]* **And what about the Lucky Charms? What evidence did you see or hear that tells you it might have a lot of sugar in it? What clues did you notice?** **Ss:** It has marshmallows in it! **T:** That's right. **Any other clues?** **S12:** It has a cartoon character in it! **T:** Good observation! **So do you need to have that sugary cereal in order to have a good breakfast?**	*The second commercial provides students with a chance to practice observation and listening skills, further building their own ability to inquire and analyze.* *This commercial is all cartoon, featuring an Irish leprechaun who wants to keep the kids from stealing his Lucky Charms. He uses his magic to create an amusement park, and he rides the Ferris wheel and hides in a giant balloon while describing the different marshmallow shapes in the cereal. The complete breakfast shot shows a huge bowl of cereal with a huge glass of milk, an orange, and a muffin while the leprechaun says, "That would make Lucky Charms a delicious part of this good breakfast." He bursts out of a balloon and falls into a boy's arms, saying "They're magically delicious!"* *In a more advanced class, you might want to pause here to ask if the claim that Lucky Charms is "delicious" is a fact or an opinion, underscoring that just because a student might agree that it is true does not mean it is a fact.*

(Continued)

(Continued)

Decoding Demonstration Example 2	Notes
Ss: No! **T:** In fact, as long as you have other healthy food in the picture, you could put in anything in the complete breakfast shot and say it was part of a good breakfast. I could take out the cereal and put in an old shoe and say, "This shoe is part of this complete breakfast!" **Ss:** *[giggling]* That's not food! You can't eat a shoe! Yuk! **T:** That's right. But I can say it's a picture of a complete breakfast as long as I keep the orange juice, fruit, milk, and toast. **Who can think of something else they could put in the picture instead of the cereal?** *[Encourage students to call out objects—the sillier the better.]* **T:** **So would an old shoe or** *[Use examples students have given; e.g., rock, candy bar, smelly sock, etc.]* **be good for you just because I say it is part of a good or complete breakfast?** **Ss:** No! **T:** So when the commercial said that Honeycomb was part of this good breakfast, it didn't mean Honeycomb was good for you. It meant that it was part of a picture that included a complete breakfast. **So, if Honeycomb or Lucky Charms isn't the "good" part of a good breakfast, could you have a different cereal instead? Is there a better choice you might make for a cereal as part of a healthy breakfast? Would you still need to eat those other foods too?** *[Probe and discuss so the students understand what is important to eat and what isn't. End by reminding students that if they aren't sure whether a food has a lot of sugar in it or not, they can always ask an adult to check the label.]*	*This "What could be in this shot?" game not only reinforces the complete breakfast shot lesson, and does so while allowing students to exercise their natural silliness, but can also provide practice for using drawings later on as an assessment. You could find out whether or not students understood the content of this lesson and give them practice speaking by asking them to draw their own complete breakfast shot, then explain which parts of their picture are the healthy foods from various food groups and which are just included for fun as part of the picture.*

Follow-up to the Cereal Decoding

Notice that children now have skills and knowledge to look skeptically at cereal advertising aimed at them, even though the teacher never used the word *misleading*. And they know it more deeply than they would if a teacher had simply lectured the class about commercials being bad for them (which you wouldn't want to do because some commercials, like public service announcements, promote positive behaviors).

Also note that the goal is not to cover every detail of the commercial (e.g., there is no discussion here of the fact that we see the boy eat the cereal but not any other part of the complete breakfast, although that would be an interesting thing to explore with an older group of students). What you choose to emphasize will depend on the goal(s) of the particular lesson. For example, in another Project Look Sharp elementary health kit lesson, the emphasis is on helping children understand that just because a product has the word *fruit* in the product name, shows pictures of fruit on the box or in the commercial, or says it is "fruit flavored" doesn't mean that the product actually contains a lot of fruit. In that lesson, children are taught about real fruit (including fruit juices and dried fruit). Then they explore commercials for "fruit" snacks and "fruit" drinks (compared to 100% juice). Cereals are also part of that lesson (Froot Loops, Fruity Pebbles, etc.), but the focus is on whether or not they have any fruit in them, not on how much sugar they have or how they fit into a healthy, complete breakfast.

Finally, notice how doing the decoding as a class allows students to learn from one another as well as from the teacher. The collective wisdom of the class broadens observations and insights as classmates comment on things that not everyone (including the teacher) may have noticed. This opens students up to learning from all kinds of people in their lives and to valuing their own knowledge.

Extensions to the Cereal Decoding

It is very important for young children to practice what they have learned on an ongoing basis, so teachers should keep an eye out for "teachable moments." For this lesson, such moments might come during snack or meal time. Teachers can also revisit this lesson using different examples of commercials or by bringing in other cereal boxes for students to examine.

Decodings also provide a wonderful opportunity to involve families in what the students have learned. In this example, teaching nutrition using inquiry-based media literacy gives children knowledge and skills without making them feel bad about their past food choices or making them feel like their families are doing something wrong. The students often feel very empowered by what they have learned, and their experience can affect their later behaviors. In fact, teachers who have done the cereal or fruit decodings have shared stories from parents about children who come home from school talking about healthy cereals, ask their parents to check to see how much sugar is in cereal, look for "100% juice" in the grocery store, etc. This is what we mean by the "trickle up effect"—students teach their families what they have learned and perhaps change the perceptions and choices of the entire family.

In one example, after a kindergarten class had finished its nutrition lessons, we got an e-mail from a parent who said that her daughter had come home and said she couldn't eat Fruity Pebbles anymore because it had too much sugar in it and didn't have any fruit at all. Instead, she asked for Cheerios, which her mother bought for her. A few weeks later, the daughter asked for Fruity Pebbles for breakfast. Her mother said, "I thought you said that had too much sugar." And the daughter responded, "Oh, I shouldn't have told you about that!"—but then asked for the Cheerios instead.

Like adults, even media-literate children can know that a food is not the most nutritious and still want to eat it. Knowledge never guarantees that students will do the desired behavior, but it does increase the chances that they will make good decisions.

AFTER A DECODING

After leading a decoding with your students, take some time to assess how well the decoding experience worked to meet your goals. Note how the students (individually and as a whole class) responded to different documents and questions and keep that feedback in mind when planning your next decoding. Also, note whether the activity succeeded in involving students who are not typically engaged in learning as well as those who typically are. And assess whether the decoding of these documents seemed to open up important conversations that might build toward a shared understanding of different perspectives. You may find that you will need to adapt the decoding or eliminate "great" documents that just don't work as well as you thought they would.

Be prepared for students to complain that their new habits of inquiry have "ruined" their ability to watch television (or other media) because they keep thinking about how things were made and what the messages are. This is a natural consequence of literacy (once one knows how to read, it is impossible not to). Though media literacy is not intended to "ruin" media experiences, this may be one of the outcomes, at least initially. You may want to commiserate and relate it to other kinds of knowledge acquired (e.g., knowing how sausage—or political legislation—is made), or you might equate their new awareness with an increased capacity to appreciate media, in the same way that learning about music helps listeners hear things in compositions that they previously missed.

As you do more and more document decoding with your students, you will learn from your mistakes and successes. You will be able to predict the types of responses that your students are likely to have, although you'll need to continue to be flexible in cases when a class or a student responds in unexpected ways. You can also use the rubric given in Table 4.1 to assess how well the decoding went in terms of inquiry-based practice. Checking the rubric from time to time can serve as a reminder of discussion strategies that help students develop their own habits of inquiry.

Finally, don't despair if the first few times that your students participate in document decoding, they seem to have trouble getting to the "deep reading" level, only responding with fairly superficial analyses or comments. Insightful decoding—like all of media literacy—involves skills that need to be developed through practice.[CP3] We have repeatedly found that the high school students who have been doing media literacy decoding consistently for many months are much better at getting to the deeper issues than our older college students who are just being introduced to the decoding process. So remember that your students will get better at this the more they do it—and so will you. With enough practice, your students will begin decoding classroom documents without prompting from you. That's when you'll know you have succeeded.

Table 4.1 Leading a Media Literacy Decoding—Teacher Evaluation

Element	Unsatisfactory	Basic	Proficient	Distinguished*
Media Selection	Teacher selects documents that are simplistic, unrelated to curriculum or students' lives, or are primarily chosen to provide an opportunity for the teacher to convey his or her own beliefs to students.	Teacher selects curriculum-related documents, but they are not complex enough to serve well as prompts for rich discussions.	Teacher presents documents that are curriculum-related, and offer rich opportunities for multiple interpretations.	Students add relevant documents from their own experience to the initial documents supplied by the teacher.
Discussion Techniques	Teacher asks all questions and accepts or rejects student answers; exchanges are predominantly between single students (one at a time) and teacher; questions are asked in rapid succession with little time for student reflection.	Teacher makes some attempt to engage students in genuine discussion during the decoding, with uneven results.	Teacher facilitates genuine discussion among students, leaving time for students to reflect before responding and often stepping aside to allow other students to join the conversation.	Students assume considerable responsibility for the discussion, raising issues and initiating new topics.
Quality of Questions	Teacher's questions are leading (designed to come to a single, correct, foregone conclusion or to reinforce the teacher's beliefs), or offer little cognitive challenge.	Teacher asks a few of the Key Questions, mostly focused on message Content and Techniques; sometimes asks students to cite their evidence, but avoids asking deeper questions about Purposes or significance.	Teacher draws from many of the Key Question categories; follows up basic questions with more complex prompts; words questions in ways that link discussion to the curriculum; routinely asks students to back up answers with document-based evidence.	Teacher asks high quality prompts in order to model asking questions; students ask many of the questions themselves, including Key Questions and questions of their own.
Interpretation of Media Messages	Teacher presents media document and tells students what it means (or provides students with an "expert's" interpretation of what the messages are).	Teachers shares their own or an "expert's" interpretation but also leaves open the possibility of multiple interpretations.	Teacher welcomes diverse student interpretations.	Following the teacher's lead, students expect and respect diverse interpretations of the same message.
Student Participation	Teacher allows a few students to dominate the discussion.	Teacher attempts to engage all students, but only a few respond.	Teacher engages all students in the discussion; students actively participate and are responsive.	Students are clearly comfortable voicing their views and do so with clarity and respect; all voices are heard in the discussion.

Note: Based on the work of Danielson (2010).

*No matter how skilled or experienced the teacher, it would be unrealistic to expect that students would initiate questions and discussion without many opportunities to practice. And very young students will likely always need some scaffolding from teachers in order to do deep readings. So teachers (and those who evaluate performance) should expect that most of the time, even the best media literacy teachers will operate at the proficient level, and they will have to work their way towards the "distinguished" level with every new group of students with whom they work.

5

General Approaches to Teaching Media Literacy Across the Whole Curriculum

Viewing media literacy as *literacy* makes it easier to see it as part of everything we do as educators and to find a multitude of ways (large and small) to incorporate it into our daily teaching. Still, at conferences and schools, when we suggest that media literacy can be integrated into any curriculum area and at every grade level, we get more than a few skeptical glances. But over the course of more than a decade of Project Look Sharp workshops in which participants create their own lesson plans, we have witnessed professionals from across the educational spectrum producing a huge variety of lessons. We know that it is possible to integrate media literacy into any subject area and grade level because we have seen it.

In this chapter and the following one, we provide both general and content-specific suggestions for integrating media literacy into teaching. Many of the strategies are simple tweaks to existing practice, and most can be adapted for different grade levels.

An important reminder as we begin this process: Simply *using* nonprint media or new technologies with your students does not necessarily mean you are *doing* media literacy education. In the same vein, teaching students to use new media technologies to communicate their own messages, while a useful goal, doesn't necessarily mean that the class involves media literacy. Media literacy activities are distinguished from general integration of technology or pop culture by their emphasis on inquiry and student reflection. And in our approach to media literacy, activities also start with curriculum goals and the needs of learners.

GENERAL WAYS TO INTEGRATE MEDIA LITERACY

We start with some tweaks that can be adapted to many curriculum areas and grade levels.

- **Replace generic exercises or questions with media-related examples.** A math teacher demonstrating calculation with decimals might replace an existing word problem with one related to media and then follow up with a brief discussion about the issues raised by the problem (e.g., "A soda company paid $500,000 to produce a 30-second TV commercial and $2.5 million to have it air during the Super Bowl. If cans of soda average 50¢ each, how many cans would the company have to sell before it pays for the ad?"[1] Or an elementary school teacher working with students to recognize adjectives could replace the standard worksheet of sentences with the script of a sales pitch. Students circle the adjectives, discussing the definition of each, and then read the script with the adjectives changed or removed, comparing the different impressions of the product reflected in the two versions.

- **Identify "teachable moments" that occur when students are describing media they have encountered.** Instead of dismissing or staying out of student conversations about films or TV shows they've seen, for example, use these as opportunities to learn about your students' media use and to raise their own awareness of their media choices. Without being judgmental, encourage them to ask the kinds of questions that will help them think critically about their media experiences.

- **Model using nonprint along with print media as information sources.** When you use video, audio, or digital applications, take care to demonstrate that these media can be important sources for active learning and listening, in addition to being entertainment. [CP2.5]

  o Expect students to take notes and/or be prepared to discuss content.

o Help students focus on what you want them to learn by sharing with them ahead of time your purpose for spending class time using particular media. This is especially important with media that students are accustomed to using for entertainment, because the way that students' choose to focus their attention influences what they learn and remember, and people are more likely to be in the habit of using entertainment media to relax their brains than to put their brains in learning mode.[2] The right kinds of prompts can direct students' attention to particular material and foster active engagement.

o Use short segments from full-length video or audio materials, focusing only on the key portions that best illustrate or reinforce your lesson goals. Pause longer pieces frequently to discuss and invite questions, the same way that you might assign and discuss a book a chapter at a time.

o When you project media in class, leave the lights on if possible. Nothing sends the signal that it is naptime like turning off the lights (and it makes taking notes difficult).

o Avoid using screen media as a reward. Not only does this reinforce the notion that printed texts are more serious than other types of media, but it makes screen media seem like dessert and printed texts seem like veggies. We want students to see all types of media as valuable sources of information and insight.

o Teach students how to properly cite nonprint sources.

- **Have students apply Key Questions to their writing and other creative projects.** Ask students to reflect on (both in class discussions and in writing) their own creative, informative, and persuasive written assignments, as well as projects that involve other types of communication forms (e.g., posters, dioramas, videos, PowerPoint or Prezi presentations) and media that they create outside of class (e.g., instant messages or social-networking pages).

- **Incorporate media literacy into the study of a new topic by adding media literacy questions to a K-W-L[3] approach.**

o After asking, "What do you already *Know* about this topic?" follow up by asking, "Where did you get your information or ideas? What were your sources?"

Encourage reflection about the answers. Be sure to note when the answers include media and discuss the role of popular media in influencing our beliefs or what we think we know.

o After asking, "What do we *Want* to know about this topic?" ask, "Where might we find credible information about this topic to be able to answer our questions about it?"

Explore different types of sources, discussing the advantages for learning from each. When might a person be more helpful than a media source, or an audiovisual or web resource be a better choice than a published text-based one (e.g., due to currency, importance of visual characteristics, or ability to illustrate an action)? Develop an information plan with the students regarding where and how the class might find the best sources for their exploration.

○ After asking, "What did we *Learn* about this topic?" ask, "Which sources were the most helpful and most credible about this topic?"

As a class, reflect on the usefulness of the different sources you used and the advantages and limitations of each.

- **Have students (or the class as a whole) develop a "media literacy toolbox."** This will include the frameworks, terms, concepts, and resources that will help them in their ongoing process of inquiry about media messages. This would likely include the Key Questions grids (both for analysis and production), as well as frameworks like the Key Concepts about media messages (see Chapter 1), all of which are available as handouts on the book's website. It is also likely to include rubrics for judging the credibility of information in various types of media documents (including websites), terms and concepts that have been learned as part of media literacy lessons, and resources such as http://snopes.com. This "toolbox" can be physical (e.g., a notebook in which students keep relevant handouts or a chart of the Key Questions on the wall of the classroom) or conceptual. Teachers might also incorporate the "toolbox" idea as part of assessments or assignments (e.g., "Using at least three of the media literacy concepts or questions in your toolbox, evaluate the arguments made in the president's speech about nuclear energy.").

- **Discuss the relative advantages and disadvantages of different communication formats students might use to present their work.** When would video or PowerPoint be the best mode for conveying information, and when might a written paper be a better choice? When would the inclusion of visual elements be important, and when would they be unnecessary? When would a personal (face-to-face) presentation have the advantage over one conveyed primarily through media? When is "text-speak" effective, and when is it inappropriate? How do audience size, presentation context, and the need to provide clear citations influence those decisions?

- **Have the class collectively critique examples of visual presentations in preparation for creating their own.** Using past student work (with any names or identifying information deleted) on a curriculum-related topic or examples from the book's website, deconstruct and evaluate the production choices made by the creator of the message. How well did the color and font choices work? Was the text clear and readable? Was there too much print content (or too little)? Could more visual images or video footage have helped as examples? Were there visual elements that distracted from the message? Was information presented in tables or graphs clear, with appropriate labeling for categories and axes? How could the presentation have been improved?

- **Provide opportunities for students to communicate and collaborate with individuals outside of their school community through new media modalities.** Encourage students to find experts on a topic whom they might interview or discuss issues with as part of their exploration of the topic. Identify ways in which your students might interact or collaborate with students from another school—or even another country—to deepen their understanding of perspective and cultural differences. Help students develop strategies to assess the credibility of these sources, including when it is reasonable to accept a source as representative of a larger group of people and when they should seek multiple perspectives. Discuss "netiquette," asking students to share and reflect on rules and guidelines for communicating in mediated formats in ways that are respectful.

- **Use media examples as part of the assessment at the end of a unit.** Get into the habit of collecting examples of media documents that include both accurate and inaccurate information or portrayals about topics that you cover in your classes. As part of your standard assessment at the end of a unit on that topic, include one or more of those examples, asking students to note things that are true and things that are not true based on what they have learned in the class. Be sure to leave time to discuss the media documents after students have completed the assessment.[4]

- **Use a video game–scoring framework for activities involving decision making.** Have students assign points to various choices (e.g., which actions would best preserve biodiversity in a particular region or which snack choices would be most nutritious). As in games, the best choices would be awarded the most points. Once students have made the link between scoring and values, it is easy to involve them in an analysis of the values expressed in their favorite video games.

- **Identify ways in which your students can publish or share their work with a wider audience using new media technologies.** Encourage students to publish their written work or post their videos or photographs online and discuss which sites might provide the best venue. Develop a class blog or newsletter to share projects with families and other classes. Involve students in the decisions about what content to include and how the material is presented (keeping in mind the purpose, target audience, and other Key Questions for producing media messages).

- **Use visual and audiovisual media as part of parent-teacher conferences and open houses.** Involve students in creating short video presentations or photographic displays describing a typical day in the classroom or representing their learning progress, asking students to weigh in on the decisions made about what to include and what to leave out. For an example of how to do this with very young students, see Rogow (2011).

VOICES FROM THE FIELD: *MEDIA LITERACY AND OPEN HOUSE*

Elementary school librarian June Locke created open-house videos with students in third- through fifth-grade classes. While the students weren't able to handle all of the technology involved in video editing, they participated fully in scripting what the final video would look like, deciding what content to include and exclude, selecting transitions and title slides, creating voiceovers, and other technology decisions. Locke held numerous discussions with the students and teacher regarding these production choices. One class felt that what they were doing in science at that time (which mostly involved reading and library research) didn't really "look like science," so they decided to create new activities for the videotape that "looked more like science," like using microscopes and testing batteries. Their discussions included the ethical aspects of including footage of activities that don't really happen during the school day and the opportunity to rearrange the order of the typical class schedule because it would make a more interesting video. The finished product was tremendously useful for the teacher to show during the open house, and it was also a powerful way for students to participate and be represented in that event even when they couldn't be there in person. It provided students with an opportunity to reflect on how best to represent their typical day as well as a concrete understanding of the media literacy concept that "all media are constructed."

- **Actively facilitate "writing" in multiple media modes:**

  ○ Be flexible in assignments, allowing students to choose which media formats are the most effective way for them to communicate the required information.

  ○ Have students incorporate multiple media formats into standard written reports (e.g., inserting photographs or computer illustrations).

  ○ Ask students to design their written work as if it was a chapter in their textbook, using headings, subheadings, illustrations, sidebars, charts, etc. Help them think about which information is important enough to highlight and why.

- **Involve students in local community or service projects in which they can put their media literacy skills into action:**

  ○ Find collaborative possibilities for projects with community institutions (e.g., museums, libraries, galleries, service agencies) that involve students in analyzing or creating media messages.

  ○ Encourage older students to teach production techniques or media literacy principles to younger students.

  ○ Use media forums (e.g., local community access TV, newspapers, social networking sites, or electronic mailing lists such as Listservs) to solicit input or share research about a topic.

○ Help students see the power of media by encouraging them to use media to give people in their community a voice (e.g., record and share oral histories, interviews, local events, etc.).

FEATURED EXAMPLE

Developing Student "Noticings"

A fundamental goal for inquiry-based media literacy education is for students to develop habits of inquiry that extend beyond the classroom into their daily lives. As an educator, you can make that goal explicit as part of the ongoing classroom culture, encouraging students to keep their eyes and ears open for examples in media and pop culture that reflect the curriculum content and media literacy principles they've been learning. These "noticings" could be related to a number of topics:

- **Curriculum content**—As students navigate their daily lives outside of school, they are likely to come across media content that reflects what they are learning (or have already learned) that year in class. For example, they may

  ○ see a music video dealing with a social issue that came up in class discussion.
  ○ encounter a news report related to a science issue.
  ○ play a video game with heroes or a story arc that parallels a novel the class is reading.
  ○ hear dialogue that includes a joke about or historical reference to a person or time period they've just studied.

  Encourage students to look for media that are examples of excellence as well as those that contradict classroom lessons. You might also ask students to keep an eye out for particular themes related to classwork (e.g., media messages about family, respect, war, math, conservation, success, etc.).

- **Misleading or inaccurate information**—Media content often contains errors or misleading representations of real-world situations. For example, students may see a sign that misuses grammar or misspells a word, a video that purports to be real but includes action that defies logic or the laws of physics, or an e-mail containing an urban legend.

- **Ad spotting**—Advertising is now infused into media content, popular culture, and even educational materials in "stealth" ways. Recognizing the commercial nature of these types of messages is an important way to empower students to take actions based on conscious decision making. Advertising may occur in numerous forms:

  ○ Product placements, which are brand names or products that have been included in the media content because of a payment or quid pro quo deal with the advertiser. These are common in TV shows and films, video games, sporting events, young adult books (like the *Clique* novels by Lisi Harrison), and even educational videos (like films about puberty supplied by makers of the featured brand of sanitary napkins).

(Continued)

(Continued)

VOICES FROM THE FIELD: *SPOTTING PRODUCT PLACEMENTS*

When the movie *Antz* (1998) was first released, a local elementary school was invited to bring its students to see a special pre-winter holiday screening. Prior to the field trip, teachers took the time to teach their students some facts about real ants so they could discuss what was accurate and inaccurate in the animated film's portrayal of ants. They also took a few minutes to explain the concept of product placements and told the students that they would be seeing some product placements in the film. When the first bottle of Pepsi appeared in the scene of Insectopia, there was a rousing shout from the children in the audience—"product placement!"—and students continued to identify product placements in videos and other media for the remainder of the school year. This is a terrific example of how teachers can use media literacy to develop both skills and knowledge.

- o **Sponsorships and cross-marketing** (e.g., money paid to a sports star to use a particular brand of sports equipment, underwriting of programs or educational materials in exchange for brand exposure, giving away "free" gifts or special discounts in exchange for entering a contest or opening a credit card account, collaboration between films and restaurants to market each other at both sites, etc.)
- o **Viral marketing** (e.g., paying teens to log in to chat rooms or social networking sites and casually drop product names or music references into their conversations, providing free products to college students to have available at their parties, online "advergames" that incorporate logos and other brand elements into the game's settings or action, etc.)

Examples of noticings can be collected and shared in many different ways: during circle time, by emptying a box and discussing its contents during what typically might be unproductive class time (e.g., late Friday afternoon), or on a class discussion board. You could have formal sheets for recording noticings (see handout on the website or periodically ask if anyone has any noticings to share.

By encouraging the practice of noticings, you can bridge home and school experiences; build habits of inquiry that may transfer to other arenas; provide ongoing practice in observation, writing, and speaking; and reinforce the relevance of school for students' lives.

INFORMATION LITERACY

No matter what subject area you are teaching, if you want students to develop the habits of inquiry that are at the core of media literacy, it is vitally important for students to be able to identify information sources and judge their credibility.

Sources of Information

As educators, we are often the gatekeepers for classroom information sources (e.g., which websites can be used for assignments). If we want students to be able to make decisions themselves about what sources of information are best to use when learning about a topic—inside and outside of school—then we must explicitly teach them how to make those judgments and why their criteria matter. To accomplish this, teachers and library media specialists can

- **make their own decisions more transparent by explaining why they selected certain resources and why they find those sources credible.** For the youngest students, that might mean just getting in the habit of saying, "The source of this story is . . ." or "This information is from. . . ." For older students, more detailed explanations would be appropriate: "This story is based on the work of a historian who used primary sources from multiple eyewitnesses with differing perspectives."

- **involve students in the decision about what information sources to use and encourage them to think about what kinds of sources the class can or should use to learn about a new topic** (e.g., When might we learn more from video footage than from simply reading about a topic in a book? When would a website or newspaper provide more up-to-date information than a standard encyclopedia?).

- **encourage students to view their textbook as a media document:**
  - Have students look at the cover of their textbook and discuss what ideas it conveys about the topics inside and why the publisher might have chosen those images.
  - Note that publishers, not authors, choose covers and ask why that might be the case.
  - Have students glance through the book and make educated guesses (based on the use of graphics) about what topics or ideas are most important to the author(s).
  - At the end of a course or year, have students review what they learned by asking whether or not they agreed with the book's editing choices about what to feature and what to omit; older students might even discuss the distinction between "omit" and "exclude."

- **help students reflect on how and when sources are included for claims presented in different media sources.** Also, help students to notice when sources are *not* given and to understand why that matters.

- **assign students to create annotated bibliographies for research reports.** These will include information on where students found their sources and why they believe them to be reliable.

- **frame lessons about how to create citations.** Educators can explain that the purpose of citations is to help other people find and analyze their sources the same way that students analyze media sources. Helpful questions might include these:
  - Why is the year or date important?
  - What assumptions can we make about the credibility of a source based on its type (e.g., journal versus magazine articles, dissertations versus edited books, encyclopedias versus wikis)?
  - Why are page numbers important to include?
  - Why isn't the URL enough when referencing a website, and how can you identify a particular section when there are no page numbers?

○ What do you learn about a web source from all of the different parts of its URL (not just the suffix)?[5]

○ Students using tools such as Noodlebib (www.noodletools.com), which create citations automatically from information that users plug in, could be asked why the application asks for particular kinds of information.

Media Gatekeepers

Teaching about citations is also an excellent time to introduce different search engines, asking students to compare results for search terms entered into search engines with different purposes.[6] A discussion of gatekeepers—people or institutions that control access to information—also provides a way to begin a lesson on source credibility that empowers students rather than lecturing them.

Try starting a research assignment with this tweak. Ask, "If someone was given the same assignment 25 years ago, where would they go to find information? What about 50 years ago? 100 years ago? "The answer to all of these is likely to include going to the library and looking in the encyclopedia. But what about today—how many of our students would go to a library instead of doing a web search for the information? Follow this by introducing the concept of "gatekeepers." When librarians, teachers, or encyclopedia editors were the primary gatekeepers for most information, students relied on them to decide which resources could be trusted and which ones couldn't. But on the Internet, those gatekeepers don't exist. That means students need to take responsibility for themselves to make good decisions about sources and assess the credibility of information (beginning at least in upper elementary school).[7] Older students might be asked to think about who the existing gatekeepers of information are (Google? Newscasters? Talk radio hosts? Comedians?) and what role tags or RSS feeds play. For all students, a discussion of gatekeepers provides a rich opportunity to think about how we seek out information and the advantages—and disadvantages—we face today with virtually unlimited access to all information on the Internet.

REFLECTION: *WIKIPEDIA*

How do you feel about using Wikipedia as a source? Do you ever use it yourself when researching information online? How would you explain its advantages and drawbacks to students? Would you allow—or even encourage—your students to use it when researching information about a topic or cite it as a source on a reference list? Why or why not?

One of the suggested assignments in this chapter involves having students revise an entry on Wikipedia to make it more thorough and accurate. What media literacy skills and concepts would that address? Would you feel comfortable having your students do that assignment? Why or why not?

Internet Credibility

One of the most important aspects of media literacy follows from this discussion: How can we judge the credibility of information we read or see on the Internet? When we ask our college students how they know if a website is credible or not, they almost always respond by saying they look at the URL. They view sites with a suffix of *.edu, .gov,* and *.org* as credible but sites with suffixes of *.com* and *.net* as not credible.

There are several ways to clearly demonstrate the limitations in this approach.[8] One of the most powerful involves the website http://martinlutherking.org. At the time we are writing this book, that site always comes up on the first page of a Google search for "Martin Luther King," and its description says "A True Historical Examination." Clicking that link would take you to the homepage, which is shown in Figure 5.1. Take a few minutes to examine the figure. Who is the target audience, and what's your evidence? What elements of the site are likely to give the impression that it is an educational resource, especially to an elementary or middle school student? What elements of the site might indicate that its claims are questionable?[9]

These are the kinds of media literacy questions that students should be encouraged to ask when evaluating the credibility of a website. They should also ask Authorship questions: Who made this website, and what is their purpose?[10] In fact, this website was created by Stormfront, a Nazi white supremacist group that seeks to indoctrinate students into its racist view of Martin Luther King and civil rights.[11]

After guiding students to question and understand the purpose of the website, you might wrap up the decoding by asking students, "What did you learn from this activity about using URLs to determine credibility? If a URL is not a reliable indicator of credibility, how will you know if a site is credible or not?"[12] The answer is to ask Key Questions about Authorship, Purpose, Context, Content, and Credibility; you can remind students that they already know several of those questions.

Figure 5.1   Homepage of the Website http://martinlutherking.org

Leading an analysis of the Stormfront website with students can be a powerful experience, but it should be approached with some caution, given the sensitive and potentially harmful nature of its content.[13] We recommend that you use screen grabs of relevant pages rather than going to the site itself, because it is in part the number of hits that keeps a website in the top ten search results and we don't want to encourage thousands of hits by teachers using the hate site as a teaching tool.

After teaching students how to evaluate the credibility of information on websites, you can assess understanding by assigning each student to find two websites on the same topic, one that he or she judges to be very credible and one not credible. Students'written evaluations of each website should include the search process they used to find it (and more than just "Googled it"—they should include where it fell on the list and why they selected that site to look at), as well as answers to the relevant media literacy questions. Their analyses should include specific evidence in support of the websites' credibility (or lack of credibility). This should include content from the websites themselves but might also include follow-up research to investigate the credentials of the authors or identify other information that could shed light on credibility issues.

Students can also gain powerful insights about the credibility of information on websites like Wikipedia by actually contributing content to them. Ask students to find a topic they know a lot about and then read what the Wikipedia entry says about it. Have them identify information that might be inaccurate or incomplete and then ask them to upgrade the entry by adding to or changing it. They will need to be able to justify their own sources of information to support the credibility of their post, and they will reflect on the process of contributing to the collective knowledge about that topic or issue "known" around the world.

Another way in which students can gain a powerful—and sometimes disconcerting—understanding of how information gets put up on the Internet is to have them "Google themselves" by searching their names to see what comes up (in both text and images), then reflecting on how their cyber images compare to who they are in the physical world. Older students might discuss the common practice of college admissions offices and employers doing this type of Internet search to find out more about their applicants, including issues of ethics and control. And while students can't usually delete what's already there, they can work to alter their cyber footprint by altering their Facebook pages, posting to blogs, making sure that volunteer activities they are involved in are posted online (e.g., by offering to write up a report for the organization's website), etc.

NEWS LITERACY, JOURNALISM, AND CURRENT EVENTS

Like information literacy, the analysis and creation of news cuts across many curriculum areas. Through the course of their lives, most students will get much of their information about the world from news reports. As Thomas Jefferson argued 200 years ago, an informed citizenry made possible by a free press is essential to the workings of a healthy democracy. Much more recently, the Knight Commission's 2009 report *Informing Communities: Sustaining Democracy in the Digital Age* stressed the importance of news literacy, and one of its key recommendations was to "integrate digital and media literacy as critical elements for education at all levels" (p. xvii). Learning how to analyze news stories is clearly essential to helping students become prepared to be "active citizens."

By the time they graduate from high school, students who are "news literate" should be able to distinguish between factual news and opinion and among journalists, pundits, and commentators. They should also

- know what makes a news report reliable (e.g., verification of facts, presentation of evidence, source citation);
- recognize the problems inherent in using anonymous sources;
- be aware that photographs can be digitally manipulated (e.g., cropped, Photoshopped);
- recognize the ways in which editing and other production choices influence the messages; and
- understand the value of letting events or individuals speak for themselves.

The multiple forms of news and commentary that populate the Internet today make all of this increasingly challenging for both students and adults. Blogs, in particular, are often mistaken for news reports, and there is increasing pressure to report stories quickly, without taking the necessary time to verify the information or reflect on the impact of a news story on the individuals involved.

The Nature of News

To determine how you might help students achieve these goals in ways that are integral to your core curriculum, it is helpful to know a bit about news. Depending on the age of your students, you may want to build these concepts into your discussion of news.

The Agenda-Setting Function of News

The news media certainly influence what we think about the issues that they cover. But perhaps more important, the news media influence which issues we think about at all. Like the person in charge of the agenda in a meeting, the news media have considerable power in determining what people, events, and topics are important enough to consider each day. Traditional journalistic criteria such as "What will have the greatest impact on the largest number of people?" are often offset by other criteria, such as "What has the best pictures?" or "What will be dramatic enough (or salacious or frightening enough) to sell the most copy?" For example, a headline like "Senate Overhauls Social Security" refers to a story with more important implications than "Congressman Caught Sucking Toes of Secretary in Hotel Tryst," but the latter is likely to generate more web hits than the former. In the United States, the pressures to generate revenue also lead to a preference for coverage of items that are directly related to Americans, so international news is often ignored unless something especially explosive has happened.[14] For an exercise that highlights the agenda-setting function of news media, see the companion

website.

News as Paradox

Another important thing to know about the impact of news on our "knowledge" about the world is that we tend to believe the most that which we know the least about. The more we know about a person, place, or topic, the greater our ability to question what we read or hear about him, her, or it. So we are better able to assess whether a report about the neighborhood we live in is accurate than a report about someplace across the globe that neither we—nor anyone we know—has personally visited. By definition, most news is about things that are unusual—so it's not a good source for learning about daily life in other places, though we often take it that way. Also, because news media cover and repeat those unusual stories (e.g., shark attacks, murders), we think they happen more often than they actually do (Ruscio, 2006), and we rarely hear about daily occurrences even when they are dramatic (e.g., thousands of children worldwide don't have access to clean drinking water or enough to eat).

"Parasocial Relationships"

We only "know" many celebrities and other people through the media, but we feel as though we actually know what they are like (their personalities and preferences) and that we have some kind of relationship with them. We even make judgments about whether news stories about them are believable based on "knowing" their character. This tendency can also occur with fictional characters; actors, for example, often tell stories about fans treating them as though they are the characters they play.[15]

VNRs and Other News Sources

Today's news creation often involves the use of video news releases (VNRs), PR pieces created by outside organizations (e.g., advertisers, lobbyists, government groups) and provided free of charge to cash-strapped news organizations for use in stories. Television news outlets—especially local news stations— increasingly use excerpts from VNRs. Though there are discussions about changing the rules, stations are not now required to label or identify the source of these clips, leaving the impression that the content reflects the more "objective" viewpoint of the news station rather than the biases of a promotional piece.[16]

Humorous Media Content as a Source of News

Adolescents and young adults are increasingly likely to turn to late-night comedy shows for news, especially regarding political candidates and issues.[17]

While editorial cartoons have long been important sources of humorous and pointed commentary about news and politics and satirical publications like the *Onion* have a rich history of spoofing news, digital media technologies now allow all sorts of individuals and organizations to do the same, and in a fairly sophisticated way. When students don't distinguish among journalism, satire, comedy, and commentary, they can easily become misinformed. For example, in 2008, the *New Yorker* ran a cover portraying presidential candidate Barack Obama as a Muslim (complete with a picture of Osama bin Laden on the wall and flag burning in the fireplace). While the cover's title—noted only inside the magazine—was "The Politics of Fear," some who were unfamiliar with the magazine's long history of using satirical covers thought the magazine was confirming that Obama was indeed a Muslim.

REFLECTION: *YOUR OWN NEWS SOURCES*

Where do you get *your* news, and why? How do you know those sources are reliable? Do you regularly go to more than one source? Would anything lead you to reconsider the sources you typically turn to for news?

Resources for Teaching News Literacy

Two wonderful resources for news analysis are Newspapers in Education (whose website at http://nieonline.com includes lesson plans and other resources for educators) and the Newseum (whose website at http://newseum .org includes more than 800 front pages of newspapers from around the world every day). Also, http://gradethenews.org offers a printable scorecard for evaluating news on several quality measures, and the book *Detecting Bull: How to Identify Bias and Junk Journalism in Print, Broadcast, and on the Wild Web* by the site's founder John McManus (2009) is also an excellent resource for learning to think more deeply about news.[18]

Lesson Ideas

There are many ways to combine coursework with news literacy, often by selecting news stories whose content directly relates to your curriculum.

Customizing or Extending the Key Questions

Start with any news report related to what you are teaching and apply the Key Questions to a discussion of its content.

- **Authorship**—Is this story from a wire service? Did the reporter actually investigate the story, or did she or he receive the information from another source? Where was the journalist (e.g., at the event or reporting from a regional bureau or remote location)? Who played a role in deciding how the story was edited; what headline and images accompanied it; and where it appeared in the newspaper, news program, or website?

- **Content**—How does this compare to what you have learned in class or from other sources?
- **Credibility**—Which parts of this story are factual, and how do I know? How is it rated by fact-checking web resources like http://factcheck.org or http://newstrust.net?
- **Response**—What perspectives are expressed in comments posted to online news stories or letters to the editors? (See, for example, the final lesson in Project Look Sharp's *Media Constructions of Martin Luther King, Jr.* kit.)
- **Economics**—Whom do the reporters and photographers/videographers work for? Where does the money come from that paid for this story?
- **Purpose**—What are the links between Purpose (e.g., to support a political position or to generate revenue for corporate owners) and Content (including Techniques used to attract attention)?
- **Techniques**—Might the photographs included in this story have been digitally altered, and why? What is it about the way that this looks that makes me think it is news? To increase Awareness of the formal features of news, ask students to draw a picture of a typical TV news report. You may be amazed at how similar their pictures will be: a single commentator (often male), seated, only head and shoulders showing, with a screen or graphic shown in the upper right corner and a "crawl" along the bottom of the page. Recognizing the techniques that quickly establish that "this is a news story" can help students recognize when an advertisement or other persuasive message is co-opting those techniques to imply credibility about its claims.[19] This occurs frequently in newspapers, and papers are bound by ethics requirements to label such "stories" as advertisements (although they don't always do so).
- **Context** and **Content** questions can also help students better understand the structure of the news media by

  o identifying different types of news articles (feature stories, commentary, investigative stories, international news feeds, human interest stories, etc.).
  o comparing the way news is reported in different media formats (newspapers, newsmagazines, radio, TV, the Internet) and distinguishing between news and opinion (editorials, blogs, letters to the editor, etc.) or fact-checked news and reports coming live (or nearly live) from observers' (or participants') phones, Twitter accounts, or social-networking sites.
  o discussing the importance of photographs and captions and the role that headlines and magazine covers play in framing a news story.

Exploring International News Sources

These basic Key Questions can also help students recognize and reflect on the fact that in the United States we receive almost all of our news from US sources. This might seem obvious, but it's not true for much of the world—people in most other countries read and hear televised and print news stories from a much broader range of international sources. This relates again to the issue of gatekeepers and the "lens" through which we view other countries and their people. One way teachers can increase students' understanding of the impact of this issue is to have them read and/or watch news from other countries. Before the Internet, this would have been a daunting task—but now it's fairly easy to access English-language versions of newspapers and televised stories from dozens of countries around the world. Leading students through an analysis and discussion of which stories are covered—and how they are covered—on the same day in different countries can be eye opening.

Analyzing Headlines and Magazines Covers

Headlines and magazine covers are useful for discussing Key Questions of Authorship, Purpose, and Credibility. Magazine covers are considered advertising for the magazine, so they are not subject to the same accuracy and ethical guidelines that apply to articles and photographs inside the magazine.[20] Headlines are typically written by the copy editor rather than the writer of the news article, and are designed to briefly inform and attract attention to the article. Because of this, sometimes headlines are misleading or just plain wrong. Consider the newspaper article shown in Figure 5.2; since IQ is always based on a written test, unless these are exceptionally smart mice, the use of the term

Figure 5.2 IQ in Mice?

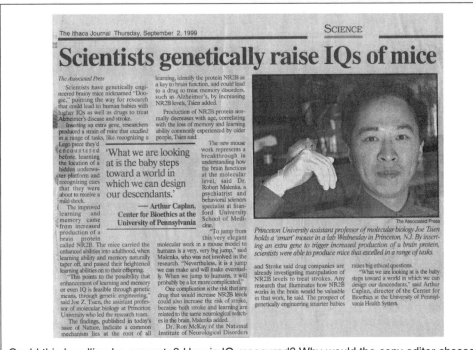

Could this headline be accurate? How is IQ measured? Why would the copy editor choose to use "raise IQ" in the headline instead of "improve memory"? Why did the newspaper include this photo? Might it unintentionally reinforce stereotypes?

Source: Ithaca Journal, September 2, 1999.

IQ is incorrect. The article describes research that demonstrates ways to increase *memory* ability in mice; why might the copy editor have chosen to use "IQ" instead of "memory" in the headline?

Analyzing headlines in online news reports is particularly intriguing because they are usually written specifically to draw the attention of search engines rather than to accurately describe stories (Carr, 2010). Students might compare and contrast the same story reported in the print and online versions of a particular newspaper or use http://newseum.org to compare the use of the same photographs with different headlines on the same day in different newspapers. And with the rise of Twitter, analyzing the tweets that news media send to draw readers to a story—in comparison to the headlines created with the same purpose—can highlight the power of certain words and phrases to convey drama and importance when space and time are *really* short.

Supporting Student-Produced News

Creating student newspapers, magazines, documentaries, or radio programs, while time consuming, provides wonderful opportunities to develop and demonstrate all of the capabilities that define media literacy. Have students reflect on—and even report on—the decisions they continuously make regarding which stories to cover, whom to interview, what to edit out, and which techniques to use. This can generate powerful insights into effective communication and the ways in which decisions can distort or bias information.

News publications or programs also provide natural opportunities for interdisciplinary cooperation (e.g., science students reporting on science-related matters, art students providing photography and graphic support, civics classes covering political issues, etc.). And journalism provides enough variables to adapt to nearly any subject area and skill level. For example, in history classes, students can demonstrate both an understanding of the various components of news and the time period, people, and place they are studying by creating a newspaper for, say, ancient Egypt, the Aztecs, or colonial America. An English teacher may opt to have students create podcasts rather than video because radio news requires more descriptive language than narration for a video.

Teachers can also scaffold experiences by engaging students in short projects (e.g., creating a still ad for a magazine) before moving on to more complex productions that involve decisions about wording, tone of voice, sound effects, music, research, fact-checking, and editing.

Before students begin to create their own news stories, it is a good idea to engage them in activities that help them work through some of the challenges that journalists typically encounter. For example, at the high school level, to increase Awareness about how editing influences news content, take a printed news story (or the transcript of a radio or TV story—something that is no more than a single printed page and is related to your curriculum works best) and put students in the role of editor. Tell them they need to cut the story in half to fit it into available airtime (or column space). It is important that you give no other instructions so that students are completely free to determine how they will make their cuts. Divide the class into small groups of four to five and let them work for about ten minutes (things happen quickly in news). In the follow-up discussion, focus on what criteria each group used to make their cuts. The actual edits they made are less important than what individual group members said to convince their classmates to make a particular cut or save a sentence. Wrap up the discussion by noting that since no story can include all of the available information or full quotes from every interviewee, news stories are always edited, and there are many possible (and valid) criteria for making editing decisions. Knowing something about the source or perspective of a news story can help students see how editing criteria might have influenced what they are seeing or hearing.

Another related lesson idea involves noticing the language choices to see how they change the impression of the story. Discuss the differences among common verbs like *said, claimed, pointed out, admitted, asserted,* or *argued,* etc. Ask students to notice the use of euphemisms, labels, "code words," and generalizations (i.e., attributing a statement or action to an entire group instead of specific individuals, such as "the black community is up in arms . . ."),[21] and discuss how they impact the reader's understanding of the issues and events being reported.

Students can also begin to get a feel for real-world journalism by posting comments on an Internet news blog or submitting letters to the editor and monitoring the responses. All of these suggestions help students develop a better sense of how professionally produced news stories are created and edited, building awareness and reflection on issues of credibility, bias, ethics, and epistemology.

Discussing Current Events

In an effort to get students interested in current events by reading newspapers, teachers often have students do something like this: find three newspaper articles about current events (local, national, and international), summarize each one on a note card, and then present them to the rest of the class. When Cyndy's daughter was asked to do that, she always found the shortest articles possible and copied the information without really thinking about it, and neither she nor the other students remembered much about the events afterwards. So while the goal was an admirable one, the assignment didn't really work to meet it.

A media literacy tweak to the same assignment might be to have each student find three newspaper articles all about the same current event (from different newspapers), summarize the event by drawing on information in all three articles (including information inferred from the headlines and accompanying photographs), present the information about the event to the class, and comment on the similarities and differences among the sources in the ways they reported on the event. CP1.4, 2.2 This takes the same amount of class time but offers a much deeper experience for the students because they've had to use analytical and synthesis skills. This approach has the added benefit of serving as a parallel task in preparation for answering the document-based questions frequently found on social studies assessments.

Another way to incorporate media literacy into both news and current events is to have students apply the Key Questions to news stories designed especially for children, such as those found in *Time for Kids, Weekly Reader,* and on *Nick News.* Older students could also compare stories in those news outlets to stories on the same topic in local or national newspapers, identifying similarities and differences in the way the stories were reported.

6

Integrating Media Literacy Into Specific Content Areas

The curriculum-driven approach that we have adopted in this book provides a framework for using media literacy education to teach core content and skills in specific content areas. Like reading and writing, media literacy can—and should—be integrated across the curriculum. As the US Department of Education (2010) puts it: "Whether the domain is English language arts, mathematics, sciences, social studies, history, art, or music, 21st-century competencies and expertise such as critical thinking, complex problem solving, collaboration, and multimedia communication should be woven into all content areas" (p. xi).

This chapter suggests integration strategies designed to get you started and then have you take off on your own, adding modifications and new ideas as they occur to you in your daily teaching. Educators have been integrating media literacy into English/language arts (ELA), health, and social studies for several decades, so it isn't surprising that the sections devoted to those areas contain a much larger array of examples than for, say, physical education or mathematics. This doesn't mean that there aren't possibilities in those areas, only that teachers in those subjects are just beginning to look at the potential of media literacy. A decade from now, as media literacy education continues to grow, we expect the suggestions to be more evenly distributed, and we are eager to see the ideas that emerge.

ENGLISH LANGUAGE ARTS

Because we consider books and other mass-produced print documents to be "media," on some level much of ELA already involves media literacy, and media literacy strategies address most ELA standards even when that phrase is not explicitly used. So, integrating media literacy often requires no more than tweaking existing practice.

Teachers can—and many already do, to some extent—incorporate the wording of media literacy questions and concepts on an ongoing basis into their discussions about stories, poems, novels, and other "traditional" content, identifying the Author (source), Purpose (and target audience), Context, Content, and Impact. In the same way, students can be encouraged to see their writing through the lens of the Key Questions, reflecting on their own Purpose, Audience, available Techniques, and potential Impact. In both instances, ELA teachers can point out grammatical and literary elements employed across a wide spectrum of media formats, helping students see parallels between how they read, write, and discuss print media in school and how they approach media they use outside of school.

Lesson Ideas

*Combine Different Media Forms in Order
to Enhance Analysis and Discussion*

- **Link plays, books, and novels to film.**

    Use selected scenes from one or more versions of the many required classic plays and novels that have been made into films to do a deep reading of both texts. Integrating movie scenes during the reading of the book, rather than saving the film to be a "reward" at the end, often takes no more class time and leads to complex discussion. By contrasting how the story is presented in different formats (including how a scene is interpreted by different directors), students will get a much deeper appreciation for literary elements such as character development, point of view, symbolism, and setting. This also works well to draw in students who are not strong readers; discussion of the film scenes may help build understanding of the characters and plot that will then support them in reading the play or novel. CP3.3

    For elementary-level students, try using graphic organizers to help students sequence, compare, and contrast books and film. For example, Wan and Cheng (2004) describe a lesson plan using Venn diagrams to study the acclaimed children's folktale *The Ballad of Mulan* (Zhang, 1998)[1] and the Disney film *Mulan* (1998), identifying similarities and differences in those two versions of the original Mulan story. Using popular media content to create graphic organizers is likely to engage students in the process in ways that more traditional content may not, making it easier for students to understand how to create Venn diagrams for other purposes.

- **Contrast similar characters and storylines from different media formats.**

    Students might compare traditional novels and graphic novels, poems and music videos, or short stories and comic strips, in each case contrasting the two formats in terms of both use of literary elements and also production/format elements.

For example, in a 2010 NCTE Conference presentation, teachers Leslie Burns and Stergios Botzakis asked attendees to compare an excerpt from the book *The Joy Luck Club* (a recommended text from the ELA Common Core Standards) and several panels from the highly acclaimed graphic novel *American Born Chinese*. Like the book excerpt (and unlike a film or video clip), the panels from the graphic novel could be easily distributed and studied during small-group discussion, and several groups could read different texts at the same time. The ensuing compare-and-contrast provided deep insights about both art forms, revealing how the graphic artist used drawings and the novelist used words to evoke similar emotions, plot elements, and characters, including struggles with stereotypes and life as an immigrant. It also generated insights into multicultural experiences that would have been unlikely had the discussion solely focused on the *Joy Luck Club* excerpt.

- **Experience or create the same message in different modalities.**

    Have different groups of students in the class "experience" the same audio-visual media message in different formats (video only, video and audio, audio only, printed text), comparing impressions and interpretations of the messages, then discussing and reflecting on the relative influence of each format. Music videos are especially good for this activity, since they always incorporate words, music, and visual elements and the content of the visuals is often different from the words of the song.[2] The same idea can be used when students create messages of their own: a poem can be handwritten on paper and illustrated with images, read as a recording with music in the background, or presented as a voiceover on a video with still or moving images. Students can then reflect on the impressions created in different modes and evaluate the effectiveness of each mode to decide which one best suits their purpose and audience.

VOICES FROM THE FIELD: *MULTIMEDIA POETRY*

About ten years ago, we were working with a long-time middle school ELA teacher who was excited about learning media literacy approaches but terrified about using any form of digital technology. For years he had taught a creative poetry writing lesson that included having students illustrate their own poems (and other poems they liked) with images and collages created from pictures found in magazines; their final projects included an anthology of these illustrated poems bound in a book. We suggested that he could add other options using digital technologies, including PowerPoint and digital videos (with students providing their own voiceovers, reading the poems to accompany the visual images they had chosen).

With much trepidation, he did so, and for the first time he met with the school's technology support teacher (whom he had been avoiding for years). Many students chose the PowerPoint or video options and—to his astonishment—they were able to easily learn the technologies from the support teacher and each other. In fact, several expanded on his original assignment, creating more poems than he had originally required. The resulting final presentations were so effective and engaging that it prompted the teacher to learn how to create his own PowerPoint and video presentations—and at the end of the year, the principal and his department chair told us that his teaching had been transformed.

Use Media Literacy to Teach Shakespeare

Shakespeare's plays are often core parts of the ELA curriculum, and though in many places it has become sacrosanct for students to only read the Bard's works, we would remind teachers that Shakespeare wrote plays, which—unlike novels—were never intended to be read but rather to be watched. So Shakespeare offers an excellent opportunity to use nonprint or nontraditional media. You might

- have students compare film versions of *Romeo and Juliet* that were made at different points in history, discussing how cinematic interpretations of the play reflect societal norms and preoccupations during each time period.

- have the class demonstrate comprehension of a play by creating a movie trailer or poster for a film version of it, making choices about which scenes, characters, and events to emphasize (or leave out); what music or sound effects to add (for the movie trailer); and what content would be most likely to attract their desired audience.

- assign each student to create a mock social network page for one of the play's characters, developing bios and pictures, deciding which of the other characters he or she would "friend," and creating sample chats about the events and characters. In class discussions, ask students to reflect on the role that social-networking sites play in today's world and how they might have influenced the character relationships and events in the play had those forms of communication been available.

Other Examples of Media Literacy Applications in English Language Arts

You might also

- have young children create picture storybooks or their own customized alphabet books using pictures taken with a digital camera. Discuss the pictures with students to provide practice in speaking and description as well as enhance their awareness of the ways in which photographs can be framed or cropped to convey certain impressions.[3]

- engage students in discussions about why certain books or poems are considered important enough to be included as part of the required reading list (by the teacher, school district, or state) and/or why certain books are given awards for excellence (e.g., Caldecott, Newberry, Coretta Scott King). Who decides? What criteria are used? What types of outstanding or favorite books are *not* likely to be included in these lists, and why? What makes a book, play, or poem "great" according to consensus over time? You will also want to share why you selected the books and other media examples the students are using in your class.

- discuss basic literacy elements (plot, setting, character, sequence, etc.) by using TV commercials, narrative children's smartphone apps, or film scenes,[4] which can serve as rich media documents that work well for students with a wide range of learning styles and are short enough to be shown several times for a deeper analysis. Including the audio elements (voiceover, music, sound effects) in your discussion helps to build critical listening skills.

- show covers of classic novels over time and different printings, discussing the changes in design, fonts, images—and sometimes even title—as reflections of editorial choices, historical preoccupations, and the increasing need to attract an audience. As part of an assessment after reading a novel, have students analyze the front and back covers of the book, discussing how they reflect the content of the story (e.g., which parts of the story were shown or described and why, or whether anything was said or shown that was inaccurate or misleading in terms of what the story was actually about).

NCTE's compilations *Lesson Plans for Creating Media-Rich Classrooms* (Christel & Sullivan, 2007) and *Lesson Plans for Developing Digital Literacies* (Christel & Sullivan, 2010)[5] provide many other excellent ideas, including using video games to teach about plot elements and stereotypes, and using "word clouds" as part of the writing and revision process.

SOCIAL STUDIES (HISTORY, GLOBAL STUDIES, GOVERNMENT/CIVICS, ECONOMICS)

Studying the impact of the news media (and media messages in general) on historical events, government, politics, global events, and other cultures—and on our understanding of those things—is so core to social studies that it's hard to imagine teaching a social studies class without media literacy. In fact, even though they don't always use the term *media literacy*, many social studies teachers have already been using media literacy inquiry methods—especially when discussing current events and politics or preparing students to answer document-based questions (DBQs) on exams. Students who have had ongoing practice analyzing and discussing the messages in media documents are well prepared to synthesize information from multiple sources and to draw the types of conclusions about perspective, conflicting viewpoints, credibility, and value of content often required in social studies courses and assessments.

The integration of media literacy into social studies can often occur through small changes to existing practice. The Key Questions, for example, provide students with a standard framework to analyze and think critically about historical documents or cultural artifacts. Media literacy can also provide the basis for more extensive projects that immerse students in the study of complicated events and issues, building core skills and knowledge while also developing analysis and communication skills (such as the "Middle East Debates" described in Chapter 7).

Using Project Look Sharp's Curriculum Kits

Project Look Sharp has long focused on social studies issues, and its curriculum kits (available free online) provide hundreds of current and historical documents for analysis, as well as dozens of activity ideas, including

- exploring how current and historical events are framed in the covers of news magazines and/or newspaper headlines, using decodings to introduce or review core content (e.g., using *Media Construction of War* to study the Vietnam War, the Gulf War of 1991, and the War in Afghanistan following 9/11 through analysis of *Newsweek* covers and photo spreads during each war).

- decoding government propaganda posters to introduce or compare and contrast the political agenda and perspectives of different nations, especially during times of war (e.g., using *Soviet History through Posters* or *Media Construction of Peace*).

- discussing ways in which available media in particular places and times influenced lawmaking and the political process (e.g., using *Media Construction of Presidential Campaigns,* with lessons covering the year 1800 to the present and ranging from topics such as the innovative uses of campaign songs and rallies as part of the early populist campaigns to the use of new media such as YouTube, text messages, and social networking to attract young voters).

- exploring the roles that media have played in furthering (or hindering) social justice and activism, historically and across the world (e.g., using *Media Construction of Social Justice* and *Media Constructions of Martin Luther King, Jr.*).

Weaving Media Literacy Into Social Studies Throughout the Year

One ongoing approach to the incorporation of media literacy relates to epistemology: How do we know what we know (about historical events, other cultures, current social issues, etc.)? You can use media literacy to help students understand that history is a construction (rather than a set of names, dates, and places to memorize) by engaging students in activities where they identify whose stories are told—and whose stories are *not* told—on an ongoing basis:

- Discuss what is meant by the expression "History is written by the winners."[6]

- Compare descriptions or reenactments of the same events using different popular media and educational sources (see, for example, Voices from the Field: *Thanksgiving*).

- Have students compare the topics and treatments in their textbook with counter-histories (e.g., Zinn's *A People's History of the United States* (1980), Loewen's *Lies My Teacher Told Me: Everything Your American History Textbook Got Wrong* (1995), or *History Lessons: How Textbooks from Around the World Portray U.S. History* (2004) by Lindaman and Ward, which includes excerpts from history textbooks around the world concerning historical events involving the United States).

VOICES FROM THE FIELD: *THANKSGIVING*

Veteran fifth-grade teacher Betty House decided to transform her annual Thanksgiving unit—which had gotten pretty tired and boring after twenty years—by adding an overlay of media literacy. She gathered five media examples that told the story of the first Thanksgiving: a children's book, a short documentary film from her school library, excerpts from pilgrim Edward Winslow's journal, an account told from a Native American perspective, and the 1994 Disney film *Squanto: A Warrior's Tale.* The students studied all of the sources and made lists of the events and information that were common across them—as well as elements that only occurred in one or two of them. Somewhat to their surprise, the students discovered that the accounts that were *most* similar were the Native American source and Winslow's original journal. After some investigation, they discovered that the Native American author had used Winslow's journal as one of his primary sources. In contrast, the account that had the *least* in common with the others was the Disney film; it emphasized conflict between the Native Americans and the pilgrims, contained a great deal of violence, and featured Squanto's "daring escape" from the British. As a group, the students concluded that while the Disney film was the most fun to watch, it was probably the least accurate of the sources. These students discovered an important lesson in credibility without the teacher giving a lecture about why a Disney film might not provide the most historically accurate account. That is the power of inquiry-based media literacy education—and the lesson didn't stop there. House said that the students were so engaged in this unit that many said they had shared their findings with their families at Thanksgiving dinner, an example of the "trickle-up" effect of media literacy education.

- Have students analyze the pronouns and generalizations made in news reports and political speeches. When are *we/us* or *they/them* or generalizations like "Americans believe..." used appropriately, and when is the speaker functioning as an unelected representative of a group? How do you determine whether or not someone is a legitimate spokesperson for a nation, political movement, religious (or ethnic or racial) group, and how do journalists decide whom to interview?

Taking Advantage of New Media

- Establish a class wiki or encourage the use of social-bookmarking sites to help students share information and resources as they study other cultures or historical events.

- Analyze political cartoons and then have students create their own comics to retell an historical event, to imagine what a contemporary observer at a historical event would have said, or to comment on a current issue. Use the opportunity to talk about visual representation, target audience, and the use of symbols.[7]

- Identify ways for students to communicate with experts at museums or in other countries through websites or video conferencing.

- Access international news sources online as part of lessons in global studies to provide a broader understanding of events and issues in those countries as well as insights about how journalists in other countries see the United States.

Other Examples of Media Literacy Applications in Social Studies

- **Hollywood history**—As part of an end-of-unit assessment, have students identify accurate or inaccurate historical content in popular films (e.g., *The Patriot* [1990], *Saving Private Ryan* [1998], *or Gone with the Wind* [1939]).

- **Country reports**—Tweak the common elementary school "country" report by adding media to the typical list of information about exports, form of government, flag, and so on. Have students find out how much of the country's popular media are imported from the United States and discuss with students what difference it makes if media are government controlled, independent, or commercial; if people get news primarily from print and radio as opposed to TV or the Internet; or if people have cell phones. As we mentioned in Chapter 1, students might also include an analysis of the country's money as an important source of media messages.

- **Word cloud analyses**—"Word clouds" (which can easily be created using websites such as www.wordle.net or www.tagxedo.com) allow you to import a section of text that is then turned into a graphical representation based on the frequency of different words (see Figure 6.1 for examples from two speeches by Martin Luther King Jr.). This provides a dramatic summary illustrating the terms and ideas emphasized in the text, which teachers can use to introduce or summarize a speech or historical document and students can use to graphically compare and analyze the content of different speeches.

- **Media and government**—Have students look at the ways in which government regulation influences or has influenced the media they use. Explore how the courts have interpreted the concepts of free speech and freedom of the press or the content of the Telecommunications Act of 1996 (see http://transition.fcc.gov/telecom.html). Discuss the differences between commercial speech and other speech—and the legal restrictions covering each. Look at the role of government agencies that oversee media, including the Federal Communications Commission and the Federal Trade Commission, and the regulations they have instituted at different points in history.

- **Historical re-creations of the news**—Students might demonstrate their understanding of an important historical event by creating a newspaper front page (or hypothetical TV newscast) from a particular city on a particular date, including headlines and news stories, photographs, sidebars, and even advertisements

Figure 6.1   Martin Luther King Jr.'s Speeches in Word Clouds

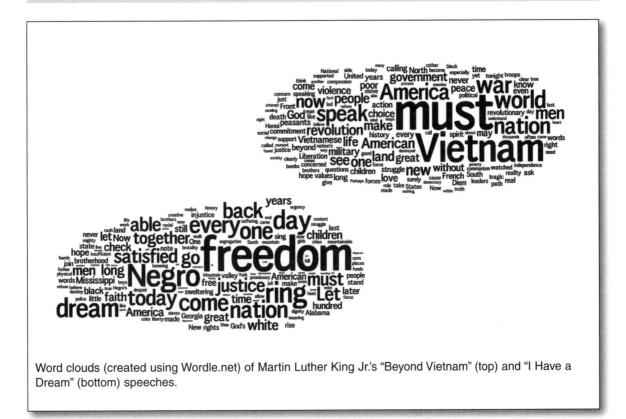

Word clouds (created using Wordle.net) of Martin Luther King Jr.'s "Beyond Vietnam" (top) and "I Have a Dream" (bottom) speeches.

that would reflect the time period. Or different groups of students might create newspaper pages or newscasts from different cities that would reflect different perspectives and sides of a controversy (e.g., a Northern versus Southern newspaper during the Civil War; TV newscasts from Honolulu and Tokyo about the bombing of Pearl Harbor or Hiroshima).

SCIENCE AND ENVIRONMENTAL STUDIES

Science and media literacy education share a deep grounding in the process of inquiry. Like media literacy, science emphasizes careful observation and the use of evidence to support conclusions. In their book *Developing Scientific Literacy: Using News Media in the Classroom* (2007), Irish educators Ruth Jarman and Billy McClune suggest other parallels:

- Both involve skillful analysis and interpretation of data plus the application of logical reasoning.
- Conclusions don't emerge from data; they are explanations based on prior knowledge, evidence, and even the exercise of creative imagination. Thus, individuals (including scientists) can come to different conclusions from the same data.

- Interpretations are open to revision in light of new information, and you must be able to clearly lay out reasoning so that others can test your arguments.
- Credibility of sources is very important, including the credentials of the authors and the institutions or organizations that they are from.

It is easy to use media documents to practice many of these skills. A class decoding of ads, film clips, magazine articles, or newspaper stories can provide an opportunity to engage in careful observation, make reasoned arguments about evidence-based conclusions, identify accuracies and inaccuracies related to science content, and even look for examples of terminology that is used differently in science than in popular culture (e.g., a chemist's use of the term *organic* in contrast to the use of that word on a food label). The exercise could end with a discussion of the quality of science information in popular media and why the quality of available information might matter.

Using Project Look Sharp's Curriculum Kits

A good source of relevant media documents related to science is Project Look Sharp's curriculum kit series on environmental issues, which incorporates content from biology, chemistry, earth science, and physics. In addition to hundreds of rich media examples, the kits include activity ideas like

- **examining media messages about a science issue over time**. Students analyze a selection of advertisements and articles that appeared in popular magazines like *Life, Look,* or *Popular Science* over the course of many years to explore changes in attitudes about things like the value of science, the consequences of human actions on the environment, or the advisability of continued use of chemical and medical innovations once deemed "wonder products."

- **contrasting media messages from different sources**. Each message draws different conclusions about the same set of scientific data and concepts. Students can explore scientific controversies by comparing information on the topic in documentary films, blog posts, academic journal articles, advocacy websites, government websites, traditional news organizations, alternative or independent news sources, and the popular press (e.g., *Rolling Stone* magazine). This is a powerful way for teachers to introduce controversial topics without imposing their own views on the discussion.

- **identifying the ways in which scientific ideas and information are conveyed to the public**. These include the roles played by the news media and the US government. Students examine factors that influence public awareness, including how research is reported, the credentials of science reporters, and what rights employees of the government or corporations have to share their research findings without prior approval.

Other Lesson Ideas

- Encourage students to research the veracity of science-related urban legends (see the "Fact or Fiction?" lesson in Chapter 7).

- Kick off the year by asking students, working individually, to draw a picture of a "scientist." At a designated moment, have everyone hold up their pictures. If your students are typical, you'll see a lot of pictures of skinny, nerdy white guys in glasses and lab coats or mad scientists with crazy hair. Discuss where these stereotypes come from and what role popular media play in creating or perpetuating them. As you progress through the year, encourage students to bring in counter-images of what real scientists look like.

- Conduct experiments to test the claims in ads and on product labels.[8] How much toothpaste or shampoo do you really need, and why would they consistently show people using more than that in the TV commercials? What is really meant by saying that "four out of five doctors" recommend a certain product, and how might the advertisers have gone about collecting those data?

- Create scientific reports using data and graphs that convey different messages for different audiences (e.g., bottled water companies, environmental action groups, government regulators). Scientific data can often be manipulated to imply different conclusions, and students can develop a keen awareness of this by summarizing their own data (collected as part of a regular classroom experiment) in ways that might support different arguments. Their "production choices" might include how to the scale or labeling of the axes in a graph, how to categorize the data or describe the groups, what steps in the research methods to include and what to leave out in the description, and the specific wording used to summarize their findings.

MATH

Applying media literacy to mathematics may seem like a stretch, but current math curricula and core standards increasingly recognize the importance of students being able to talk through their reasoning and use evidence to support conclusions in ways that parallel typical media literacy discussions. Media also provide an ample supply of real-world application opportunities for students to practice and apply mathematical skills.

For example, graphs and statistics in advertisements and news reports provide excellent examples for analyzing mathematical information while also taking into account who made the message and that person's or organization's purpose and identifying biases that led to distortions in the way the data were reported (e.g., by leaving out key labels or definitions). Consider, for example, the cover of a free newspaper (supported by advertising) reporting on the rising cost of college tuition shown in Figure 6.2. What messages about colleges does this graph convey? Since the line for Cornell University's tuition is going up and the line for Cornell's ranking is going down, the overall impression is that Cornell students aren't getting enough bang for their buck. But look more closely: How much is tuition actually going up? We don't know, because the y-axis isn't labeled with a scale. The same is true for ranking. When we read the accompanying article inside the paper, we discover something astonishing: the final "drop" in ranking represents Cornell going from fourteenth place to

Figure 6.2 Graphs Can Be Both Accurate and Misleading

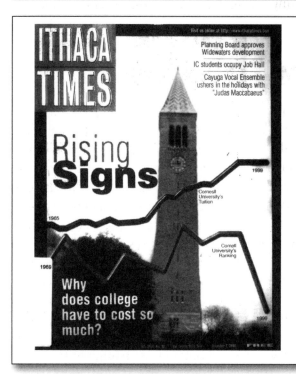

What are the messages about today's colleges in this cover story about Cornell University's tuition (top line) and ranking (bottom line)? What information is missing that might be important in determining the accuracy of this graph?

Source: The Ithaca Times, December 7, 2000.

sixth place in a national ranking poll—which is good! Cornell's tuition is going up, and its ranking is also going up—so why didn't the paper show it that way? Because then there would be no story. It's the controversy implied by rising costs and decreasing quality that drives the reader to pick up and read the paper—and its advertisements—which is the underlying purpose of this cover story.

Lesson Ideas

- Collect and summarize data on the amount of time students spend using different types of media. This provides practice in math skills and in reflecting on their media choices (see, for example, the lesson plan for "Media & Activity Diaries" in Chapter 7).

- Hunt for examples of misleading ways in which mathematical information or quantitative data are presented in the media (e.g, citing statistics selectively to exclude contradictory evidence, using percentages or implying comparison without identifying the whole that the example is measured against, asking leading survey questions).

- Practice different types of calculations to assess the implications of the language used in specific advertising claims (e.g., the difference between "buy one for $10, get one free" and "two for $10"; the meaning of "one third less fat" or "gets clothes 20 percent whiter").

- Pose research questions about media content that require different types of mathematical calculations to be answered. Which type of media has the most advertising? What types of news stories get the most coverage? In order to gather data to answer those questions, students would need to calculate proportions (for advertising in media formats that involve time) or area (for print media).

HEALTH AND CONSUMER EDUCATION

In many ways, this is one of the easiest content areas into which to integrate media literacy, since it is usually where we find the study of advertising, body image, media effects, tobacco and alcohol education, conflict resolution, nutrition, and other topics heavily influenced by media messages. However, discussions about these types of media messages often are conducted using a "danger cluck" approach—with the teacher pointing out the harmful media messages to his or her students (while making noises of disgust or concern). An inquiry-based media literacy approach would deal with these topics very differently.

For example, a middle school health teacher might divide the class into groups and have each group do a content analysis of the articles and advertisements appearing in a different teen magazine. Each group would summarize what they found (including the number of ads for different types of products, the types of topics covered in the articles, and the characteristics of the people shown in the magazine), reporting back to the rest of the class about their findings. The teacher would then guide the students through a discussion about what types of messages were most frequent and what topics and messages were rarely included. By applying Key Questions about target audience, Techniques, and Impact, students will draw their own, evidence-based conclusions about the potentially harmful messages found in these magazines—rather than simply adopting (or rebelling against) the teacher's interpretations.

Other Lesson Ideas

- Address bullying, violence, and conflict resolution by having students analyze media messages about those issues across a range of popular media (e.g., comics, films, books, sports, news, cartoons, video games, advertising), in particular noting the kinds of conflicts that arise and the roles that the "good guys" and "bad guys" play in resolving the conflicts. The ensuing discussion could include reflections on what would happen if the behaviors shown in the different media examples occurred in real life (e.g., Who would be hurt, and who might benefit? Who would be most likely to get arrested? How successful would the "resolution" be in the long run?).

- Have students create short video animations or public service announcements that demonstrate healthy decisions and behaviors (e.g., nonviolent conflict resolution, safety rules, healthy eating and exercise), reflecting on the target audience and techniques likely to be most persuasive to them.

- Analyze and discuss the types of nutritional messages in the media, including overt messages (e.g., the nutritional makeup of foods and beverages most commonly advertised) and mixed messages (e.g., film and TV portrayals of attractive, thin people who appear to only eat junk food; "don't drink and drive" PSAs shown during a broadcast of a drag race sponsored by a beer company), as well as the techniques used to convey nutritional messages (e.g., products with "fruit" in their name that actually contain little or no fruit; statements like "all natural," "light," or "low-fat") and other persuasive devices.

- Have students create counter-ads as a means of talking back to advertisers who are portraying messages they consider stereotypical or harmful. Using low-tech or digital techniques, students create parodies of magazine advertisements by changing the wording and/or images to communicate a totally different message that comments on or highlights the problematic aspects of the advertisement (see Figure 6.3 and the book's website for examples).[9]

FINE ARTS (MUSIC, ART, DRAMA, PHOTOGRAPHY)

Fine arts classes provide wonderful opportunities to create and analyze music and visual elements in media messages. Music, in particular, often goes unnoticed in TV commercials and dramas, films, and children's cartoons; rich discussions can result from identifying specific musical instruments and phrasing designed to evoke certain emotional responses or otherwise add to the overall impression of a scene. Teachers (or students) might create video scenes with different types of musical backgrounds, analyzing the impact on the viewer's impressions and expectations of what is going to happen next, or teachers might play an audio track with the picture off and have students use the music to predict what is happening on screen.

Students can also explore context through debates about the relationship between art and politics, comparing assertions that "true" art is only about aesthetics and expression to examples of explicitly political art. Discuss why music with overtly political messages rarely makes the charts and find historical examples of time periods when this was not the case. What accounts for the change?

Teachers also might arrange for students to debate issues of copyright, file sharing, and sampling related to commercial and traditional music, including identifying how technologies have influenced practice over time.

Paintings, photographs, and other artwork also represent rich media documents for analysis (see Chapter 4). Teachers can provide various contexts for discussion of art, including the historical period in which it was created. For example, how would your interpretation of a painting be different if you understand what "Madonna and child" means in Christian theology versus simply seeing the picture as a mother holding a baby?

Young children can begin to explore the constructed nature of media by drawing pictures of their neighborhood, home, or bedroom and then talking about what things in the picture (set elements) make it clear that this is their place (and not someone else's) or what sounds they would hear if they were standing in the picture.

Art teacher Duane Neil has developed a number of creative art lessons that incorporate media content and analysis. One involves having students

Figure 6.3 Counter-ads

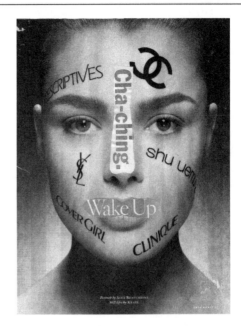

Examples of student-created counter-ads created in a college media literacy course. Students were also asked to describe in detail the original message and how it was conveyed, what they did to alter the message, and what their new message conveyed.

Original messages and counter-ad creators:

a) Illustration for magazine article on makeup brands (Dan Jones)
b) Can you really find satisfying taste at lower tar? You know it—you've got Merit. (Ross Orenstein)
c) Ever see a grown man cry? (Kristin Lucy)
d) Cash—lots and lots of cash; get a start on your story today (Morgan Ehlers)

How did the students' alterations change the message of each advertisement?

Source: Created by students from Ithaca College in a course on media literacy and popular culture taught by professor Cyndy Scheibe.

create "ransom poems" by cutting out words from magazines (in different sizes, colors, and fonts), then piecing them together to form poems and other messages, similar to old-fashioned ransom notes. Students convey impressions not only through the words of their poems but also through the emphasis and style conveyed by the size, color, and font of each word and the overall layout of the poem. Students might also investigate the processes used in photograph manipulation by analyzing and creating examples for different purposes.

PHYSICAL EDUCATION AND SPORTS

On the face of it, the idea of incorporating media literacy into physical education classes may seem counterintuitive, especially if media use is viewed as competition for time spent in physical activity. In fact, helping students to become more aware of the choices they make about how they spend their time—as we do in the "Media & Activity Diaries" lesson in Chapter 7—can advance the goals of both media literacy and physical education, as well as health. And media messages certainly influence our perceptions about sports and exercise, our choices of sports heroes and role models, and our beliefs about what constitutes healthy activity. Where better to analyze weight-loss reality shows or infomercials for exercise equipment than in a physical education class?

Lesson Ideas

- Have students move to different types of music during warm-ups or drills, reflecting on how their speed or performance was influenced by the style of the music.

- Incorporate popular dance forms (e.g., salsa, swing, hip-hop) and exercise approaches (e.g., aerobics, Zumba, Pilates) into physical education activities, discussing the role of media in promoting or popularizing each type.

- Provide opportunities for students to analyze ads and infomercials for exercise equipment and fitness programs, comparing the promised outcomes to benefits from regular, nonaided exercises. If possible, get some of these products for students to try out (from secondhand stores or families who will donate them) so students can evaluate how easy they are to use and other claims from the ads.

- Have students investigate and report on the ways that media shape school and professional sports. Students are often surprised to learn that televised football games, for example, incorporate a mandatory number of timed breaks for commercials and if the normal game play goes on too long without a break, the referees will call a special time-out so advertising can be shown. Students might discuss this practice and its impact on network television's hesitancy to cover sports like soccer, where there aren't a sufficient number of breaks to satisfy advertisers. Students might also use Key Questions to analyze sports figures' endorsements of products, sales of team uniforms and logo paraphernalia, issues related to team mascots, and the creation of fan identity.

MODERN LANGUAGES

Teachers of Spanish, French, and other languages often draw on popular media (films, songs, advertisements) to provide interesting opportunities for students to translate vocabulary and explore the cultural messages in countries where a language is spoken. This practice can easily be tweaked to include media literacy by applying the Key Questions (translated into that language, of course).

Using the Internet in general or SCOLA (www.scola.org) in particular, to follow news stories from other countries can provide both practice in reading and listening to other languages and insight into cultural norms. Using the http://newseum.org website to see the front pages of newspapers in countries where the language is spoken could make a great daily exercise or final assessment. Students who correspond with pen pals in other countries (e.g., through www.epals.com) might make discussion of daily news stories a regular topic of conversation, which can develop awareness and appreciation for how their understanding of the world—and each other's cultures—is influenced by the media they see and hear.

ENGLISH-LANGUAGE LEARNERS

Because they provide a way to integrate image-based material into teaching, media literacy activities can be especially effective for students with limited English skills. In addition to production opportunities (e.g., making and sharing videos in which students reflect on how to represent their cultures or countries of origin), media literacy approaches lend themselves well to unpacking differences in cultural norms and understanding that can be very challenging for students who are new to the United States. Using the Key Questions can help to acknowledge and affirm an English language learner's interpretation of a media message that may be quite different from that of a native English speaker (see, for example, the follow-up to the de Soto decoding in Chapter 4).

INTERDISCIPLINARY APPROACHES

Media literacy lends itself beautifully to collaboration among teachers from different disciplines, providing a common lens for creating and analyzing media messages that relate to each curricular area. For example, Jarman and McClune (2007) argue strongly for using "science in the news" as a means of developing interdisciplinary approaches linking ELA and science. Other opportunities for cross-curricular collaboration are reflected in many of the content area suggestions above, and some topics that cut across many disciplines—like stereotyping—can be effectively explored using media literacy.

Teaching About Stereotyping

Teaching about stereotypes can be very challenging, especially with younger students. Teachers need to unpack (often unconscious) stereotypical beliefs and attitudes without unintentionally reinforcing them. Also, by showing or discussing examples of stereotypes, teachers run the risk of actually introducing students to stereotypes about which they were previously unaware. In order to effectively discuss stereotypes, teachers need to make sure that the classroom is perceived as a safe place for all students to express their opinions, but they must also find ways to challenge those stereotypes and prejudicial attitudes when they arise (e.g., in students' comments or media content).

Inquiry-based media literacy approaches can facilitate this process in several ways. First, by leading such discussions with questions (rather than by scolding or lecturing), teachers are often able to identify misperceptions and stereotypes of which they were previously unaware (see, for example, the Notes on Pedagogy in the lesson plan "Introducing Africa" in Chapter 7). Second, by creating the expectation that students *always* need to back up their statements and interpretations with evidence, teachers can challenge students about their stereotypical beliefs without labeling them as "wrong" or backing them into a corner where they feel they must defend their beliefs with irrational arguments. Third, as students practice analyzing media messages in different curricular contexts, they learn to question their own assumptions and to reflect on their sources of information (illustrated by the lesson plan "Fact or Fiction?" in Chapter 7), so they are likely to be more willing to acknowledge that their previously held beliefs and assumptions might have been wrong. If students are already asking, "How do I know about them?" and, "How do they know about me?" then they are primed for a conversation about stereotypes.

In leading discussions about stereotyping, the Key Questions related to Content, Impact, and Credibility provide a useful starting point; in fact, for students who have already been introduced to the Key Questions, you might ask *them* which questions they feel are most relevant to the discussion of stereotypes. Other questions that can guide discussions about stereotypes come from exploring the power dynamics that lie at the root of many stereotypes:

- Who is the main character, leader, authority, or decision maker?
- Who is doing work, and who is served by the work?
- Whose body language or clothing expresses power?
- Who is perceived as setting the standards by which others are measured?

Finally, numerous media literacy lessons and curriculum materials deal directly with stereotypes; some are appropriate for elementary grades, while others deal with subtler and more challenging aspects of stereotyping. Some of our favorites include

- a TV commercial for "Real Bugs" that contains both obvious and subtle stereotypes about boys (as well as stereotypical portrayals of girls, fathers, science, school, and people of color). See the lesson plan and commercial under "General Media Literacy" at www.projectlooksharp.org.
- *The Basic Skills: Caucasian Americans Workbook,* created by Native American author Beverly Slapin (1994). This work demonstrates, through a highly effective parody of traditional children's workbook activities,

the inappropriateness of viewing other cultures and peoples as entities to be examined for exotic differences.

- the lesson "The Magic of Stereotypes" in Project Look Sharp's *Media Construction of the Middle East,* through decoding the opening scenes from Disney's *Aladdin.*
- suggested questions for analyzing depictions of Muslim girls on covers of young adult novels, developed and described by Özlem Sensoy and Elizabeth Marshall in the article "Save the Muslim Girl!" (2009).
- the technique of analyzing body language of males and females in advertisements and other visual examples to talk about gender. How would you describe someone of the opposite sex if they were shown in a given pose?[10]

The lesson plan "White Towel" in Chapter 7 also unpacks stereotypes as students design TV commercials for different target audiences. This exercise provides the opportunity to discuss our own unconscious tendencies to fall back on certain age and gender stereotypes and how they are influenced by the media messages we receive.

Linking Content Areas Through Inquiry

Regardless of the content area, inquiry-based media literacy fosters active learning and engaged discussion. Once this process of inquiry is well established, it almost becomes second nature, and you may find that you and your students apply a media literacy lens as a matter of common practice throughout the school day (and beyond). When media literacy becomes an automatic habit—just like reading and writing—then you'll know that you've transformed the process of student learning in ways that really do cut across the entire curriculum.

7

Media Literacy
Lesson Plans

This chapter features seven complete lesson plans, each demonstrating the application of the curriculum-driven, inquiry-based approach to media literacy described in the preceding chapters. Each is designed to build critical thinking and/or effective communication skills while at the same time teaching core content. We've selected these specific lesson plans because

- they are all classroom-tested lessons that have been developed and taught by us, our colleagues at Project Look Sharp, or teachers who have had extensive training in media literacy education with us.
- they provide examples for a wide range of curriculum areas and grade levels.
- as a set, they address all eight of the media literacy capabilities described in Chapter 2 and all of the elements of the NAMLE statement on the purpose of media literacy education.
- they utilize many different types of media and provide examples of a variety of media literacy education strategies, including document decoding, high- and low-tech production, and student activism.
- they are easily adaptable to suit an individual teacher's goals, context, and students, while still retaining the basic elements of inquiry-based media literacy education.

To quickly identify particular lesson plan features that apply to your educational context, see Table 7.1. However, we encourage you to look at all the examples because they demonstrate different aspects of media literacy education, and one that isn't designed for your specific subject or grade level might just be the one that sparks an idea for something that would work in your classroom. Also check the book's website for additional lesson-extension ideas, which may apply. As you review the lesson plans, keep in mind that they are not meant to be "out-of-the-box" templates to be followed precisely as written. Rather they demonstrate in different contexts and subject areas how inquiry-based media literacy approaches can address multiple goals that teachers and schools have (including teaching core content), while engaging students in the empowering processes of analysis, creation, reflection, and discovery.

There are many other excellent sources for media literacy lesson plans, both in print and online, including the free online curriculum-specific kits published by Project Look Sharp (available at www.projectlooksharp.org). As you search for additional ideas, it is helpful to be aware of some of the common strengths and weaknesses you are likely to find in collections of media literacy lessons.

Some, like NCTE's outstanding series *Lesson Plans for Creating Media-Rich Classrooms* (2007) and *Lesson Plans for Developing Digital Literacies* (2010), edited by Mary T. Christel and Scott Sullivan (for ELA), and *Developing Scientific Literacy: Using News Media in the Classroom* (2007) by Irish educators Ruth Jarman and Billy McClune, incorporate lessons focused on only one particular curriculum area.[1] Others, like Bill Kist's *The Socially Networked Classroom* (2010), incorporate lesson and activity plans that can be used in multiple subject areas but only address one particular type of media or technology.

Some wonderful resources for lesson plans, like Selma Wassermann's *Teaching for Thinking Today: Theory, Strategies, and Activities for the K–8 Classroom* (2009) and Michael Opitz's *Literacy Lessons to Help Kids Get Fit & Healthy* (2010), employ inquiry-based pedagogies to build the same critical thinking, analysis, and reflection skills that we've been describing—but never actually mention or use media literacy approaches, even when they incorporate media content in their analysis.[2] These lessons could easily be tweaked to incorporate media literacy by adding or rephrasing some questions.

And there are websites like Frank Baker's Media Literacy Clearinghouse (http://frankwbaker.com) that, true to its name, gathers an amazing array of sources, many of which reflect the inquiry-based approach we are advocating. Also, websites from other countries, like Canada's Media Awareness Network (http://media-awareness.ca), include many brilliant lesson plans, though some don't mesh with our approach to media literacy or the specific curriculum needs of US classrooms.

Many media literacy teacher guides and web resources contain lesson plans or rich media documents dealing with different types of media formats, new digital technologies, or media-related topics (e.g., stereotyping, body image, media violence) in creative and interesting ways. But while they employ discussion about media messages (including those they create themselves using new technologies), they don't use a probing, inquiry-based approach to unpack the students' own interpretations of media messages, nor do they encourage students to reflect on their own roles as communicators and their impact on a particular audience. The discussions are entirely teacher driven, and the interpretations are predetermined. These lessons and activities could be strengthened by incorporating the inquiry-based approaches

Table 7.1 Lesson Plans in Chapter 7

Lesson Number	Title	Mass Media Forms Included	Materials Available on Website	Media Literacy Skills	Grade Levels	Curriculum Areas	Other Notes
1	Introducing Africa	photographs	PowerPoint slides, student worksheet, answer key	analysis, reflection	middle/ upper elementary	social studiies	deals with cross-cultural issues and stereotyping
2	Media Diaries	all	diary templates for different grade levels	awareness, reflection	middle elementary through college	social studies, health, physical education, math	can incorporate recording of nonmedia activities, including exercise
3	Fact or Fiction	websites, e-mail, TV shows, documertary films	video clip, Internet links, PowerPoint, worksheets	understanding, analysis, evaluation	middle school through college	science, information literacy	includes analysis of urban legends and Disney's documentary about lemmings
4	Twister	popular films	video clips, student worksheets	analysis, evaluation	middle school through college	science	evaluating accuracy and credibility of scientific content in films
5	White Towel	TV commercials	storyboard forms	creation, reflection	middle school through college	ELA	low-tech production activity, also addresses stereotypes
6	News Spin	newpaper articles	print news articles	creation, evalution, reflection	high school through college	ELA, journalism	incorporates both analysis and creation of news stories
7	Middle East Debates	newspapers, Internet, new technologies	Internet links, student worksheets, and more	creation, reflection, participation	high school through college	social studies, global studies	incorporates current events, stereotyping, journalism

we've described in this book, placing more emphasis on the evidence students give to back up their responses, reflection on their own and others' perspectives and interpretations, and participation in a collective process rather than leader-led analysis and evaluation.[3]

LESSON PLAN #1

"Introducing Africa"

Overview

Designed to kickoff a new social studies unit, this lesson—developed by elementary teacher Carrie LaZarre in Ithaca, New York—uses a media literacy activity as both a needs assessment (to help a teacher determine what students already know and where there are gaps or mistaken ideas that need to be corrected) and as an exercise to help students gain awareness about where their ideas about other countries come from. The lesson also provides students with a foundation for challenging stereotypes and introduces them to methods for finding good sources of information when learning about another continent, country, or culture. This example uses Africa, but it could be adapted to nearly any social studies unit about which students have media-based preexisting ideas.

Curriculum Areas

- Social studies
- English language arts
- Global studies

Grade Levels

- Grades 3–5
- This idea could be adapted for older grades by using additional or more complex photographs (presenting greater geographical and social diversity) and adding a deeper discussion.

Suggested Frameworks (Curriculum Context)

- Studying other countries/cultures
- Diversity education
- Stereotypes
- Researching information

Learning Objectives

Students will

- learn that Africa is a continent with many nations.
- learn that the continent is geologically and culturally diverse.
- recognize and challenge preconceived notions about Africa. [CP4.5, 5.3]
- identify the origins of their stereotypes/preconceived notions. [CP6.2, 5.3]
- recognize the similarities and differences between cultures and communities in the United States and those of other nations and continents.
- understand that representations made by the popular media are not always accurate or complete. [CP5]
- use group discussion and analysis of media messages to see that people can interpret the same media message differently. [CP6.6, 1.4]

Vocabulary

continent, geography, diversity, culture, stereotype, perspective

Preparation and Prerequisites

- Prior to this lesson, the teacher should introduce the concept of continents and help the students find the continent of Africa on a globe or world map.
- If possible, find or have the students create a wall map of Africa that clearly shows all of the countries.

Time Needed

- Approximately two 30-minute sessions or one 50-minute session

Materials and Equipment

- *Introducing Africa* PowerPoint slide show—available on the Project Look Sharp website—or your own collection of pictures showing the diversity of life on the African continent; the equipment on which to project the slides
- *Introducing Africa* teacher guide, available on the book's website
- *Introducing Africa* student worksheet with thumbnail images (see Figure 7.1); worksheets available on the book's website
- Pencil (one per student)

Step-by-Step Procedures

1. Explain that the class is going to be studying the continent of Africa and that you are going to start by finding out what they already know about Africa.

2. Hand out the student worksheets with thumbnail images (see Figure 7.1).

3. Explain that you will be showing twelve color pictures on the screen that match the black-and-white images on their worksheet and that, as you show each one, you want them to decide if it is a picture that could be from Africa (yes or no) and to write a few words underneath the image about why they think it could or could not be from Africa. Stress that they should just write down what they think and not call out the answers until after everyone sees all of the images, and then you'll be talking about them as a whole class.

4. Show each of the twelve images, giving the students a couple of minutes with each one to write down their reasons on the worksheet. As you show each slide, be careful not to ask the students what they are thinking and writing. This should be a relatively quiet activity so that students are not influenced by each other's responses. If they do say anything, make sure not to confirm or negate their perceptions.

Figure 7.1 "Introducing Africa" Student Worksheet *Page from student worksheet with thumbnails of images shown on the Power Point slides.*

1.

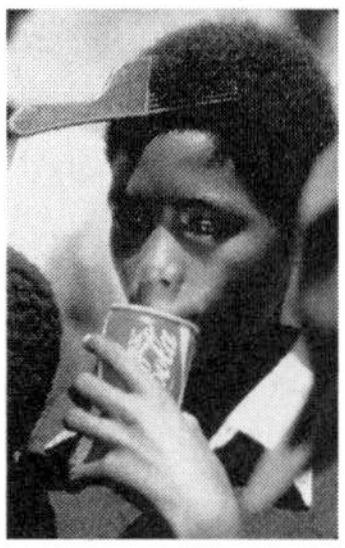

Yes ☐

No ☐

2.

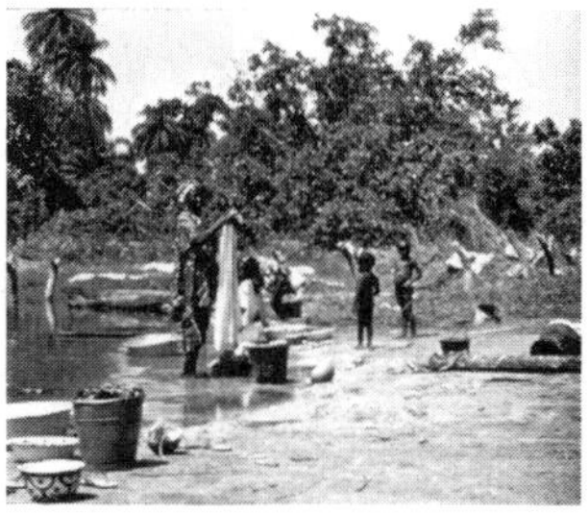

Yes ☐

No ☐

3.

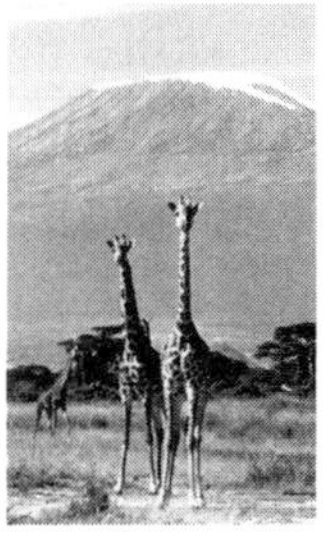

Yes ☐

No ☐

4.

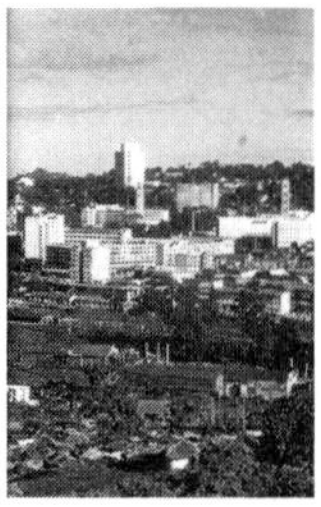

Yes ☐

No ☐

5.

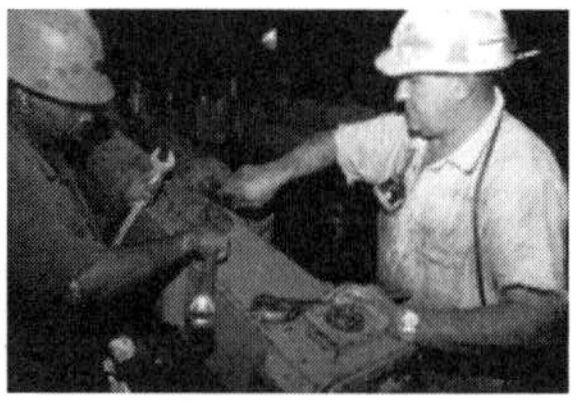

Yes ☐

No ☐

6.

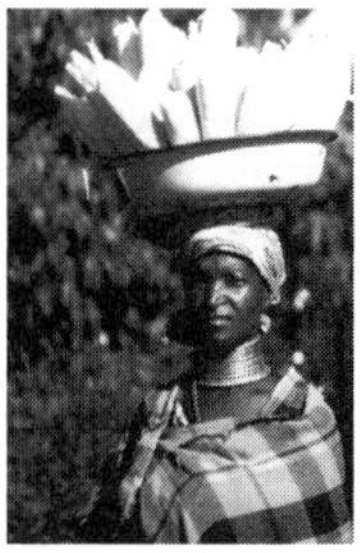

Yes ☐

No ☐

Is this a picture of Africa? Why or why not?

Source: Used by permission from Project Look Sharp, Ithaca College, Division of Interdisciplinary and International Studies.

5. As you show each photograph briefly a second time, ask students to raise their hands if they thought it could come from Africa. Lead a discussion about the images, asking them what clues or evidence they used to decide if it could or could not be from Africa. After all of the photographs are shown the second time, tell the students that all of the photographs are from Africa and note their responses. Follow up on their comments and questions by asking them why they thought some pictures couldn't be from Africa and how they "knew" that.

6. Ask the students how they felt and what they think they might have learned when you told them that all of these pictures are from Africa.

   Note: Step 6 could end the first session. If so, tell the students that you will be talking about this more during your next class.

Note: The activities described in steps 7–13 may not necessarily occur in the order given, depending on the student responses and the goals of the teacher. For example, a teacher might want to combine steps 7 and 8 when going through the photographs a second time, taking a longer time with each photograph; or the teacher might start with step 7 during the second pass through the photographs and then do step 8 separately, going back through the photographs a third time.

7. Go through each photograph again, this time more slowly, discussing the people and their clothing, the geographical features, and other elements seen in the pictures. Point out the diversity across the slides in terms of geography, urban versus rural settings, skin colors and dress of the people shown, activities, etc. Encourage children to draw connections between the lives and cultures they are seeing from Africa and those they see in their own world, noticing both the similarities and the differences. Give the background information about each slide as you discuss the images (e.g., what country the photograph was from, what is being portrayed in the photograph). This information can be found in the *Introducing Africa* Teacher Guide, available on the book's website.

8. As you go through the photographs, it is especially important to discuss the specific clues or evidence in the photographs that gave students the impression that this could or couldn't be from Africa, including the words they wrote on their worksheets. It is not uncommon for stereotypical ideas to emerge from these words. The follow-up discussion is your opportunity to challenge stereotypes about Africa and Africans in a way that models respect.

9. Ask the students if they have a sense of where they might have gotten their ideas about what Africa is like. Brainstorm and make a list of all of the sources that they might have used to get their information (including personal experiences such as visiting African countries or meeting someone from Africa, as well as media sources like books, magazines, movies, and TV shows).

10. Ask students if they know what a stereotype is. Explain that a stereotype is an idea or set of ideas that someone might have about a whole group of people who share something in common (e.g., they are from the same country or culture, the same gender, the same age, the same religion). These ideas rarely apply to all, or even most, or even some of the people who are in that group, but often others believe that everyone from that group is like that, and it makes them prejudge a person from the group before they even get to know him or her.

11. Discuss their responses to the photographs of Africa and remind them of some of the things they said that might have reflected stereotypes that Americans often have about Africa. Explain that as we learn about something new, one of the most important things is to challenge what we already believe to be true and to be open-minded about questioning our beliefs if they might be wrong.

12. Ask them what they can do to guard against relying on stereotypes about other people and other countries. Brainstorm suggestions that they can put

into place as a class (e.g., notice the images that we see of groups of people and countries and think about whether they are only stereotyped images; be careful about the things we say and think about groups of people and countries).

Notes on Pedagogy

- This lesson nicely illustrates the application of media literacy to the K-W-L approach to starting a new unit, especially in exploring what students already *Know* (or believe) about the topic and sources of information that led them to hold those beliefs.

- It is important to approach this activity with sensitivity, given that students are likely to be astonished that all of these pictures are from Africa and some might feel they were tricked or are being made fun of for getting the answers wrong. Stress that many people are surprised to find out that all of the pictures are from Africa, because most Americans have not visited any of the countries in Africa and media images are often incomplete.

- This activity not only unpacks what students know and don't know about Africa, it also makes it clear to teachers what misconceptions their students have about Africa and African people. For example, one third-grade teacher showed us one of her student's worksheets. Under the image of a mother and children washing their clothes in the river, the student had checked "Yes" (it was from Africa) and for evidence had written "naked" and "dirty." For this teacher, the lesson functioned as a needs assessment. She found out that her curriculum would need to counter students' confidently held (but inaccurate) beliefs as well provide information about Africa.

  The lesson also provided her with an opportunity to model respect, even as she challenged negative stereotypes. Rather than making the child who made the comment feel self-conscious or guilty (which could discourage a student from participating in future discussions), a media literacy teacher can thank the youngster for raising such an important issue as she guides students to think about where their ideas originated and where they might locate more reliable sources.

- Use the insights that students learn from this lesson throughout their subsequent exploration of Africa (and other countries/cultures). Encourage students to get in the habit of asking how accurate the information they read/see/hear is in different sources and whether the images they see in books, films, on posters, or so on. reflect only stereotypes of Africa.

- An important issue in media literacy involves recognizing the power of repetition of images and messages—so we think of Africans as poor, rural, and dressed in tribal attire (or nothing) because those are the images we see most often. Teachers can do important work that disrupts the power of this repetition by providing counter-images (e.g., showing the white man working in the factory, the image of the city, etc.).

- For the rest of the year, let the students know that they will be asked (and should ask each other) "How do you know that?""What is your source?" and

"Is that a good source of information *on this topic*?" They should come away from this exercise knowing that a source can be accurate without giving a full picture (e.g., there are poor people in Africa, but that doesn't mean that all Africans are poor) and that a source that is credible on some topics isn't necessarily credible on all topics (e.g., the film *The Lion King*, 1994, might convey some good lessons about courage, but that doesn't automatically make it a good source on what life is like in Africa). If *The Lion King, Madagascar* (2005), or another animated film comes up as a source, you might discuss the strengths and weaknesses of using cartoons as sources of factual information (but take care not to suggest that just because a media source uses pictures of "real" people that it is automatically credible).

Assessments

- Since this lesson often serves as the introduction to a more in-depth study of the continent of Africa, one way to assess the effectiveness of this lesson is through the evaluation of the individual country reports. Do the students go beyond stereotypes about Africa? Identify ways in which the culture and geography are both similar to and different from our own? Evaluate the sources they chose to use as part of their country research for both credibility and stereotypes?

- While a teacher could assess this lesson by using a fairly standard set of knowledge-based test questions about Africa (e.g., identifying Africa as a continent rather than a country, recognizing different geographical features of Africa, naming and locating specific countries on a map of Africa), another way to assess students' understanding is to have them read a story (made up by the teacher) about Africa that contains some accurate and some inaccurate information about African cultures and identify what is true and what is not true in the story. In creating the story, the teacher would want to embed some of the content shown in the photographs that many students had initially said was not true of Africa but actually is true of Africa.

Extensions and Adaptations

- Have students cut out the pictures from one of the student worksheets and place them on the wall map of Africa where the correct country is.

- For upper elementary students, introduce a lesson about the Nacirema. In a paper titled "Body Ritual Among the Nacirema" (in the anthology edited by Spradley & Rynkiewich, 1975, *The Nacirema: Readings on American Culture,* available very inexpensively in paperback), Horace Miner describes a culture with very odd and exotic behaviors, manners of dress, and habitats—and students gradually realize that he is describing American (*Nacirema* spelled backwards) culture. Lesson plans are available through many sources, including the book *Engaging Students Through Global Issues: Activity-Based Lessons and Action Projects* (Facing the Future, 2006).

LESSON PLAN #2

"Media & Activity Diaries"

Overview

This lesson introduces the concept and categories of "media" and raises students' awareness of their own media use, especially in relation to other activities (like learning, exercise/sports, hobbies, face-to-face conversations with peers and family, and sleep). It is also a very rich activity that relates to many different curricular areas, including math and science (incorporating prediction and estimation, categorization, research, and graphing skills), ELA (writing about and reflecting on one's activity choices), and social studies (comparing different groups and time periods). It also has implications for the students' health-related choices and physical education. It can be combined with examinations of national studies of current media use by children and teens done by such organizations as the Kaiser Family Foundation (www.kff.org) and the Pew Internet & American Life Project (http://pewinternet.org).

Curriculum Areas

- Health
- Math
- Science
- Physical education
- Social studies
- English language arts

Grade Levels

- Upper elementary through middle school (Grades 4–8)
- This idea could be simplified for younger grades by using fewer categories and preprinted pictures or stickers to represent different types of activities and by using a shorter time frame (1 or 2 days).
- Media diaries can easily be used with older students (high school through college), and different versions of media diaries are available on the book's website. With older students, the social desirability issues that are raised in Notes on Pedagogy below will increasingly show up in their own self-reports, and they probably won't report at all on some examples of media use.

Suggested Frameworks (Curriculum Context)

- Healthy choices
- Types of media
- Research and data collection
- Categories and concepts
- Quantitative measurement and graphing
- Self-reflection

Learning Objectives

Students will

- learn about different types and categories of media and the criteria that define "media."
- recognize that media include forms that are used for learning in school, as well as forms that are used primarily for entertainment and social communication.
- consider their own use of and exposure to media (both in amount of time spent and types of media) in relation to other activities (social interactions, physical activities, sleep, etc.).
- learn about the ways that television uses "program promos" to increase the amount of time children spend watching, including how that relates to exposure to advertising.
- develop awareness of how they spend their time and what they have a choice about doing (including their use of different types of media for entertainment).
- gain experience gathering scientific data using a self-report recording form.
- practice using and applying mathematical and scientific skills and concepts, including predicting and estimating, summarizing and graphing data, making comparisons across categories and groups, and reporting research findings.

Vocabulary

media, medium, mediated, technology, audiovisual, digital, social networking, print, program promos, multitasking, prediction, estimation, data

Preparation and Prerequisites

- Students should already be familiar with the concept of creating and defining categories, as well as basic quantitative skills involved in computation.
- If possible, students should be able to compute percentages and have some experience creating simple graphs of data.

Time Needed

- Approximately 3–5 sessions of 30–40 minutes each, plus 3–5 days of assignments outside of class for students to keep the media and activity diaries

Materials and Equipment

Examples of all of the following handouts are available on the book's website.

- Packets of *Media & Activity* Diary sheets for each student (with enough pages for the number of days students will be keeping their media and activity diaries)
- Prediction forms (one per student)
- Reflection sheets (one per student)

Step-by-Step Procedures

1. Explain what is meant by the terms *media* and *medium,* including grade-appropriate information from Chapter 1 of this book (e.g., the three criteria that define *media*).

2. Have students generate a list of different types of media that they use or are exposed to. Keep probing to elicit as many different types of media as possible. As they name things, list them on the board or sheets of paper. Identify why—or why not—the things they name would fit the definition of *media*.

3. Discuss and ask the students to reflect on
   - what types of media they named first;
   - what types of media that they named they think people use the most (in their class and in general);
   - whether they included books as media and, if not, why not; and
   - what types of media they use in school or for schoolwork and what types of media they use at home or with friends (and what types of media are used in both situations).

4. **Optional**—Brainstorm and discuss what types of media were available (or not available) 100 years ago, 50 years ago, 25 years ago, and 10 years ago. Hypothesize what types of media their parents or guardians probably used when they were in the same grade in school. Ask the students to reflect on how their lives would have been different if they did not have certain types of media available to them now.

   Note: Step 4 could end the first session. If so, tell the students that you will be talking about this more during your next class.

5. Have students generate a list of other activities and ways they spend their time besides using different types of media. Be sure they remember to include sleeping, eating, playing sports or games, doing hobbies, talking with friends and family, time spent traveling to and from school, etc.

6. As a class, discuss how to organize the ways in which the students spend their time into different categories, including different media forms (print, music, audiovisual, computer-based, etc.), activities (hobbies, sports, vacations, etc.) and basic living (sleeping, eating, bathing, etc.).

7. Lead a discussion about healthy choices that children can make regarding the ways in which they spend their time, identifying what activities are important to do for a healthy life, what activities are important for learning, what activities are important for helping families and other people, what activities are fun to do, etc.

8. Discuss the fact that we are often not aware of the choices we make about how we spend our time, even as adults. Include that fact that sometimes we get caught up doing something and spend far more time than we planned on it. Ask if that ever happens to them and to give some examples of when it does.

9. Discuss the techniques media use to keep you in front of the screen. You may need to explain the concept of "program promos" on television, which are short messages telling viewers about the next shows that are coming up and/or shows that will be on later that day or week. Ask students why they think TV stations show program promos, including informative motives (to let viewers know important information) and economic motives (to get people to watch more television so they will see more advertising, which is usually where the money comes from that pays for the TV shows). Ask students to think of other examples (e.g., in advergames, on social networking sites, in videogames).

10. **Optional**—Explore the idea of "what gets sold" that provides the financial basis for media content. Students are likely to say that it is products—but explain that advertisers are the ones who pay the money, so what are they buying? Discuss the fact that advertisers pay by the second for the time to show their commercials on TV or by the click for banners on websites, but that they also pay more money for the same amount of time during different shows and the same space on different sites. For example, during the Super Bowl, advertisers might pay as much as $2 million to $3 million a minute—why? Explain that the advertisers are actually buying the audience that is watching their commercials, so the more people who watch, the more money they have to pay. Discuss what it means for the TV shows that students watch that advertisers are buying them as an audience. Note that some stations—like PBS—are not based on this model but instead get their money through contributions from people who like their shows and other organizations.

    Note: This might end the second session. Before assigning students to keep their *Media & Activity Diaries*, it is important to notify the students' families about this assignment and to request their help with reminding students and helping them to fill out the diaries. See Notes on Pedagogy below.

11. Introduce the *Media & Activity Diaries*. Explain how to keep them and the period during which the students are going to keep track of their time. Have them write down as many individual activities as they can (e.g., playing baseball, reading a book, eating, traveling in the car, watching TV) and explain that they will be summarizing the activities into categories after the diaries are completed. Reassure them that they don't need to keep track of exact minutes but can estimate how much time they spent on different activities; however, the more accurate they can be, the better.

12. Discuss the challenges they are likely to face, including being aware of what they are doing during the day and the time they spent doing different activities.

Identify ways to help students remember to keep track of their activities and how to get help from family members. Discuss how to record overlap and multitasking (e.g., playing video games while talking with friends, listening to music while reading, eating while watching TV).

13. Before starting the *Media & Activity Diaries*, have the students make predictions about how much time they typically spend on different activities in a day or a week. Remind them how many hours are in a day (24) and week (168). Their answers are probably not even close, but that's okay because they will be comparing their predictions to the actual data they collect in their diaries.

    Note: This is when the students will begin keeping their *Media & Activity Diaries*.

14. Check in with students every day to make sure they are remembering to keep the diaries. If they forget, ask them to think back and try to remember what they did. Remind students at the end of the day. In class, comment on when they are doing different types of activities and using different types of media that they would include.

    Optional—Have students bring diaries daily and have them complete parts in class or at the end of each day.

15. Collect completed diaries (see Assessments below). Generate a list of all the activities that students recorded and come up with categories that each activity could fall into. Have students tally up the amount of time they spent on different types of activities each day and over the total time that they kept the diaries. Ask them to compare their media use on the different days to see how similar it was from day to day and when it was unusual. Have students discuss or reflect on whether their activity during the time period that they kept the diaries was typical of how they usually spend their time and, if not, why not (it could be an unusual week for reasons like trips, snow days, or holidays).

16. **Optional**—Have them multiply their total time spent on each type of activity by the number that would allow them to see how much time they would spend in a year on each activity. Alternatively or in addition, have them calculate their average time spent over several days.

17. Using the categories that the students developed earlier (see step 6), have the students create some simple graphs (e.g., a bar or pie chart) and written statements summarizing their own media use. What did they spend the most time doing? If they have already learned how to do percentages, have them compute the percentage of time they spent on an average day doing different types of activities.

18. Discuss and/or have students write about and reflect on what they learned about themselves and their choices. Have them compare the actual findings with their earlier predictions. What was most surprising? What activities did

they have a choice about doing, and what activities did they not have a choice about? Ask them to reflect on whether they might change anything about how they spend their time, given what they learned. Also ask them to share their findings with their families.

Notes on Pedagogy

- It is very important to notify families ahead of time that this activity is going to be done and when (and the goals behind it, especially in terms of increasing healthy activity choices and as a way to create a rich set of information that can be used to practice math and science skills). Ask for family participation in helping students keep track of their time doing various activities. However, it's important to note that the social-desirability issues involved are very powerful; family members may not want teachers (or other adults) to know how much television their child watches or how little time their child spends reading, etc. So in letting families know ahead of time and asking them to help students keep these diaries, you run the risk that parents or guardians will try to (consciously or unconsciously) influence the findings by encouraging students to engage in some activities and discourage them from others—even if that means their diaries don't reflect how they typically spend their time. But this isn't meant to be an accurate research study, and it's crucial for elementary students to have family support in keeping their diaries.

- Keep in mind social-class issues that might come up during this process (e.g., related to the types of media that different students have access to outside of school or the types of vacations or trips that students might take) and avoid comparisons across individuals. Keep the focus on types of media and activities, not specific activities or media examples, in order to keep these comparisons in check.

Assessments

- In assessing how well the students completed their media diaries, teachers will want to look for evidence that the students actually wrote in their diaries at different times and on different days and that they are remembering to include different kinds of activities. So, for example, the teacher might ask students to turn in their diaries after two days just to be checked to make sure they are in the process of keeping them.

- Part of the assessment for this lesson should be based on the students' participation in the discussions about developing of the media and activity categories, as well as their participation in the follow-up discussions about similarities and differences among class members and their overall engagement in the research and analysis aspects of this lesson.

- Depending on the goals of the teacher, assessment might include an evaluation of the accuracy of the data summaries and graphs that each student produces illustrating her or his own media use (or other data sets, depending on whether the teacher uses any of the optional aspects or extensions).

- One of the main goals of this lesson is to raise the students' awareness of how they spend their time (especially regarding media use and physical activity) and for them to reflect on what they learned—and perhaps plan to make some changes in how they choose to spend their time. Part of the assessment might, therefore, include having the students write a reflection paper about this immediately after they complete the diary and then again a few weeks later (including whether they made any changes in their choices of activities as a result of what they learned in the diary lesson).

Extensions and Adaptations

- Divide the students into pairs or small groups and have each group decide on a research question (e.g., "I think boys spend more time playing video games than girls."). List the research questions on the board and discuss/ revise them to make sure that they can actually be investigated with the findings from the *Media & Activity Diaries*. Have each group gather the data from all of the members of the class—including themselves—in order to answer their question (e.g., How much time did you spend playing video games, and are you a boy or girl?). Have each group compute their findings, graph them, and report back to the class. Discuss what they learned from their investigation.

LESSON PLAN #3

"Fact or Fiction? Urban Legends and False Beliefs"

Overview

Using hands-on data collection, a variety of media sources (including a nature documentary and various websites) and media literacy analysis techniques, students assess source credibility, learn about lemmings, and practice scientific thinking. They also decode a film clip, discuss the practical difficulties and ethical issues involved in the production of nature films, and explore the phenomenon and impact of urban legends. The use of group work and a lesson design in which students work through data collection and analysis themselves (rather than just hearing a lecture about Internet credibility or scientific misinformation) help them build inquiry skills that they can then apply to other coursework.

Curriculum Areas

- Information literacy
- Science
- Biology
- Communications
- Media studies

Grade Levels

- Middle school through college

Suggested Frameworks (Curriculum Context)

- Credibility of information
- Data collection
- Media production techniques
- Urban legends
- Ethics
- Scientific knowledge

Learning Objectives

Students will

- understand the concept of "urban legends" and false scientific beliefs. [CP1, 6]
- discuss and explore ways to check on the validity of scientific claims, rumors, and urban legends (through scientific investigation, logical thinking and common sense, information gathering and evaluation, and resources like Snopes.com). [CP1, 2, 4, 6]
- practice data collection through surveys. [CP3.4, 6]
- practice detailed observation and providing evidence-based answers. [CP1]
- practice analyzing audiovisual media messages. [CP1, 2.5, 6]
- build awareness of production techniques used in film and television (including nature documentaries) to create action sequences and portray animal behavior. [CP1, 2.5]
- reflect on the influence of the media on people's beliefs about science and about the real world. [CP5, 6]
- learn about lemmings, including where they live and their behaviors.

Vocabulary

urban legends, consensus, lemmings, tundra, arctic, migration, precipice, avalanche, tarantulas, Snopes.com

Preparation and Prerequisites

This lesson revolves around popular urban legends that students at your school are likely to be familiar with and that relate to science. Students will be conducting surveys regarding these urban legends, and sample survey forms are available on the book's website (see Figure 7.3 for examples of those urban legends). However, you should modify or substitute urban legends to match your curriculum goals as much as possible (e.g., by selecting other science-related urban legends from Snopes.com).

Time Needed

- 45–60 minutes in two sessions, plus time to investigate the credibility of urban legends through Internet searches (15–30 minutes in class or as a homework assignment)

Materials and Technology

- Copies of survey sheets with descriptions and/or images of different urban legends
- Clipboards (if possible) and pencils or pens
- PowerPoint slides or print examples of media illustrating beliefs about lemmings as suicidal and related pages from Snopes.com (see Figure 7.2)
- *Fact or Fiction* Teacher Guide, available on the book's website
- Video clip from *White Wilderness* (1958)
- (Preferably) Internet access (for Snopes.com and other websites)
- (Optional) Student access to computers to investigate urban legends and explore Snopes.com (either during class or as a homework assignment)

Step-by-Step Procedures

1. Ask students if they know what an urban legend is (a widespread rumor or story that is typically believed by the teller to be true without any evidence that it actually is, often spread via the Internet and e-mail). Have the students give examples of urban legends they have heard before, discussing whether they think the stories are true (and why or why not).

2. Ask if they have ever heard of lemmings, which are small animals that look a little like guinea pigs. Probe to find out what they have heard about lemmings (which is likely to include the idea that lemmings follow each other blindly and commit suicide by jumping off cliffs into the sea). Show examples of popular media portraying lemmings in that way (on PowerPoint slides or printed handouts, available on the book's website; see Figure 7.2). Ask the students if they think this is really true and how they might be able to find out.

Figure 7.2 Popular Images of Lemmings

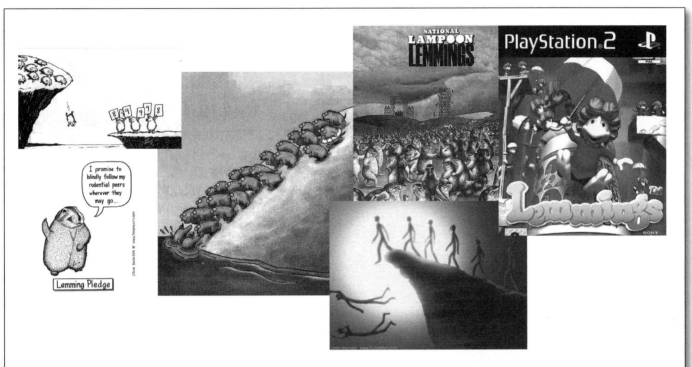

Examples of media messages about lemmings from comics, a book cover, a painting, and a video game. What is consistently implied about the appearance and behavior of lemmings in these images?

3. Divide the class into pairs or small groups (with one group for each urban legend to be investigated). Give each group one of the sheets with the image or description of a different urban legend and the places to gather data from ten people (using the survey sheets available on the book's website; see Figure 7.3). Explain the procedure they will be using to gather their data. This could involve surveying ten other students in the classroom or completing an assignment outside of class (e.g., during lunch or study hall).

4. After groups have surveyed ten people, have them calculate their results in percentages (i.e., by multiplying the number of each type of response by 10) to draw conclusions about the percentage of respondents who thought the urban legend was true, false, or mixed or were unsure. Have the pairs or groups discuss among themselves whether they agree with their survey results and, if not, why not. They should then complete the bottom of the survey describing their own judgment about the truthfulness of the urban legend.

5. When all groups are finished, discuss their findings. Which urban legends had the highest percentages of believability? Which ones had the lowest? What was each group's judgment about the credibility of the urban legend, and how much weight did "public opinion" carry in their decision? (Upper-level students might be asked to comment on the

Figure 7.3 True or False? Popular Urban Legends

Lemmings are small animals that commit suicide by jumping off cliffs.

Tarantulas are poisonous, and their bites can kill humans.

Poppy seeds on bagels and muffins can result in positive drug tests.

Coca-Cola used to contain cocaine.

Rice thrown at weddings is dangerous to birds.

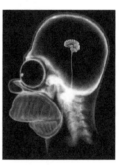

We only use ten percent of our brains.

These images reflect some popular urban legends that have appeared in the media. Which of these are true? (Hint: Only two of them are.) What's your evidence? Do the images reinforce the credibility of the legend and, if so, how? Who might benefit from—and who might be harmed by—these images? For those that are false, why might the creators have chosen to use these images?

relationship between sample size and validity.) If they disagreed with the consensus in their survey, what did they base their judgment on? Make a list on the board of the different sources of evidence or reasoning that could be used to support one's judgments about stories like these, which could include

- a lot of people believe it (consensus);
- I've always heard that—you hear it a lot;
- I've read about it or seen it somewhere (probe to find out the source);
- someone I trust told me; or
- thinking logically about it, given what we know scientifically about the topic.

6. Point out that news and video documentaries are often used as sources of credible information. Suggest that the class examine the urban legend about lemmings that was included in the survey. Explain that in 1958, Disney made a nature documentary about animals and birds in the arctic tundra. It was called *White Wilderness*, and it won an Academy Award for Best Documentary Feature. It included a segment about lemmings that showed their behavior during migration.

VOICEOVER DIALOGUE

White Wilderness

(accompanied by dramatic music)

By now the lemmings have forgotten the original idea of food.
   They've become victims of an obsession, a one-track thought: move on, move on, keep moving on.
   If they come to a tiny stream, they plunge right in; water doesn't faze them.
   Indeed they will swim sizable rivers and even lakes in their determination to push on.

Ahead lies the arctic shore, and beyond the sea,
   and still the little animals surge forward.
   Their frenzy takes them tumbling down the terraced cliffs, creating tiny
   avalanches of soil and rocks
   and the seemingly indestructible lemmings.

They reach the final precipice.
   This is the last chance to turn back.
   Yet over they go, casting themselves bodily out into space . . .

---

7. Show the 2-minute video clip, asking students to carefully listen to the voiceover and the music, as well as to observe the behaviors of the lemmings that are shown.

8. Review what the film showed and said about lemmings (see Voiceover Dialogue box), clarifying some of the vocabulary and noting the roles of the

dramatic music and tone of the voiceover in portraying the lemmings as suicidal. Ask the students what they think about this as evidence. Does the documentary present proof that lemmings commit suicide by jumping off cliffs? Is there any way that it could be untrue? How could students find out the truth about lemmings?

9. **Recommended**—Have the students, working in small groups, go online to research whether lemmings actually commit suicide by jumping off cliffs as the media examples and the nature documentary showed. Give them 10 minutes to investigate and then have the groups report back on what they found. As part of their report out, they should include the search terms they used to investigate and which websites they used for information. Alternatively, assign each group of students to investigate the credibility of the urban legend they had in the survey (online in class or as a homework assignment). Have each group report back on what they found, including the search terms and sources they used. Have the class as a whole discuss the credibility of those sources (compared to the documentary). See Extensions (and Chapter 5) for more information and suggestions for how to discuss the credibility of Internet websites.

   Note: In doing these investigations, students are likely to have come upon the website Snopes.com, which will lead nicely into the continued discussion in Step 10.

10. Introduce Snopes.com as a source of information about urban legends. Show the Snopes page about lemmings and the Disney movie *White Wilderness* (www.snopes.com/disney/films/lemmings.asp) or use the still images provided on the PowerPoint slides on the book's website. Have the students read what the website says about the film and the false beliefs about lemming suicide that have been perpetuated by the filmmakers' decision to push the lemmings off the cliff in order to include that behavior in the film.

11. Confirm that lemmings actually do not follow each other blindly or commit suicide by jumping off cliffs. This is a false belief of long standing that popular media have perpetuated as an urban legend. Show the film clip again, having the students describe the camera angles used to show the lemmings jumping off the cliff and to consider where the camera must have been in order to get those shots. Note that the film never actually includes a shot that shows a lemming running up and jumping off the cliff.

12. Discuss the filmmakers' decision to push the lemmings off the cliff in terms of ethics. If the filmmakers believed that lemming suicide was really true, was it okay for them to stage this in order to demonstrate that behavior?

13. Show other examples of urban legends reported on Snopes.com (by going to the website or using the still images on the PowerPoint slides), including other examples of inaccurate beliefs about animals (e.g., opossums hanging by their tails) and urban legends that are actually true (e.g., the Marlboro Man died of lung cancer). Encourage students to use Snopes.com to investigate urban legends they hear and to bring in what they find for future class discussions.

14. Discuss the credibility of each of the other urban legends included in the survey (see the Teacher Guide on the book's website), including the relevant web reference from Snopes.com or other sources. Identify other sources where students could go to confirm whether the urban legend is true or not and stress the importance of applying their own common sense/critical thinking as well as prior knowledge from science or general experience.

15. During the discussion, raise possibilities for how the urban legend came to exist and/or why people would believe it. Frame the discussion around these questions:

- Could it be that this was true at one time but now it isn't (because something has changed)?
- Could it be that it was once believed to be true but then better scientific investigation and tools have proven it to be false?
- Was this perpetuated by a particular group for a particular reason (e.g., as propaganda)?
- Is it the result of a mistaken inference on the part of the audience?
- Is its widespread acceptance due to lack of scientific knowledge on the part of most people?

Discuss how students might consider other claims and urban legends in the future. Using the urban legends in their survey (or on the book's website) as examples, frame the discussion around what questions they could have asked about the claim. Here are some examples:

- Does cocoa mulch actually have chocolate in it? And is the chemical present similar to that found in dark or baker's chocolate (which is known to be harmful to dogs)?
- Do they mean seeing the Great Wall of China (from the moon) with the naked eye or with a telescope?
- What amount (e.g., of poppy seeds) would be necessary for that effect?
- How could they possibly know or measure what men think about and how often?

16. Make clear connections between this activity and the general process of scientific discovery, evaluation of evidence, and information gathering about a topic. Refer again to this lesson as the students investigate other scientific topics throughout the school year.

Extensions and Adaptations

- Have the students collect survey results from all other students in the class or in several classes (i.e., more than just ten students) and graph the results for different urban legends to illustrate which legends are most heavily believed and which are not. Create a display in the hallway reporting these results, including the "truth" about each urban legend. Include in the display information about Snopes.com.

> ### VOICES FROM THE FIELD: *TARANTULAS*
>
> When Cyndy was in graduate school, her professor John Condry raised the issue of credibility of media information by saying that—despite popular belief—tarantula spiders are not highly poisonous and can't kill you. Even though she trusted her professor in general, she didn't believe him about this; she "knew" that tarantulas were deadly—she'd heard that all her life. When she went to the library to check on it, she was astonished to discover that he was right—tarantulas are no more poisonous than bees, and while they might give you a painful bite, it won't kill you unless you are specifically allergic to tarantula venom. Later in the course, Condry showed examples of films and TV shows portraying tarantulas as deadly, pointing out the reasons why film and television makers might choose to use tarantulas instead of actual deadly spiders like black widows or brown recluse spiders (e.g., their large size and hairy legs, the fact that they aren't highly poisonous and therefore don't endanger the lives of the actors).
>
> Years later, when Cyndy asked students in her classes whether they thought tarantulas were deadly, there was high consensus that they were. When she probed for evidence, it was often from fictional media sources (like the episode "Pass the Tabu" from the TV sitcom *The Brady Bunch* [1972]). Even though the students clearly knew the show was fiction, on this point (tarantulas being highly poisonous), the show was viewed as a credible source.

- When discussing specific urban legends, delve into the sources of those legends and widespread beliefs in them, along with media portrayals that have reinforced them. Here are some examples:
  - Concerning *lemmings,* show the clip from Disney's *White Wilderness*, which you can access through Project Look Sharp. Discuss why the filmmakers might have made the lemmings jump off the cliff.
  - Concerning *tarantulas,* discuss why makers of TV shows and movies might use the relatively safe tarantula spider to portray a dangerous bug instead of using other spiders that actually are dangerous.
  - Concerning *hair and fingernail growth,* discuss why this might be included in horror stories or films to increase the horror or fear created in the reader or viewer.

- To help students learn that they always need to use their critical thinking skills no matter what the source, you can ask students to read about the talking horse on the 1960s television series *Mister Ed* (1961–1966) on the "Lost Legends" section of Snopes.com. The "Lost Legends" section is cleverly devoted to presenting "the truth" in misleading ways, so what Snopes.com says is actually wrong—but there are lots of clues in the explanation that indicate that the information is wrong for a reader who applies common sense or critical thinking skills. The site explains that it was possible to use a zebra instead of a horse because the program was shown in black and white and therefore the stripes wouldn't show up. But common sense and observation should cue readers to the fact that even if a person was viewing a program in black and white, it would be possible to distinguish between a horse and a zebra and that a zebra's stripes wouldn't somehow disappear. While this seems obvious, the power of a website—especially one like Snopes.com—to generate unquestioning acceptance of its claims is remarkable.[4]

At the bottom of each Lost Legends page site, a link says, "Additional Information," and if you open and read it, it says that you should never blindly believe anything you read and accept it as truth without question, even if it's on this website. This is a brilliant and important lesson—but be cautious in how you use it. You don't want to make students who fall for the wrong answer feel stupid or wrong. If you ask students to look at this site in class or as a homework assignment, begin the discussion by asking:

o What did Snopes.com say about Mister Ed?
o Do you think that is true?

Probe for specific clues in the explanation that are questionable, like the claim that because the TV show was in black and white, viewers couldn't tell that the horse was a zebra, or the picture you can click on to show how the zebra would look in black and white (which is identical to the original picture of the horse).

o Could Snopes.com be wrong about this?
o Did anyone read the attachment at the bottom? What did it say?
o What was Snopes.com's purpose in creating this section of the website?
o What's the lesson about trusting sources?

• Let students (especially at the middle school level) practice their new analysis skills by looking at the purposeful hoax websites for the Pacific Northwest tree octopus (http://zapatopi.net/treeoctopus/) or dihydrogenmonoxide (www.dhmo.org). Focus on the ways in which the sites use scientific-sounding language and arguments to persuade people.

LESSON PLAN #4

"Twister"

Overview

In a lesson that merges science, observation, special effects, and film analysis, students discuss and/or analyze in writing a clip from a popular Hollywood film, making note of what was presented accurately and what was presented inaccurately or in a misleading way. In this example, we use the film *Twister* (1996) to examine tornadoes, but the lesson's techniques could be applied to a range of films and topics in any area where films give an impression of being factual but use creative license (e.g., depicting events as historical when they are not). The lesson design draws its power from the fact that students are doing the investigative work instead of the teacher providing all the information and answers in a lecture (i.e., doing the work for them).

Curriculum Areas

- Earth science
- Meteorology
- General science
- Communications
- Media studies

Grade Levels

- Middle school through college

Suggested Frameworks (Curriculum Context)

- Tornadoes/meteorology
- Credibility/accuracy of scientific content shown in the media
- Observation
- Logical thinking
- Media production techniques
- Assessment of knowledge after completion of a unit

Learning Objectives

Students will

- identify specific actions and vocabulary related to tornadoes.
- identify accurate, inaccurate, and misleading information about tornadoes (and science in general) in popular media portrayals. [CP2.5]
- practice making detailed observations and giving evidence-based answers. [CP1.4]
- practice analyzing audiovisual media messages. [CP1]
- build awareness of techniques used in film and television to create action sequences and portray the movement of things like tornadoes. [CP1]
- develop understanding of and appreciation for different production techniques used in audiovisual messages (characters, dialogue, music, lighting, pace, camera angles, special visual and auditory effects, etc.). [CP1]

- reflect on the influence of popular fictional media portrayals on people's beliefs about science and scientific topics like tornadoes. ^{CP5}

Vocabulary

tornado, twister, sisters, the core, flanking line, waterspout, funnel

Preparation and Prerequisites

This exercise can be used either to begin a discussion of tornadoes or as part of an assessment following a unit about tornadoes.

- If using this as an introduction to tornadoes, it would be helpful to have the students read some material (from their textbook or another source) about tornadoes prior to class.
- If using this as an assessment, it would be important to cover all of the information that the student will need to answer the questions about terminology and accuracy on the Student Assessment Sheet.

Time Needed

- 10 minutes (assessment)
- 15 minutes (introducing tornadoes, including terminology used in the video segment)

Materials

- Video clip from *Twister* on YouTube (or entire film on video or DVD); if using the actual film, this clip occurs at 58:25 minutes into the movie— and the equipment with which to screen it
- Student Response Sheet (for whole class discussions) or Student Assessment Sheet (if using as an individual assessment at the end of a unit on tornadoes), both available on the book's website

Step-by-Step Procedures

1. Pass out the Student Response or Student Assessment sheets.

2. Explain to the students that they will be seeing a short clip from the popular movie *Twister*, which came out in 1996. Ask them to note any scientific terms they hear and decide what aspects of what they see and hear are true about tornadoes and what aspects are not true.

   Note: If this is conducted as an assessment, tell the students how many terms, accuracies, and inaccuracies they will be expected to identify and whether they need to define each of the terms they hear. The Student Assessment Sheet can be modified to fit your goals for assessment.

3. Show the 1-minute video clip.

VOICEOVER DIALOGUE

Twister

Jesus, Bill, I've never seen it clouded like this.

I don't think anybody has.

The angle's too high.

Bill, we're in the core.

OK, we got sisters.

Oh my God. [phone rings] What? Yes? Julia, I can't talk to you right now.

We're running into the flanking line.

I realize that.

We can't attack this thing from the south—we're going to get rolled.

Watch me.

Julia, I know you're upset, you just gotta breathe, we both just gotta breathe.

Cow.

I gotta go Julia, we've got cows.

Another cow.

Actually I think that's the same one.

---

4. Give the students 3 or 4 minutes to write.

5a. If using this as an assessment, show the film clip two or three times (with time to write between each showing). After the students have completed the assessment and turned it in, continue with the discussion about accuracy and misleading content that is described in steps 7–10.

5b. If the clip is being used to introduce the topic or generate discussion, ask the students to describe the terms and images that they saw. Use this as an opportunity to clarify or introduce other terms and concepts, including the characteristics of tornadoes (size and funnel shape, the center or core), the types of tornadoes (e.g., "sisters," waterspouts, the different levels on the Fujita scale), and any other concepts that relate to the level of understanding appropriate for the class.

6. Ask the students to give examples of other content they saw or heard that they believe to be accurate about tornadoes. For each example, ask the rest of the class if they agree and then discuss it in terms of the material the class has already learned. If the class is unsure, ask how they could find out whether something they saw or heard in the movie was true or not. There are good websites that can help identify scientific inaccuracies in films, including the Internet Movie Database (www.imdb.com). For links on that site and others regarding this specific film, see the companion website.

7. Ask the students to give examples of other content they saw or heard that they believed to be inaccurate or misleading about tornadoes. For each

example, ask the rest of the class if they agree and then discuss it in terms of the material the class has already learned, if possible. Students are very likely to raise the issue of whether or not a cow could go flying past the car while still alive and mooing; this is an example of a portrayal that is partially true (cows and other animals have been known to be lifted up by tornadoes and dropped a distance away without being harmed) but also partially untrue (if they were really in the core of the tornado, then the winds wouldn't blow the cow so close to the car, but if the cow did blow past, then the roar of the tornado would mask the mooing sound and the wind would be blowing the truck off the road). Again, ask how they could find out whether something they saw or heard in the movie was true or not and review good sources for checking on accuracy of scientific information.

8. Discuss why the filmmakers presented this kind of inaccurate or misleading information about tornadoes and how it might influence viewers' beliefs about actual tornadoes.

9. Summarize the "facts" and the misleading/inaccurate information presented in this fictional film.

Extensions and Adaptations

- Teachers may want to use a longer segment or other segments from *Twister* to get at different meteorological concepts or other inaccuracies about tornadoes shown in the film. If so, it may be useful to search the script for scientific concepts and information (see link to the script on companion website).

  For example, at an earlier point in the movie, a character says:

  Rotation is increasing. Sheer is 90 knots. 50 outbound, 40 inbound. Good southeast gusts at 40 miles an hour, approaching 150 in the funnel. The storm motion is 225 degrees, coming straight out of the southwest.

  At several points, there are discussions about different classifications of tornadoes (F2 through F5) on the Fujita scale. Other concepts that are mentioned include horizontal rain, *rain b*ands, backbuilding, the caps, dry line, debris, and NSSL.

- Analyze newspaper and magazine articles that highlight the danger, death, and destruction resulting from tornadoes (which is often exaggerated, making readers feel that they are more at risk than is actually the case). As part of this discussion, it's important to include why enhanced fear would attract people to news. The concept of the "FUD factor" (Jackson & Jamieson, 2007) could be introduced here, which refers to the tendency of the news media to emphasize (or even create) fear, uncertainty, and doubt as a way of attracting an audience who will come to them for information (see the glossary on the companion *websi*te). The same has been found to be true of advertising.

- Compare *Twister* with a traditional instructional video or documentary on tornadoes. Ask students to note the differences in production techniques and discuss the advantages and drawbacks of each format for informing viewers and for exciting viewers about science. Have students compare the credits from the two films and note any differences in the types of people or organizations involved.[5]

- The issue of media consolidation is an important one to explore, especially in the context of journalism and the implications for who controls what gets reported as "news" and how stories are reported in the popular press (see "The Agenda-Setting Function of News" in Chapter 5, pp. 113–114).

Use the cover of *Time* magazine in Figure 7.4 to help students explore the links among different media outlets owned by the same company and the relationship among news, entertainment, and advertising. That *Time* cover (May 1996) appeared a week after the movie *Twister* was released by Warner Brothers, and the cover story, "Unraveling the Mysteries of Twisters" (Nash, 1996) referenced the film; the issue also included a review of *Twister*. Since at the time Warner Brothers and *Time* magazine were owned by the same parent company (Time-Warner), this raises the question of the extent to which the *Time* cover story was designed primarily as advertising for the movie. Ask students to answer the questions in the caption and to generate their own questions about the *Time* cover.

Optional—Help students identify how to find release dates for different types of media and how they can track down the ownership of most commercial media companies by a small number of large corporations. Ask them to find similar examples of news outlets (e.g., the morning network news programs) reporting on movie, book, or song releases by sources related to their parent company.

Figure 7.4   Cover of *Time* Magazine

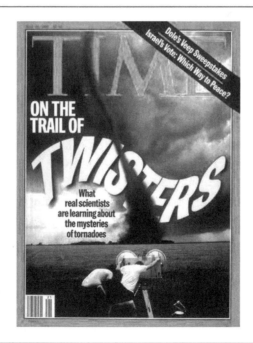

The same week that the film *Twister* (Warner Brothers) was released, *Time* magazine ran a cover story on twisters. Since both were owned by the same parent company (Time-Warner), what questions would you ask about this cover and the accompanying article?

Source: Time, May 20, 1996.

LESSON PLAN #5

"White Towel"

Overview

In this low-tech production activity, students work in small groups to design TV commercials, all for the same product but each with a different target audience. Students grapple with basic elements of a narrative (character, setting, dialogue, plot) as well as multimodal aspects of communication (visuals, text, voiceovers, music), and because their product is nearly a blank slate (a white towel6), they can't help but impose their own values and assumptions about the target group on their task. Each group presents their commercial design to the class, and the ensuing discussion quickly raises consciousness about stereotypes, persuasive techniques, and divergent points of view.

Curriculum Areas

- English/language arts
- Communications
- Business
- Economics
- Social studies
- Media studies

Grade Levels

- Upper middle school through college
- May work well in earlier grades with additional teacher guidance and/ or when students have experience working in small groups on creative projects.

Suggested Frameworks (Curriculum Context)

- Story narratives
- Persuasive messages
- Stereotyping
- Media production
- Target audience
- Advertising

Learning Objectives

Students will

- practice creating an effective, persuasive message. [CP2.1]
- build awareness of persuasive techniques often used in advertising. [CP1]
- appreciate narrative elements (plot, character, setting, dialogue, etc.). [CP1, 2]
- develop understanding of the different elements of an audiovisual message (visuals, printed text, dialogue, voiceover, music, sound effects, editing transitions, etc.). [CP1]
- understand and appreciate importance of "target audience." [CP1]

- understand the concept of a "unique selling proposition" (USP) in an advertisement (promoting something unique about the product that makes it memorable or desirable) and how to incorporate it into their own advertising design. [CP1]
- understand the process of media production (planning and design). [CP2]
- practice the use of storyboard forms to plan out the elements and sequence of scenes (visual, text, audio). [CP2]
- participate in small-group collaboration and decision making.
- practice effective speaking and listening skills.
- reflect on stereotypes and assumptions about specific groups. [CP5.3, 6.2, 6.6]

Vocabulary

target audience, stereotype, voiceover, unique selling proposition (USP)

Preparation and Prerequisites

- This works best in classes of 12–60 students.
- The teacher will probably want to make sure students are already familiar with story and production elements commonly used in advertising (target audience, USP, voiceover, dialogue, editing, etc.).
- This lesson often works well to follow up a prior discussion about stereotypes (recognizing how easily people fall into relying on stereotypes about specific genders and age groups in designing their commercials).

Time Needed

- *Small group work* (designing commercial): Minimum of 15–20 minutes (more in cases where additional teacher guidance is needed or if more detail and depth are desired in the commercial's design)
- *Presentations:* 1–3 minutes per group (including some discussion for each)
- *Follow-up discussion:* 5–15 minutes

Materials

- Storyboard forms (see Figure 7.5). Complete forms are available on the book's website.
- Note cards with names of different target audiences (could be told verbally to each group). It is important that the other students don't know the target audience for each group prior to the presentations.
- If possible, several identical plain white towels (ideally, one for each group). It is important that the towels be completely white with no patterns or words, lacking any inherent characteristic that would make a given towel desirable or different.

Step-by-Step Procedures

1. Divide the class into small groups of three to five students. If possible, have each group work around a table or with desks in a circle, separated from the other groups as much as possible.

Figure 7.5 Storyboard Form

Target Audience = _____   USP = _____

Visuals

☐	☐	☐	☐	☐

Printed Text

Audio Voiceover

Music/ Sound

Visuals

☐	☐	☐	☐	☐

Printed Text

Audio Voiceover

Music/ Sound

Used to design TV commercials or other audiovisual content.

Source: Used by permission from Project Look Sharp, Ithaca College.

2. Give each group a storyboard form.

3. Explain that each group will be designing a TV commercial to sell a white towel. They'll need to come up with a name for their product, decide what characters (if any) will be in the commercial (and if so, a description of what they would look like, including any particularly notable factors such as gender, race, age, body type, costume, hairstyle, etc.), what the background or scenery will be like, how the "story" will unfold, what the voiceover will say, what kind of music will be playing, whether there will be words on the screen or sound effects, and so on. They will fill out all of this on their Storyboard Form, sketching in the visuals as well as they can.

But the trick is that each group will be designing their commercial for a *different* target audience.

4. Assign a target audience privately to each group by handing out note cards with the target audiences on them (or telling each group verbally but taking care to make sure that other groups don't overhear). Basic target audiences that work well (depending on the number of groups):

Adult women	*Adult men*	*Older adults*
College students	*Teenagers (13–17)*	*Children (5–12)*
Infants/Toddlers (either directly or targeted to a parent to buy for them)		

For large classes, you might also use specific occupations (e.g., doctors, athletic trainers, lifeguards, janitors, teachers, scientists). See additional suggestions in Extensions and Adaptations below.

5. Explain to all the groups that they'll have 15–20 minutes to design their commercials and then each group will present their commercial design to the rest of the class. (This could involve acting it out or just describing what is on the storyboard.)

6. As the groups work, remind them that they need to have a name for their product. The naming adds a richness to the activity that is both instructive and fun; names sometimes reflect stereotypes and often reveal creativity and humor. Some of our favorites over the years include "Totally Towel" (for teens), "Tuff Towel" (for men), and "The Blood Bib" (for doctors). Also remind students of other elements they should be considering (background, lighting, voiceover, music, etc.). This could be done by writing those elements on the board or on a PowerPoint slide or by listing them on a separate handout for each group. Periodically remind students of the time (or how much time is left).

7. Each group presents their commercial *without naming the target audience they were assigned*. After each group is finished, ask the class who they think the target audience was and what the USP (unique selling proposition) was, and what their evidence is for those conclusions. Ask the group presenting to identify their actual USP, to name the actual target audience they were assigned, and to identify the elements of the commercial they designed to appeal specifically to that target audience. Then briefly discuss with the group and the class what worked well and what suggestions other students might have for strengthening the commercial's design to better target the appropriate audience. If the focus of the lesson is persuasive writing, start that discussion by asking, "Do you think this ad would persuade that target audience? Why or why not?"

8. Have each group turn their storyboards in to the teacher when they are finished.

9. Either after each group's presentation or after all of the groups have presented, raise the issue of what stereotypes (if any) appeared in the commercials. In those discussions, include

- age and gender stereotypes that people might have and/or that are sometimes reflected in advertising;

- who might benefit from and who might be harmed by such stereotyped messages; and
- why advertisers frequently use stereotypes (e.g., because they have limited time or space to get across their message, because they want people to quickly recognize what is happening).

Notes on Pedagogy

- The emphasis for this lesson should be on understanding the process used in creating advertisements (or persuasive messages in general) and decisions that are made in designing advertising messages. Students should also reflect on the potential impact of such messages—rather than simply being taught how to do successful marketing.

- Teachers will need to be sensitive in handling the discussion when the members of the class cannot correctly identify the target audience assigned to the group, being careful not to make the group members feel that they have failed. Instead, focus on what aspects of the commercial might have indicated a different target audience and what the group might have done differently to more clearly target the audience assigned (e.g., using different phrasing, characters, settings, voiceovers).

- A plain white towel is so generic that it forces students to insert their own assumptions into their advertising designs. They are likely to gain some insights about their unconscious assumptions but in a way that is not confrontational. For example, at the end of all of the presentations, we sometimes ask all of the students to close their eyes and imagine each commercial as we do a brief summary of each one. Then with their eyes still closed, we ask them to raise their hands if any of the commercials included main characters who were people of color. In classes where most students are white, often no hands go up. We can then have a deep and enlightening conversation about why that is the case (including the fact that most advertisements still feature only white characters). Because we have used a media literacy frame for this exercise, we can have that substantive discussion without accusing anyone of being racist, homophobic, sexist, or prejudiced in some other way, which would only serve to shut down the conversation.

- Notice the advantages of using an activity like this to unpack unconscious attitudes and assumptions about different groups of people and to get students to recognize the choices that advertisers make in creating their ads (compared to trying to accomplish the same thing just by analyzing production techniques and stereotypes in existing ads):
  - It transforms the teacher role from "expert mode" (pointing out things in an ad that students don't know) into facilitator mode for a hands-on activity.
  - This example of a low-tech media production activity is much more likely to actively involve all of the students rather than just those comfortable speaking up in class.
  - It requires self-reflection in a way that analyzing something that someone else makes doesn't (which is especially important to address stereotyping).

Assessments

- The assessments for this lesson depend a lot on the context and course in which the lesson occurs. In an advertising or media production class, the teacher may want to evaluate the quality of the production design and elements used and how successful the students were in identifying an appropriate USP and appealing to their assigned target audience. In an English class, the assessment might focus more on narrative and character development, accuracy of grammar and language, and elements of persuasion.

- In all classes, the assessment should also focus on the extent to which the students can articulate what elements they put in to appeal to their target audience and the attention they paid to the product name, the production details, and the character descriptions. Students may also be assessed on their participation in the analysis of each group's commercial (which could be done in writing as well as through the whole-class discussion).

- A follow-up assessment might focus on the students' ability to correctly identify target audience and a USP for professionally created commercials (or advertisements in magazines) and to give evidence from the commercial or advertisement and the context in which it appeared. Accurate identification of the target audience(s) is likely to be based on the program during which the commercial was shown (or magazine in which it appeared), USP, characters, setting, product name, elements of the narrative, and specific production elements (like choice of music).

Extensions and Adaptations

- Other possibilities for target audiences (if you have a larger number of groups) include
  - o athletes (professional or amateur) and
  - o more specific age groups (young adults, 22–30; middle-aged adults, 30–50)

  You could also have more than one group design a commercial for the same target audience and ask the class to compare how similar or different the two commercials are.

- Students could design political commercials, all supporting the same political candidate but for different target audiences (e.g., men, women, families, urban poor, conservatives, independents, liberals).

- Relate the discussion to particular parts of your curriculum by deepening the exploration of why particular images or concepts are or are not appropriate for particular groups. For example, connect to a lesson about modern US history by asking if an advertiser trying to reach urban youth would be more likely to use ethnically Asian actors than an advertiser whose target audience came of age during World War II? Why or why not? Or have target audience assignments be groups of people in a particular time period. For the Civil War, as an example, use target audiences of Confederate soldiers, slaves, residents of Northern towns reliant on the cotton and rum trade, abolitionists, etc.

LESSON PLAN #6

"News Spin"

Overview

Because news serves as a vital source of information in our world, mastery of news literacy is important to nearly every curriculum area. This lesson addresses that need with an activity that focuses on how news-reporting methods and word choices create impressions that go beyond the facts. Students analyze different news articles about the same event designed to convey positive or negative impressions without saying anything that is factually untrue. They then write their own news stories to convey specific impressions. In doing so, students learn to pay attention to the use of language, grammar, and layout, as well as gain awareness of how news writing and editing choices influence what readers think of as "truth."

Curriculum Areas

- English/language arts
- Journalism

Note: There could be ties to other curriculum areas by having students report on events in curriculum-specific areas, such as science fairs, plays, political debates, or sporting events.

Grade Levels

- High school through college

Suggested Frameworks (Curriculum Context)

- Current events
- Vocabulary and grammar
- News reporting
- Media literacy
- Transactive writing[7]

Learning Objectives

Students will

- identify production and editing choices in newspaper reporting that create different impressions of events, organizations, and people. [CP1, 4]
- increase awareness of the "spin"(i.e., a special point of view, emphasis, or interpretation presented for the purpose of influencing opinion) that news stories can put on an event through language choice and other production techniques. [CP1, 2]
- reflect on the influence news reporting can have on our understanding and beliefs about the world. [CP4, 5]

- practice writing for the purpose of conveying factual information and skills related to layout and design. CP2
- practice writing to create specific impressions based on word choice and grammar. CP2

Vocabulary

production techniques, spin, headline, caption, slant, bias, qualifier words, active and passive verbs, direct quotes, plenary session

Preparation and Prerequisites

- It would be best if students undertook this activity after having done a good deal of media decoding using the media literacy approaches described in Chapter 4. That way, students will have experience drawing conclusions about production techniques and messages while providing evidence from the media document to back up their conclusions.
- Teachers should make sure that students are already familiar with basic grammar terms and concepts (e.g., adverbs, adjectives, passive versus active verbs or voice) that might support their analysis of the language choices in the articles.

- While not absolutely necessary, it may also be helpful if the students are familiar with some of the terms and concepts that are frequently used to create impressions and spin in news and advertising (e.g., that were included in the section on the Media Literacy Toolbox in Chapter 5, page 104, and in the glossary on the companion website). These include *glittering generalities, framing,* and *ambiguous language.*

Time Needed

- One 30–40 minute session, plus time for the students to create their own news stories from two different perspectives (which could be done as a homework assignment or as part of in-class work).

Materials and Equipment

- Handouts of the two news articles written by Emily Brown (available on the book's website): one copy of both articles for each student (as one double-sided handout), plus an extra copy of one of the stories for each pair of students. The original articles contain color images, but they can work just as well duplicated in black and white.
- For the news story creation component, students will need access to basic computer software that will allow them to do some simple word-processing layout in columns with a headline and embed a picture with a caption. They will also need some means of capturing digital photographs or images of the event (e.g., a digital camera or cell phone with a built-in camera) that can be uploaded to a computer for embedding into their articles.

Step-by-Step Procedures

1. Explain that you are going to have them work in pairs to read various newspaper articles about media literacy conferences. Together the pairs should make a list of what they learned about media literacy and about the organization and individuals that put on this conference. They should also note whether they think this sounded like a good conference for educators to attend or not and identify specific evidence from the article's content (including the headline and any accompanying images) to back up their conclusion. They can write on or circle things in the article if they want.

2. Hand out newspaper articles, one article for each pair of students. There are two different articles (available on the book's website); make sure that each pair of students only gets *one* of the articles and that roughly an even number of pairs have each article. You may want to create a specific handout for them to record their observations, which they can then hand in with their marked-up copy of the article.

3. Give the students 8–10 minutes to analyze their article, with a 1-minute warning that they should finish up.

4. Ask the students to share first what they learned about media literacy from their articles, aside from reporting about the conferences themselves. If you think there will be time, you may want to discuss whether any of the articles effectively conveyed factual information about media literacy or whether readers were left to interpret what that term means by themselves.

5. Ask students to raise their hands if they thought the conference their article described sounded like a good one for educators to attend (probably half of the hands will go up). Call on each group to provide one piece of specific evidence to back up their impression, probing for specific wording or other evidence as necessary. If no pairs mention the pictures, captions, or headlines, ask about those specifically.

   Note: During the conversation, some students may start to notice that there are similarities in wording or information in their articles, but you can respond noncommittally by saying something like "I believe that Key Qs has held a number of conferences," or "We'll get to similarities that we often find across news articles in a minute."

6. Then ask students to raise their hands if they thought the conference their article described sounded like it was pretty bad and probably not worthwhile for educators to attend. Again, call on each group to provide evidence to back up their impressions. As the pairs share, students are likely to catch on that all of the articles are reporting on the same conference. When someone asks directly, confirm that is the case and that there are two different articles, both written by the same reporter, who specifically wrote one to make the conference sound great and one to make it sound awful. Also tell the students that everything she wrote in both articles is true and that the quotes she included are accurate.

7. Hand out clean copies of both articles to all students and have them compare their original article with the other version by laying them side by side. Continue the discussion about the production techniques and wording choices that the reporter used to convey positive or negative impressions, in addition to those already mentioned.

 8. Share Emily Brown's "Production Notes"[8] (see Figure 7.6) or the more detailed list of changes available on the book's website, describing how she went about crafting these two different versions of the same event (as a separate handout or by reading it aloud). Have the students find examples of the techniques she describes (e.g., active versus passive verbs), including how the headlines and pictures were crafted to enhance the positive or negative impressions created in the articles. Have students suggest other techniques that could have been used to manipulate the impressions about the conference (e.g., typeface font, other word choices).

Figure 7.6   Production Notes by Emily Brown

Production Notes on Spin 1 and Spin 2

Emily Brown, Journalism, Ithaca College '05

In some ways, I approached the conference the way I would any reporting assignment: I didn't plan what I would write before I talked to people and took copious notes on the plenary session and keynote speakers. And I had the same basic questions in mind: what are the people in this situation trying to accomplish and how successful are they? I was on the lookout for scenes I could describe, and wrote down both positive and negative details. I thought about what kind of mistakes someone would make if they hadn't seen everything I had—if they didn't have the whole story—and how I could represent those misconceptions. When I was writing the scenes, I considered the effect of specific versus general details and active versus passive verbs.

When I was talking to people, I was careful to ask them neutral questions, but when I sat down to write, I thought about how I could frame the quotes to highlight positive or negative aspects. I also thought about how I could give authority to different sources and how I could enhance or question their credibility. In particular, I considered how to identify them—what experience and titles to use to describe them. I also thought about how to use data, like numbers of attendees. Numbers by themselves mean nothing—their significance depends on what you compare them to.

My headline and pictures choices were obvious: bigger means more important. I also gave the more flattering story a generally upbeat tone with a cheerful headline. I wanted to people to feel interested and encouraged. For the less flattering story, I tried to phrase things in the negative and give the story a "gloom and doom" tone, so people would be turned off, rather than motivated to learn more or take action. The layout for the less flattering story was blocky, while the more flattering story had narrower columns and a column-crossing photo that broke up the lines between items and gave the story a more graceful flow.

Production notes from Ithaca College student intern Emily Brown regarding how she used "spin" to create different versions of the same news story.

Source: Used by permission from Project Look Sharp, Ithaca College.

9. Discuss the extent to which this type of spin occurs in actual news reporting—intentionally or unintentionally—and the role that reporter bias might play in the way news stories are covered (e.g., who gets interviewed, how the interviewee's comments are edited, word choices, what aspects or information gets included and what is left out).[9] You might also note that editors, not reporters, generally choose the headlines and pictures and that photographs are often taken by someone other than the reporter, so the complete impression is an amalgam of decisions from several journalists.

10. Tell the students that their assignment is now to do the same thing: pick an event to cover and write two different newspaper articles about it—one making it look positive, one making it look negative, but making sure not to say or show anything that is untrue. Explain the options for different kinds of events they might cover (see Notes on Pedagogy below), the suggested length of each news story (e.g., 500–700 words), and the deadline for the assignment. Note that their news stories must include a headline and at least one picture and caption. Tell them that part of their assignment—in addition to the two news stories themselves—is to write up their own production notes describing the techniques they used to spin each story (following the example from Emily Brown).

11. With the class's input, summarize the techniques they might use to spin their stories.

12. **Optional**—After the students have submitted their pairs of news stories, put them all together into an anthology that is distributed to each student in the class. Ask students to read each pair of stories, noting the spin techniques used. As a class, discuss the issue of spin in the news (see Extensions and Adaptations, below).

Notes on Pedagogy

- Teachers might want to have students work in pairs or small groups to create the two news stories. If that's the case, it should be clear in the students' write-up about the articles what role each student played (e.g., attending the event, conducting interviews, writing, editing, layout, photography).

- If it seems too challenging for students to cover a local event at the school or in the community, another possibility is that they could cover a televised or webcast event—such as a political debate, sports competition, or awards show—and find images from that event online to include in their articles. Or pick something related to your curriculum area (e.g., the announcement of grant recipients for science research, the induction of members to a hall of fame, an engineering contest, an Earth Day webinar, etc.). If students use this option, it's important that they actually view the event itself and write their own analysis of it—not just take information from another news report.

- The suggested option in step 12 is highly recommended. When students know their writing is going to be seen by their peers or a wider audience—instead of only by the teacher—our experience has been that the quality of the writing improves enormously. It will also give students a broader sense of how spin techniques—and biased reporting in general—can play out in the news.

Assessments

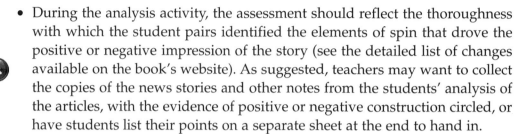

- During the analysis activity, the assessment should reflect the thoroughness with which the student pairs identified the elements of spin that drove the positive or negative impression of the story (see the detailed list of changes available on the book's website). As suggested, teachers may want to collect the copies of the news stories and other notes from the students' analysis of the articles, with the evidence of positive or negative construction circled, or have students list their points on a separate sheet at the end to hand in.

- For the news-writing activity, the final pairs of news stories should be evaluated for how well they addressed the assignment:
  o Do both cover the same event?
  o Do they include a headline and image with caption?
  o Do they make effective use of language, quotes, and image choices to drive the positive and negative impressions?
  o How reflective are the production notes about the process the students used and the production choices they made?

Extensions and Adaptations

- For another example of spin in news coverage, teachers might have students read excerpts from four newspaper articles reporting on the Gettysburg Address in 1864 that are included in Project Look Sharp's *Media Construction of Presidential Campaigns* kit. Two of the articles are from Republican newspapers, and two are from Democratic newspapers. Seeing how this seminal speech was described in those different newspapers is fascinating—and helps students understand that spin is not a new technique in the news or politics.

- Teachers might collaborate with the school art or photography teacher to get support for the students' inclusion of pictures or other images in their news stories. Those teachers might be able to effectively discuss how framing, lighting, angle, distance, and other elements create positive or negative impressions.

LESSON PLAN #7

"Middle East Debates"

Overview

Role-playing (e.g., through skits and mock debates) is a very powerful, although challenging, way to help students develop a deep understanding of cultural, historical, and political perspectives that are different from their own and to recognize the role that media play in shaping collective and individual views. This lesson plan utilizes that strategy as the framework for a major project that helps students develop higher-order thinking skills as it seamlessly integrates all eight of the media literacy capabilities into the teaching of core global studies content and current events. Based on the work of Chris Sperry,[10] it involves students in comprehensive research and analysis about current leaders in Middle East issues, using a wide range of traditional and new media forms while employing media literacy questions, concepts, and frameworks. The research culminates in an unscripted "debate" by class members, each of whom represents one of the leaders from Middle Eastern countries and the United States, including speeches and votes on proposals brought forth by the participants.

Curriculum Areas

- Global studies
- History
- English/language arts
- Politics
- Media studies
- Government

Grade Levels

- High school through college

Note: While the extensive nature of this lesson may seem daunting for many high school students, Chris Sperry has successfully led this project annually for nearly twenty years in tenth-grade classes that included English-language learners, special education students, and students who struggled with proficiency in reading and writing, as well as students who went on to become National Merit Scholars.

Suggested Frameworks (Curriculum Context)

- Studying other countries/cultures
- Current events/news literacy
- Researching information
- Writing and synthesis of ideas
- Diversity education

- Epistemology
- Humanities education
- Speaking and listening
- Literature (*optional activities*)

Learning Objectives

Students will

- Develop an in-depth understanding of current events; conflicting identities; and the complexity of historical, multicultural, and international disputes and perspectives. ^{CP4, 5.2, 5.3}
- Learn core content about current and historical issues and leaders in the Middle East and about US policy related to the Middle East. ^{CP4,5.2}
- Develop and practice skills in researching information using traditional and new media forms (including social bookmarking, online newspapers, YouTube, etc.). ^{CP1, 2, 3}
- Develop and practice skills in organizing, writing, and synthesizing ideas. ^{CP2}
- Develop and practice oral presentation skills, including giving speeches and debating. ^{CP2}
- Learn how to demonstrate knowledge and understanding through role-playing, staying "in character" while responding to unscripted statements and debate. ^{CP2}
- Develop an appreciation for global literature (*through optional activities*). ^{CP2, 5}

Vocabulary

Over the 8-week project, students will encounter and acquire a wide range of vocabulary related to the Middle East, including names of important people, places, and concepts (e.g., *ethnocentrism, totalitarianism, monotheism, militant,* and *sanctions*). See the book's website for a complete list.

Preparation and Prerequisites

- This lesson will work better if students have already experienced media decoding of news and are familiar with the *Key Questions to Ask When Analyzing Media Messages.*
- Individual teachers need help to conduct this project; we strongly recommend working with the school librarian to get assistance for the students in their individual research.
- Prior to the start of this project, teachers should access and review the *Media Construction of the Middle East* curriculum kit on the Project Look Sharp website as well as Chris Sperry's *Lesson Plans* that lay out the day-to-day details of the process and the packet of *Student Handouts*, both of which are available on the book's website, adapting them as necessary to fit your individual needs and goals for the project.

Time Needed

- Approximately 30 hours of class time over the course of about 8 weeks for student research and preparation, plus 1 week for the debate and speeches and follow-up discussion and reflection

Materials and Equipment

- *Lesson Plans* for teachers describing each of the steps and activities involved in the project (including optional global literature components)
- A copy of the *Student Handouts* for each student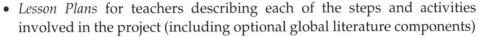
- A copy of the relevant lessons from *Media Construction of the Middle East* curriculum kit, including PowerPoint slides and video clips, as well as the technology to show them in class
- Students will need Internet access outside of class time to access international news sources and to research their characters.
- Students will need to create appropriate costumes to wear during the debates, representing their characters.
- Nameplates for each character during the debates
- (Optional) Video cameras and microphones to videotape (and possibly broadcast) the debates

General Step-by-Step Procedures

Note: Day-by-day lesson plans, downloadable student handouts, and other support materials are available on the book's website, each indicated by an asterisk (*) below. The *media literacy capabilities* that are developed at each stage are included *in italics.*

1. **Days 1–2**—Introduce the project to the students and their families with letters home* and a video of prior debates.* Introduce the possible roles for the Middle East characters* and assign a role to each student. Share a project timeline with due dates for each of the tasks* that students are responsible to complete.

2. **Weeks 1–3**—The initial stage of the project focuses on research, with particular emphasis on teaching students how to find, evaluate, and cite library and online resources* (*Access, Evaluation*). Students apply these skills as they learn them, taking initial steps to prepare their first research paper,* which is about their character's perspective on the background history of his nation. They create an annotated bibliography* identifying the utility, credibility, and bias of each source. Expectations for the paper are clarified by distributing an example outline* and sample papers* from previous years. Students create a tentative bibliography, outline, and rough draft, which the teacher collects, edits, and returns (*Creation*).

3. **Ongoing**—Throughout the project, have students follow the international news through multiple sources (domestic and foreign press, magazines, podcasts, and newspapers, etc.), discuss current events in the Middle East, and pay special attention to noticing and evaluating how different news sources

cover events (*Understanding, Awareness, Analysis, Evaluation*).[11] Consider hosting an online news portal* and giving students a weekly news quiz* (see Extensions and Adaptations).

4. **Ongoing**—Students learn about the Middle East using media literacy lessons from Project Look Sharp's *Media Construction of the Middle East* kit. The lessons address background knowledge and issues of stereotyping (Unit 1); the Arab/Israeli conflict (Unit 2); the Wars in Iraq (Unit 3); and the rise of militant Muslim movements, including the Iranian Revolution, Afghanistan, and 9/11 (Unit 4). Specific lessons explore the students' prior knowledge, preconceptions, and stereotypes about the Middle East and its peoples, including one lesson that uses an activity similar to "Introducing Africa" (Lesson Plan 1) and one that involves a decoding of the opening scenes from Disney's *Aladdin* (1992). Other lessons involve analyzing representations of Arab and Muslim people in US television and feature films, comparing regional maps and songs created from Israeli and Palestinian perspectives, and comparing and contrasting entries about "Islam" from http://islam .com and from a traditional or general online encyclopedia (*Understanding, Awareness, Analysis, Evaluation, Reflection*).

5. **Weeks 3–4**—Each student briefly introduces herself or himself to the class in character.* The short time slots force students to organize and prioritize information, and the class presentation provides practice in speaking skills (*Creation*). Classmates, as well as the teacher, provide feedback on delivery and content, keeping those who are not presenting at the moment actively engaged and providing them with practice in listening and communication skills.

 6. **Optional**—Have students read literature that reinforces the history and perspectives they are learning* (see the website for options). Remind students to evaluate the literature the same way they would evaluate any information source, using critical questions like "Who wrote this, when, and why?" (*Analysis, Evaluation*).

7. **Weeks 4–7**—Students begin to work on their second research paper,* which is about current issues and is written from the perspective of their characters. They continue learning how to conduct online research, including how to use databases, periodicals, foreign newspapers, and YouTube (for voice/ speeches) (*Access, Analysis, Evaluation, Reflection*). Students also learn how to productively use online social-networking resources, using a *Social Bookmarking site* that the teacher has created on which they enter, annotate, and tag key resources for their role.* Students may also share resources and strategies in class and/or through social networking (e.g., Facebook), including exchanging ideas and information with students from previous years (*Access, Participation, Creation*). Connecting with other students who have played their role is encouraged. Cheating is not an issue because the project is based on ever-changing current events and because the final performance requires an internalized understanding of content.

8. **Weeks 7–8**—Students prepare for the debates by responding in character (in writing and orally) to prompts, including media prompts (news clips, events, quotes, etc).* Students study* and practice writing and speaking

skills and begin to take on their roles, such as explaining whom they would and would not sit next to in a meeting (*Creation, Analysis, Reflection*). The teacher introduces the ground rules for the debate* and arranges to coach (or have a teaching assistant coach) students in small groups of related characters (30 minutes for each group), asking the types of questions that are likely to come up in the culminating debate.* Also discuss costumes (students should be able to determine appropriate dress from their research). At this point, choose and prepare a facilitator for the debates* and choose someone to collect and transcribe proposals presented during the debates.

9. **Ongoing**—Since it would be unlikely that the characters themselves would raise issues of human rights (unless to attack an opponent), there needs to be a specific structure to ensure that the debates include issues pertinent to the development of critical literacy, such as women's rights, economic development, corruption, democratic freedoms, and other non–foreign policy issues. This may be handled through the inclusion of a *Human Rights Hour* (see Extensions and Adaptations).

10. **The debates**—Set up for the debates with students seated next to allies and preferably opposite opposing characters (e.g., Palestinians facing Israelis, the United States facing Iran). Secure in place nameplates that will be visible to the debaters and audience. Students will need 10 minutes before each of the debates (more on the first day) to change into their costumes. They will also need a safe place to store the costumes. Follow the debate protocol described in the teacher lesson plan:* 90 minutes of speeches, 3 hours of debating with proposals, 45 minutes for voting, and 40 minutes for closing statements (*Awareness, Creation, Participation*).

    Collect at least one proposal from each student during the debates. Rewrite the proposals into a ballot that will help you to assess student knowledge through voting.* The voting is the one place where the teacher should play a role. After the facilitator asks for votes of yes, no, or abstention for each proposal, the teacher then calls on individual characters to explain and defend their votes. This is an opportunity both to assess student knowledge and to teach the rest of the class about critical issues. The teacher may want to arrange for photos (e.g., for the school's yearbook or website) before students change out of their costumes for the last time.

11. **Debriefing**—You will want at least two class periods to debrief. Do not cut short or skip this piece. It is critical that each student reflects on his or her feelings and thoughts about the character played (and differentiates them from his or her own feelings). It is also crucial that the other class members hear those thoughts so that they do not conflate the views of their peers with those of the characters they played. This is a great opportunity for students to reflect on how we individually and collectively develop our views of the world; the role of culture, history, and media in shaping opinions; and the possibilities for change. Students should begin the debriefing by writing self-reflections. Each student should then briefly explain to the class her or his thoughts and feelings on the character played (*Reflection, Understanding, Analysis, Creation*).

    Then discuss three or four of the central issues students wrote about (e.g., the solution to the Arab/Israeli conflict, the appropriate role for the United

States in the Middle East) through "fishbowl discussions," in which a small group of students discuss the issue, with the rest of the class listening in. This will help students to begin to differentiate their views from those of their characters (*Analysis, Reflection*). The teacher should consider following up with films and/or speakers that present alternatives to the standard political process (which they are now well schooled in) of dealing with cross-cultural conflict. These could include models of nonviolent, cross-cultural, people-to-people movements (*Awareness*).

Assessments

The teacher may choose to use any of the following for formal assessment:

- Student research papers and research process, including their annotated bibliographies (in which they identify utility, credibility, and bias for each source) and their entries into the project's social-bookmarking site.
- Multiple-choice tests on Middle East history and vocabulary (see the assessments in Project Look Sharp's kit *Media Construction of the Middle East*).
- Participation in the debates, including ability to accurately and appropriately articulate the cultural, historic, religious, national, and/or political perspective and voice of their characters.
- Student self-reflections* on their learning and learning process and self-evaluations* of their strengths and weaknesses (see Voices From the Field box "Self-Reflections on Becoming Media Literate" on page 190 in Chapter 8).

Extensions and Adaptations

- It can be very useful to have "teaching assistants" (college students or upper-level high school students who have previously taken part in this project) who can edit written work (outlines, rough drafts, etc.), pull out and coach individual students during class time, and lead small groups in discussion.

- Facilitate online connections between students and Middle East scholars and experts.

- Invite other classes, parents, educators, and the press to attend the debates* and/or invite the community to watch by videotaping—ideally using multiple cameras and microphones—and broadcast the debates (perhaps on a local cable-access channel).

- Give a weekly news quiz regarding current events and individuals related to the Middle East; see the format and teacher's guide, along with resources for news information on the book's website.*

- Have a few graduates of the class (who are longing to get back in) research human rights issues for three or four nations each and return to the debates as human rights representatives. Have a designated time (the "Human Rights Hour") when the returning students debate current characters on human rights issues. It is helpful for the (older and more experienced) graduates to give a short overview of the issues they will raise to the current students two weeks prior to the debates.*

8

Does It Work?

Does media literacy education work? This important question is impossible to answer without first asking, "Does it work to do what, exactly?" In the growing body of research on media literacy effectiveness, there is still considerable disagreement about what outcomes to expect and how to measure them.

ISSUES OF ASSESSMENT

In all high-quality education there needs to be clarity about what we want students to learn and how we (and they) will know when they have learned it. If media literacy education were simply about teaching a discrete set of facts, this would be easy. But inquiry-based media literacy is really about the process of asking questions and reflecting on production choices, and variation in student responses is the norm. To add to the challenge, in curriculum-driven media literacy education, every teacher's lessons are likely to be different. Just as document decoding isn't about uncovering a single right answer, there is not—and cannot be—a uniform set of assessment tools for media literacy education. We can, however, draw from some common approaches to suggest a few strategies.

Where to Begin

In most circumstances, you will be assessing knowledge and skills reflecting both core curriculum content and media literacy, but given the focus of this book, we'll concentrate on assessing the media literacy side of things. Though there is not yet a comprehensive set of standards and benchmarks for inquiry-based and curriculum-driven media literacy, pieces in some state standards (e.g., Texas's Viewing and Representing strand in Language Arts standards) may be helpful in terms of identifying discrete skills.

There are also online tools that may help. For example, Canadian media literacy educator Chris Worsnop has mapped out some basic rubrics and background materials in a way that would be particularly helpful to teachers who are just beginning to master assessment techniques (see http://media-awareness.ca/english/teachers/media_literacy/assess_media.cfm). At DiscoveryEducation.com, Kathy Schrock has gathered a helpful set of links to collections of rubrics as well as providing subject specific and technology integration rubrics. And to assess specific critical thinking skills, especially at the secondary level, look at the range of tools developed by CriticalThinking.org. Of course, because every classroom is different, you will want to customize your assessments to match the lessons you design.

Much of media literacy is about *skills*—like asking questions about media messages, evaluating credibility of sources, and being able to communicate effectively with a range of media tools. Since the best way to show mastery of a skill is to do it, the media literacy assessments you use will, by necessity, need to go beyond traditional pen-and-paper testing to include formal and informal opportunities for students to demonstrate progress.

VOICES FROM THE FIELD:
SELF-REFLECTIONS ON BECOMING MEDIA LITERATE

When given a formal opportunity to reflect on what they learned from a unit, either orally or in writing, students often demonstrate powerful insight. Consider these reflections from Chris Sperry's students who were involved in the "Middle East Debates" lesson plan featured in Chapter 7:

MF: I have a newfound desire to learn as well as be aware of the world, how it is presented to me and how I perceive it. I feel better prepared for school as well as life in general.

CN: This was a very powerful experience, and it made me realize just how much power people have to change or control things, for better or worse. I, however, am not passive to this change, I can be a part of it, and affect it.

NS: In other classes I learn about equations; in this class, I was the equation.

In the *Journal of Media Literacy Education*, Sperry (2010) writes, "I do not think that students could have reached these understandings and have been successful in this academic performance without extensive media literacy education. Repetitive, rich and complex content-based media-decoding practice established an environment in which the students could explore epistemology, the study of knowledge and truth.... Media literacy—be it analyzing advertising techniques, producing videos about controversial issues, or studying the ways in which their textbooks construct history—is about enabling students to decode their own truths" (p. 91).

Once you have chosen a media literacy project or activity that offers such opportunities, you can begin to determine what indicators will demonstrate to you that students have understood and can apply the skills you have taught. You might start with the foundational elements of the definition of *media literacy* discussed in Chapter 2, for example, looking at how effectively students demonstrated skills like Understanding, Analysis, and Reflection (see Voices From the Field: Self-Reflections on Becoming Media Literate). Or you could use the Key Questions categories, evaluating how well students considered things like Context, Economics, or Impact in their media analyses or creations. Or you and your colleagues might brainstorm a list of concrete things you could look for that would say to you, "This is a media-literate student." That list might include

- "Seeks out information on any given topic from more than one source before drawing conclusions."
- "Connects opinions (their own and others') to specific, document-based evidence."
- "Knows how to combine text and images to effectively communicate factual information."

You'll also want to craft developmentally appropriate expectations. To get an idea of what that might look like,[1] consider this outline for how you might determine whether a child understands the *Key Question* category of Purpose:

- **Early childhood**—Can address overt media messages present in children's media (including advertising directed at children) by accurately answering "What does this want me to do?"
- **Elementary**—Can ask and provide simple and accurate answers to the question "What does this want me to do?" as well as "Why was this created? What is its purpose?" Can identify basic purposes for many media messages: to persuade people to do things (like buy something or vote for someone), to entertain, to give information, or to make money).
- **Middle school**—Can give complex answers to questions about Purpose that clearly associate particular motives with particular media content (e.g., news is designed to inform, sitcoms are designed to entertain) and recognizes there can be multiple Purposes (e.g., a music video is intended to entertain *and* sell downloads). Can use evidence in media documents to identify target audience.
- **High school**—In addition to all of the above, can give sophisticated answers to questions about Purpose, demonstrating an understanding that there are often multiple and *interrelated* motives (e.g., news informs, entertains, and can generate profit). Understands the ways in which the profit motive can influence the availability or lack of access to media for certain Purposes (i.e., that particular media formats and topics tend to generate more profit than others).

Assessing Habits of Inquiry

Whichever assessment strategies you use, students should never have to guess what you expect of them, and the younger the student, the more explicit you need to be. Here is a rubric you could share with upper elementary–level students who are analyzing image-based media documents:

- **Inadequate**—Can name some obvious features but also misses some important details and does not draw conclusions as a result of those observations.
- **Emerging**—Notices and can name most of the important details and links them to obvious messages.
- **Proficient**—Notices most of the important details and uses them to draw conclusions about message; can describe both overt and implied messages and demonstrates an understanding of the difference between them.
- **Advanced**—Notices all or nearly all important details, uses them to draw conclusions about message, and can support conclusions with evidence from the document; extends analysis to form a hypothesis about possible impact (benefits and/or harms).
- **Exemplary**—Notices all important details; interpretation of the message is supported by document-based evidence and demonstrates original thought and/or connects the media document to other relevant subject areas or things that are happening in the world.

To use this rubric, students would need a clear idea of what you mean by *details*. Some details would be curriculum based. For example, a social studies teacher might want to highlight visual clues providing information about the likely date of a publication or broadcast (e.g., costumes, technology, or the presence of a famous historical figure). An ELA or math teacher might highlight comparison words (*more, better, 20 percent less*, etc.) and whether or not they are used correctly.

Other details would nearly always be important, regardless of content area. If the media document includes audio, then being able to describe what is heard—as well as what is seen—is an important demonstration of critical listening skills. If the analysis is of a website or informational source, noticing (or even asking about) Authorship and Purpose would be a key indication of a student's understanding. And if people or characters are present, even young children should be able to recognize and describe key aspects of their appearance or role (e.g., gender, age, race/ethnicity, costume, body type, hairstyle) and begin to connect at least some of those details to messages about things like success, beauty, or even power. In giving those descriptions, it is also important that students learn not to marginalize groups of people by using qualifiers only in front of women or minorities (e.g., "black mayor" but never "white mayor" or "female mayor" but never "male mayor") and then be assessed on whether they use qualifiers appropriately.

For a sense of what varying levels of proficiency in observing details about people or characters might look like, imagine a deodorant ad with a man in a towel looking into his bathroom mirror. Consider these examples of responses by those same upper elementary–level students when they are asked to describe the person in the advertisement:

- **Inadequate**—A man holding a can of deodorant
- **Emerging**—A strong man with black hair and his shirt off holding a can of deodorant turned so we see the brand
- **Proficient**—A strong (his shirt is off so we can see his muscles), light-skinned (white or Latino—can't tell for sure), old man with short black hair in a fancy bathroom holding a can of deodorant so we can see the label. (Note that terms like *old* are relative: what you think of as "old" and what a fourth grader thinks of as "old" may be two very different things! You might want to discuss with students what makes someone "old.")
- **Advanced**—A muscular, white man in his twenties with short dark hair is holding a can of deodorant with the top off and the label facing the viewer. The top off means he uses the product. There is a picture of a young woman holding a baby on the mirror in the background, so he might be married and have a child. He is in a big bathroom, so he is probably rich. The idea is that if we want to be like him, we should use this brand of deodorant.
- **Exemplary**—Speedster Ruiz, a famous race car driver, is holding a can of deodorant made by the company that sponsors his racing team (we can see the label). He doesn't have a shirt on, so we can see that he is in good shape. He is Latino, about thirty years old, with short black hair. We can tell that he is married from the wedding ring he is wearing and that he is a father from the picture of his wife and child on the mirror. The bathroom is big and has marble and gold, so he is probably rich. The top is off of the deodorant to show that this popular and successful guy uses this product (so if we use it, we will be popular and successful, too). Also, there is a used towel on the sink, so he probably just washed up, and the colors of the towel are the same as his racing team colors and the product.

If this was a high school–level decoding, we would expect exemplary students to explore more deeply questions about race (Why is it hard to tell if the man is Latino or white? What is the harm or benefit in viewers thinking that a Latino man is white?) and questions about financial motives (Why would a deodorant maker hire a male race car driver as a spokesperson and why would the driver accept? What are the messages being communicated about the brands—of the deodorant and of the driver? How are sports like auto racing funded?).

Looking at the frequency with which students employ media literacy techniques (e.g., cite specific evidence in the document to explain conclusions) can also be a helpful way to assess media literacy skills. These rubrics and strategies are not about students reaching particular interpretations but instead assess how well students use evidence and reason to make their case. Also, don't discount observation as an assessment tool. Sometimes students' body language, facial expression, or tone of voice can be a better indicator of comprehension, eagerness to participate, or respect than what they actually say or write.

Assessing Skills of Expression

In the same way that media literacy extends traditional literacy to include all forms of media, assessment of media production will sometimes simply be an extension of traditional assessments for writing. The means of expression may change, but the essence of concepts like how to create a believable character or the power to persuade remain the same whether one is making a video, creating a graphic novel, or writing an essay. In many instances, media literacy may require some additions to current assessments rather than wholesale change.

What may be different is the need to pay attention to the language that each means of expression uses. So, for example, if students are taking photographs, you will want to assess how well they use framing, camera angles, lighting, and the like to make their point. If you are not familiar with these concepts, look for others in your district or community who can help you conduct an authentic assessment of the students' creations. Invite a local photographer to help judge a photography project; ask the teacher who runs the video studio at the high school or the administration's IT specialist who runs your district's website to help you customize criteria for your subject area and grade level. A little coffee, chocolate, or lunch can go a long way in securing some help!

Arguably the most difficult challenge in terms of assessing communication created with new media is how to evaluate activities that use technologies or software with which you are not familiar. The primary strategy is to know the basic capabilities of what your students use. Is that really cool animation effect a one-click feature of the software, or did the student have to invest a lot of time and creativity to create it? Could the phone have taken a better picture, or is the image washed out because the student didn't think about whether she or he was facing the sun or not? Were students limited by what they could insert into an existing website creation template, or were they free to use any graphic design features they wanted? You don't have to be able to create animations, take great pictures, or design websites to know what is possible.

Aside from playing with the technology yourself, you might also ask students to tell you how they could demonstrate knowledge or mastery. Or let them help you determine where the bar should be set in terms of excellence by asking what criteria they would use to judge someone else's work (e.g., "What would a great website homepage for ____ include?"). Or assess students' skills of expression using unfamiliar technology by watching them teach it to someone else or having them teach it to you.

Integrating Media Literacy Activities Into Assessments

Finally, there are many ways to use media literacy activities to assess *both* media literacy *and* core content skills and knowledge. In addition to the obvious—like asking students to demonstrate that they can do individually the things that you have done collectively as a class (e.g., analyze a music video, lay out a newspaper with sections accurately identified)—you might

- assess reading comprehension by having students read a passage from a grade-appropriate text and asking them to write a headline, choose which headline is most accurate from a list of options, or condense a long piece into a tweet. Similarly, you can ask students which picture would best illustrate a text's main point.

- test knowledge of the sequence of historical events by having students create a comic book that puts frames from different events in proper order. To include assessment of media literacy analysis skills, have (middle or high school) students note for each frame why it is a fair (or unfair) representation of the event. Younger students might be asked to name which event is represented by each frame and how they know (i.e., What is the evidence in the picture that cues them into the fact that this is from a particular event?).

- choose a core curriculum topic and have students write their own textbook chapter (or portion of a chapter) on it, including headings, subheadings, images with captions, charts or graphs, and whatever else they see as important for the assigned topic.

These are only a few possibilities for simultaneously assessing media literacy skills and core content knowledge. You'll find additional suggestions in Chapters 5, 6, and 7 and many of Project Look Sharp's curriculum kits.

EMPIRICAL RESEARCH

In addition to our own observations (some reported in this book's examples), strong preliminary evidence shows that inquiry-based and curriculum-driven media literacy education is on the right track in terms of providing students with critical and higher-order thinking skills, applied to the analysis and creation of a variety of media forms. In other words, yes, it does work.

Critical Viewing Skills

The single most researched facet of media literacy education is acquisition of basic media analysis skills, especially as applied to TV and film. It is clear that media literacy educators in many different nations and circumstances effectively teach students to distinguish between media genres and accurately identify target audience, purpose, production techniques, and the like.

In one large study, for example, Quin and McMahon (1993) tracked 1,500 fifteen-year-olds in Australia and found that students' awareness of production processes and the constructed nature of media progressed over time in relation to the amount of media literacy instruction they received. The more instruction they received, the more open-ended and complex answers students provided when asked about media. The study also found, however, that though "students were skilled in textual analysis" and "exhibited well developed understandings about visual codes, connotation, narrative, and characterization," they nevertheless demonstrated "little understanding of the relationship among these textual elements to wider issues of representation and ideology" (Quin & McMahon, cited in Quin, 1998, p. 125). It wasn't that teachers taught this material and students didn't get it but that teachers weren't trained to help students make the connections and, by and large, they didn't. This makes clear that media literacy education without explicit instruction in critical inquiry does not automatically produce deep reading or higher-order thinking skills.

Evidence Supporting Inquiry-Based Media Literacy Education

There is evidence that when textual analysis is taught in a way that deliberately exercises higher-order thinking skills, it can have significant impact. For example, Dorr, Graves and Phelps (1980) found that elementary school children involved in just six hours of teacher-led discussions comparing TV programs to what was true in children's own lives could accurately assess how realistic TV programs were. Israeli scholar Mira Feuerstein (2007) found that critical media literacy training not only improved 10- to 12-year-olds' abilities to think critically about TV series and newspaper advertisements but also showed "that there is a tendency to transfer such learning even some time after the program has ended" (p. 3). In addition to documenting this potentially lasting impact, Feuerstein's work confirmed something commonly reported in anecdotal accounts: media literacy education is especially effective in improving the critical thinking abilities of pupils rated as low and medium school achievers.

Improvements to critical thinking skills have also been vividly described by youth media production specialists like Steve Goodman (2003) and by teachers who have done project-based media literacy in their classes like David Bruce (Pombo & Bruce, 2007). High school teacher Chris Sperry (2006b), who helped forge the approach to media literacy education described in this book, reports that the higher-order and critical thinking skills that his diverse students (about one third of whom were low skilled in reading and writing, received special education services, or had limited English proficiency) developed by doing media literacy activities even provided them with needed skills to do well on mandated state exams (averaging an 85% score, with the lowest being 77%), even though his curriculum never "teaches to the test."

Even in the field of preventative health, where—in contrast to much of media literacy education—specific outcomes are, by necessity, predetermined and not up for debate (e.g., no one should smoke cigarettes because it is never a healthy choice), research indicates that an inquiry-based media literacy approach focused on drawing attention to realistic consequences of risky behaviors, helping students see alternative points of view, and teaching students how to spot media misinformation and ask questions of popular media about Purpose and Impact can help them act less impulsively and make better decisions. Research by Erica Austin (Washington State University), Lynda Bergsma (University of Arizona), and Brian Primack (University of Pittsburgh) is particularly promising in this area (see, for example, Austin, Pinkleton, Hust, & Cohen, 2005; Bergsma, Peters, & Free, 2006; Primack, Gold, Land, & Fine, 2006).

Evidence Supporting Curriculum-Driven Media Literacy Education

In a very important US study of several hundred high school students, Renee Hobbs and Richard Frost (2003) found that regular, inquiry-based media literacy instruction in the context of an English class improved overall comprehension, analytical, and communication skills in print, audio, and visual media. Teachers reported that having a single set of Key Questions for analysis to use as a framework for diverse lessons helped them organize instruction. In a series of very important results, the study found that student performance was best when media were used almost daily; media literacy instruction was integrated across multiple subject areas; teachers made explicit connections with core subject areas; students engaged in both analysis and production; and activities were developed by the teachers, themselves, and customized for the needs of their own courses and students rather than following an "off-the-shelf" or scripted curriculum (Hobbs, 2007). These are exactly the features we describe as the core of curriculum-driven media literacy education.

The case for a curriculum-driven approach to media literacy was further bolstered by the multiyear *MEAL: Media Education Arts and Literacy* (NAMLE, 2007) project undertaken by NAMLE (formerly AMLA) and Just Think with a media arts grant from the US Department of Education. This study looked at outcomes for intervention and control groups in forty-seven middle school classes and found that inquiry-based, curriculum-driven media literacy instruction improved students' creative thinking abilities, levels of engagement, and understanding of the constructed nature of media. As did Hobbs and Frost (2003), this study also found that the greater the exposure to media literacy instruction, the stronger the results.

Student Engagement

Some of the most compelling evidence for media literacy education is anecdotal. For example, like Feuerstein, Canadian educator Irving Rother explained in *The Struggle for Literacy* (2008) that in teaching "at-risk" students, boys who had "seldom openly volunteered to participate in classroom dialog or in writing activities" were suddenly enthusiastic, engrossed in traditional ELA activities like "parody, speech, expression, and role play, the opposite of non-participation" (p. 134). Rother also reported that the boys

> produced many drafts of their work, according to our discussions: revising, editing, and revising again. Significantly, they rarely complained about having to revise their work. In fact, many of them took pride in the number of drafts they produced. That is, they felt a sense of accomplishment. This in itself is significant when we consider that writing was something that most of the ACE students greatly dislike, and in some cases, feared. (p. 134)

Or there is the glowing reflection by Edward DeRoche (2003), then a school principal, about his middle school's experience using Newspapers in Education resources to teach core content that had previously been taught without using media. DeRoche reported a decrease in the absentee rate, office referrals, and classroom disruptions and went on to observe that students seemed "more motivated and interested in class work. 'Nonreaders' were reading (if only the sports pages and the comics), and discussion of public events and political issues was more frequent, and *more fact-based* [emphasis added]." (p. 34). He also said that teachers reported a new sense of creativity in their teaching.

These two examples illustrate a common theme in many stories about media literacy in the classroom.[2] Increased interest and engagement in school-work appears to be a reliable outcome of our approach to media literacy education. That strong evidence for the benefits of inquiry-based, curriculum-driven media literacy exists at all is impressive given how little training teachers have received and how much practice it takes to master an inquiry-based pedagogy. The next step will be to confirm that pattern with more empirical research. We expect that as the field grows, the body of research will also grow and will continue to confirm the benefits.

ADDRESSING THE COUNTERARGUMENTS

Because we have witnessed such powerful results in classrooms that integrate media literacy, we are intrigued by studies that have concluded that media literacy education "doesn't work." What could lead to findings that contradict our own extensive experience and the feedback from teachers with whom we've spoken? While it could be that our experience is the exception, we think there are several possibilities, beyond the explanation that media literacy doesn't really work, that account for these negative results.

Perhaps the most obvious explanation has to do with goals of the media literacy approaches being used and evaluated. Most of the research challenging media literacy as ineffective has been focused on

1. **parents and home media use** (e.g., see Chakroff and Nathanson, 2008), which is such a different dynamic from student-teacher interactions that it doesn't apply here;

2. **serving as a counterweight to "big media"** (e.g., see McCannon, 2009), but expecting students to view corporate media and advertising as inherently bad is not—and cannot be—the goal of school-based media literacy; or

3. **negating media's potentially harmful effects** (e.g., aggression, smoking, alcohol use, negative body image, obesity, commercialization), which sets forth a predetermined goal to have students think negatively about media and is, therefore, not compatible with our inquiry-based approach. So when Chakroff and Nathanson (2008) summarized research on school-based media literacy "designed to educate children *about* [emphasis added] media and teach them to become more critical consumers" (p. 552), that is a much narrower focus than the approach we are describing in which students develop analytical skills to evaluate media messages for themselves.

In fact, almost universally, the outcomes assessed in these studies primarily focus on desired changes in attitudes about the media and in desired health- and consumer-related behaviors, rather than looking at higher-order thinking and communication skills, learning, or other educational outcomes. Expecting education to guarantee that students will choose to take particular actions is unrealistic. The causes of most behaviors are complex, involving more factors than simply what we know or understand. Even media-literate adults don't always act in their best interests; teachers can know that there are healthier snack options and still go for the chocolate chip cookies at the faculty meeting.

Education can, however, provide a foundation for action; it gives students the skills to understand things more accurately and assess them more effectively. It may even increase the likelihood of taking specific actions (like using multiple sources of information) or help people make more informed decisions, but it can't guarantee behavior. So we aren't surprised by studies that report media literacy education was not successful at producing or preventing specific actions, and we argue that—from an educational standpoint—researchers shouldn't discount the importance of increased awareness, knowledge, and understanding about any particular issue.

VOICES FROM THE FIELD:
"I KNOW THAT—BUT I STILL WANT IT!"

In conducting empirical research on the effectiveness of Project Look Sharp's lessons for early elementary grades on consumer education and nutrition, Cyndy and her students often find that the children who have experienced the media literacy training are quite savvy about what a product can or can't do and the techniques used to make it seem better than it really is—but that doesn't necessarily mean they don't still want that toy or food. As one confident five-year-old confided in the interview, "You know what? You don't really get all of those trolls, you only get one. And you can't really do that with their hair—it just turns one color and doesn't have those sparkles or stars. And you have to pay extra for all of that other stuff that they showed. But that's OK with me—I just really like those trolls!" From our perspective— if a child (or an adult) is fully aware of the puffery and tricks used in ads to sell a product, then they are media literate, irrespective of whether they still want the product or choose to buy it.

Yet another challenge is that most of the research in the field doesn't specify the actual methods of instruction. A typical description might say something like "the class spent two days (three contact hours) learning to analyze smoking in movies." But, as we have stressed throughout this book, the *way* one teaches is every bit as important as *what* one teaches. So without knowing exactly how lessons were taught, we can't tell if researchers were actually looking at inquiry-based or curriculum-driven instruction at all, and without that information it's hard to accept the validity of research showing that "media literacy doesn't work."

Finally, some recent studies by Byrne (2009) and others have suggested that there is sometimes a "boomerang effect" of media literacy—at least regarding interventions aimed at addressing media violence and advertising. Exposure to violent media content during media literacy lessons is sometimes associated with increased attraction to media violence; a similar effect has been found for advertising and desire for products. As with the other studies examined here, there is no evidence that researchers were looking at inquiry-based lessons. Without such instruction, we would expect that introducing students to a very exciting violent TV show or a very persuasive commercial might, indeed, "boomerang" and increase rather than decrease desire. That is precisely why we advise teachers to choose media documents carefully and to include Reflection along with Analysis.

CONCLUSION

As the field of media literacy education grows, so will the body of research evidence assessing its effectiveness,[3] but gaps and challenges remain. We will need strong and creative researchers to address pressing questions like these:

- How do you design research when, in a curriculum-driven approach, every teacher is doing something different?
- What measures are accurate in determining something like level of engagement or desire to question?
- How can we describe key components of instructional strategies to assess not just what lesson a teacher covers but also things like the choice of language, tone of voice, or the level of enthusiasm he or she exhibits?

We also need educators to come to agreement about realistic expectations, including developmental distinctions, and form a clearer picture of what a media-literate person looks like at different age levels and in different academic subject areas.

9

"Sounds Great, But I Don't Have Time!"

Getting Past the Barriers and Why It's Worth It

Given the potential benefits of media literacy education—for students, teachers, and the student-teacher relationship—why aren't more teachers doing it? If media literacy is clearly one of the key 21st-century skills that will empower students to succeed in school and after graduation, what are the barriers? And how can we get past them to integrate media literacy across the curriculum? We hope this book has filled part of the gap in teacher preparation that leaves so many educators without the knowledge or skills they need to integrate media literacy, but what about the other challenges?

FINDING TIME

When we first started working with teachers and librarians, we heard a consistent refrain from these dedicated and hard-working educators: "Sounds great, but I don't have time. I have so much other stuff I *have* to teach, I just can't fit in anything else." Increasing demands of testing and mandated curricula place astonishing burdens on both teachers and students, and in many schools that means that *anything* that isn't mandated or won't "appear on the test" is bound to be given short shrift, no matter how wonderful or compelling. But—as the earlier chapters have demonstrated—it doesn't have to be that way; media literacy education can provide a way to infuse inquiry into the curriculum while still meeting the needs of life within the boundaries of testing and mandates.

When media literacy is approached in the same way you would implement multicultural education—as a pedagogy rather than a separate content area—it will change your discussions with students, some content, and the activities you use, but it does not necessarily require more time than other ways of teaching. When you also adopt the curriculum-driven approach we've outlined, where media literacy and core content are taught simultaneously, then time concerns become much less problematic.

As with any new lesson or approach, integrating media literacy will initially involve more prep time. This is likely to pay off in terms of student engagement, however, and when less time is spent repeating information for students who were not paying attention, classroom time may remain unchanged. On the other hand, some teachers find that discussions involving media literacy concepts are so engaging that students don't want to stop, and so many want to join in the conversation that teachers run out of time. Compared to the common—and very frustrating—experience of feeling like it is impossible to get many students to talk at all, this is a happy challenge to face. It is important to recognize and prepare for it—by building in extra time or flexibility for these kinds of spontaneous discussions if they occur.

Certain types of projects also require allocation of significant class time. The Common Core Standards for English expects that students will learn to create their own media messages using new digital technologies. This is echoed in the growing demand for 21st-century skills. When students are simply given the option to incorporate digital technologies into individual projects, this may not mean any more classroom or prep time on the part of the teacher. However, when a teacher wants to build a media production activity into an existing unit, it is likely to take a significant amount of preparation and classroom time. On the other hand, like most project-based learning, because these kinds of activities can address so many objectives and goals, engage students with a wide range of learning styles, and involve multiple opportunities for assessment at the group and individual level, they are often well worth it. And after doing it the first time, teachers will likely find ways to make the production components more efficient while still accomplishing the same goals.

FEATURED EXAMPLE

A Second-Grade Video Project

The challenge: to cover the mandated second-grade social studies unit on urban, rural, and suburban communities. Initially, teachers[1] at three elementary schools (each representing one of those types of communities) had arranged for students to visit each other's schools to observe the differences and similarities in their communities. These field trips were tough to coordinate, however, and didn't really seem to help students better understand the nature of the communities they were visiting. So the teachers decided to experiment with a media literacy approach incorporating digital videos.

The teachers first arranged to get digital video cameras from their schools, and then they created opportunities for the students to explore their communities, taking video footage and doing interviews with people they thought represented what their communities were like. Although this took a lot of time, the children loved it. And because they were using audiovisual communication, even those with limited language skills could easily demonstrate an understanding of their type of community.

Then teachers involved students in decisions about how to edit the video clips into a story they could share with other schools; children took on various tasks (creating a storyboard, doing on-screen narratives or voiceovers, timing the segments, creating titles and credits) designed to help students build and practice ELA and math skills. Given time constraints, difficulties in making final editing decisions as a group, and an unfamiliar process, the teachers chose to do the final editing themselves (with help from technical support staff in their schools). Each video was shown at that school's special assembly.

The three schools then shared their videos with each other so the second-grade students could see what the other two types of communities were like. The students discussed what differences—and similarities—they noticed compared to their own community. In the culmination of the unit, all three grades got together for one day to watch the videos and discuss what was unique about each community and what each had in common. Teachers reported that the video component significantly enriched the experience and led to a much deeper understanding of "communities." Side benefits were the pride and empowerment the children felt when viewing their own videos and the excitement they felt when meeting another child whom they had already seen on a video. Teachers felt this experience might decrease tensions in later years when students from these communities attended the same middle school, especially if the schools develop ways for students to continue regular contact with peers from their sister schools.

Despite the success, this was a tremendously time-consuming way to address the requirements of the communities unit. In subsequent years, teachers decided to replace the video projects with narrated PowerPoint slide shows, which were technologically easier to create and edit. They used many approaches to collecting photographs, including using photos taken in earlier years, providing digital cameras for students to take home overnight to document their own homes and communities, and having students bring in photos from home. The same goals were accomplished, with much less cost—and while the project still involved significant classroom time, the prep time and outside-of-class time on the teacher's part was much less than it was the first time this unit was done.

When educators take on ambitious media production projects such as this, library media specialists and technology teachers can provide much-needed assistance—as can the students themselves. Even at the upper elementary level, you may be able to ask some students to handle aspects of the production (e.g., finding music, sound effects, or digital images) outside of class. This cuts down on in-class and teacher prep time and is also empowering for those students (who should be credited with special thanks at the end of the production).

OVERCOMING TECHNOLOGY BARRIERS

Some people still oppose using new media technologies on principle, but the fact is that students can access those technologies without us. Media literacy offers an opportunity to give them some guidance and upgrade their skills in a supportive, educational context. Otherwise, students are likely to use those technologies to play and socialize and perhaps even get themselves into some trouble, and along the way they will learn, if not from us then from people we may or may not trust. If we want students to use media with a sense of ethics, responsibility, and purpose, we have to teach them how.

More common than resistance to technology is a simple lack of knowledge combined with a lack of time to learn. Here collaboration—with students, colleagues, parents, community members—is the answer. Adding media literacy approaches and digital media production as *optional extensions* to existing lessons and student assignments is also a great way for teachers to build their own technology skills and awareness.

If it feels like you are struggling to keep up with new technologies, know that you are not alone. In less than five years after the introduction of the iPhone, for example, more than 300,000 applications were available that had been downloaded over a billion times. No one can keep track of everything new by themselves. But educators can't afford to ignore these innovations either, because they are changing the game of education. What does "Do your own work," mean in a world where collaboration using digital devices is increasingly the norm? How do teaching strategies designed for the linear nature of books and documentaries apply (or not) to nonlinear environments like the Web? In addition to your library media specialist, national experts like Will Richardson, Kathy Schrock, or Alan November keep up with the latest technologies, and their blogs are great resources for advice on specific classroom applications.

Another common technology obstacle is lack of access. Many teachers eager to embrace media literacy don't have the equipment or the high-speed Internet connection they need to use technologies in the ways they want. To them we say, keep pressing to make acquisition of technology (and the necessary tech support) a priority in your district. In the meantime, help students develop media literacy skills by using suggested activities that require little or no technology.

PARADIGM SHIFTS

The most obstinate barriers to media literacy education are those based on ingrained habits and deeply held (but often unstated) beliefs. For example, media literacy education, with decoding and communication techniques that value diverse perspectives, is not a "Just the facts, ma'am," kind of discipline. That can present a challenge to people who are comfortable teaching and learning in a system in which there is only one "right answer." This is as true for students as it is for teachers; those who perform well with hear-and-repeat instruction may resist when asked to accept more than one valid response or when they are expected to add original analysis to simple recall.

Fortunately, media literacy provides many ways to ease into more complex ways of thinking. Involving students in activities assessing credibility of sources, including fact-checking, can be a good starting place. You can help students shift from good/bad or true/false framing to a more complex "strengths and weaknesses" way of thinking by showing how it applies to real-world situations. For example, engineers and architects don't rank metals as good or bad; for each job, they take into account the available metals' varying degrees of strength, flexibility, heat tolerance, conductivity, and cost. The same could be applied to various media or information. A computer is not inherently better or worse than a book; each has strengths and weaknesses, and the same is true for most information sources.

Teachers face a different kind of obstacle when their own beliefs run counter to media literacy pedagogy. For example, media literacy challenges the traditional notion of the teacher as sole (or at least unquestionable) expert in the classroom. While this may feel a bit disconcerting—or even threatening—to teachers who design their instruction around their role as authority, those who have begun to use media literacy approaches in their classes recognize the opportunities for genuine student engagement and empowerment. These teachers quickly come to embrace co-learning. This is increasingly important in a world where seat time is no longer the only way to have direct contact with teachers and where technology makes possible synchronous, asynchronous, face-to-face, virtual, and remote interactions.

SO, WHY BOTHER?

Media literacy education provides the substantial benefits of traditional literacy, but in ways that also address technology integration and the "21st-century skills" of critical thinking and effective communication that are key to all areas of education. Time and again, we have seen media literacy education energize both teachers and students in ways that increase performance: if they are more engaged, they pay better attention, remember more, and are willing to do more on their own.[2] A media literacy–infused lesson is likely to have carryover effects that will increase efficiency and engagement in other classroom lessons. That's not an accidental by-product; it's a direct result of media literacy pedagogy.

- Media literacy intentionally brings students' own media culture into the classroom; discussing their media feels familiar and comfortable to them. Often students are excited to talk about media that bridge their lives inside and outside the classroom, and they see the teacher's willingness to acknowledge their culture in the classroom as a sign of respect (in the same way that, say, including the Latino experience in a US history class makes Latino students feel respected).

- Because the media decoding process is not based on knowing the one "right" answer, it is particularly effective in involving students who rarely share their opinions or ideas in class discussions out of fear of being wrong. Respect for evidence-based interpretations means that for some students, participating in a collective decoding of media documents will be the first time they feel confident and safe enough to publicly share their opinions. The assumption that there will be multiple points of view—and the explicit value placed on that diversity—functions, as educator and activist Nelle Morton puts it, to "hear people to speech."

- Media that incorporate image and sound as well as text often reach viewers in both affective and cognitive ways; they require involvement from more areas of the brain than reading or listening alone. When the brain is more engaged, students are more engaged. Using multiple forms of communication can also be an excellent way of differentiating instruction to reach students with reading and other learning disabilities, students with different learning strengths (especially visual learners), and English language learners.

- Media literacy education requires students to reflect on what they learn and become more self-aware, helping them make connections between media literacy tasks at which they excel and other learning requirements. For example, a student who realizes that he or she was able to memorize lines for a video may feel capable of memorizing multiplication tables, even if the student avoided that assignment in the past.

- Education professor Ladislaus Semali (1999) observed that in media literacy classes, "instead of preparing students for eventual literate behavior, teachers engage [students] in genuine acts of literacy right from the beginning" (p. 202). They aren't just watching documentaries; they are making them. They don't just read or listen to cultural critics interpreting media; they interpret for themselves. This expectation of active participation increases the chances that students will be invested in the process.

- Because we live in a media-saturated culture, media literacy education has an automatic connection to real life. It is easy for students to see the relevance of what they are studying if they are looking at media examples that have real-world impact.

- Media literacy education helps students become "effective communicators" by providing opportunities not only to create media in various forms but also to discover their own voices and have opportunities for their voices to be heard. Students who feel valued and visible are likely to invest more energy and stay on-task longer than those who don't feel good about themselves or what they are being asked to do.

For many educators, the chance to engage students is reason enough to try out media literacy strategies. In our experience, the rewards don't stop there. Media literacy education—and the culture of inquiry it creates—expects a lot from both teachers and students and provides plenty of opportunities to meet those expectations. The resulting sense of accomplishment provides a degree of satisfaction that makes media literacy education well worth the effort.

Afterword

Where Do We Go From Here?

In the decades that we have been doing media literacy education, we have been privileged to witness incredible growth in the field, especially in the United States. At least some of that growth has been driven by interest in changing media technologies and the transformative capacities they offer to students and teachers.

Media literacy education will continue to provide a natural home for those seeking to adapt to rapidly evolving digital realities. It provides reassurance regarding concerns that media technologies "dumb down" the curriculum or short-circuit thinking by demonstrating (not just theorizing) that media do not inherently distract from education's central goals but rather can serve as a means to achieve them. It provides an effective and relevant pedagogy in the face of certain change, when even schools at the leading edge find it difficult to keep up with students who continue to arrive at their doors with media innovations that provide new challenges and new opportunities.

Inquiry-based media literacy education keeps front and center questions about the purpose of all of education: to be an engaged citizen, a productive worker, and a lifelong learner—the very goals that sometimes get lost in the day-to-day details of teaching medieval history, the rules of punctuation, and the table of elements or, worse, the bureaucratic record keeping and standardized testing that eat up so much time in so many schools.

Yet, despite the fact that it is supremely well suited to meet the changing needs of digital learners, media literacy education is faced with significant challenges. The flexibility of curriculum-driven media literacy education is both its great strength and a significant weakness. It is adaptable anywhere—an important feature for educational reform in a nation with diverse communities and needs—and it holds teachers and students to high standards while allowing them to express their creativity and play to their strengths. But the diversity of practice that allows for implementation in a wide range of contexts and curriculum areas can also create confusion about the nature of media literacy education.

To help bring coherence to what is now scattered practice, the next logical step in the growth of media literacy education is to establish developmental benchmarks and sequences for media literacy skills. The field needs to come to some consensus about who should teach what and in which grades. For example, when should schools begin lessons on Internet credibility? First grade? Middle school? Later? And who is responsible to teach that skill set? The librarian? Teacher? Computer specialist? School districts need clear guidance on what makes the most sense for various curriculum areas and how to avoid repetition of the same few topics while never covering other important skills or concepts.

In the meantime, we encourage teachers to search out allies. There are people doing media literacy education in all kinds of places—schools, after-school programs, churches, community-based youth organizations, and more. They may not always label what they are doing as "media literacy," but they are sources of ideas, equipment, expertise, support, and evidence of the power of this important endeavor. On the national level, organizations like NAMLE run conferences that provide opportunities to exchange ideas, hear the latest research, and recharge your teaching "batteries." And internationally dozens of countries are offering models and ideas that can be helpful to American educators. In addition to places like Canada, the United Kingdom, and Australia, which have achieved some success in incorporating aspects of media literacy into the mandatory school curriculum, there are growing media literacy efforts in every corner of the globe from Russia, Austria, and South Africa to Japan, Israel, Italy, and beyond. International organizations like the United Nations and the European Union have developed media literacy curricula and training.

We would also encourage those who are doing (or want to do) media literacy education to stand up and be counted—in media literacy terms, to *Participate* and act. For media literacy education to get the support it needs to succeed in the United States, educators have to show up on the radar screens of policy makers and potential funders by the thousands. The United States has dozens of wonderful media literacy projects and organizations, but so far, none has grown large enough to produce those kinds of numbers. We think NAMLE is in the best position to serve as a national voice, and if just half of the readers of this book joined, it could become a powerful advocate.

 We also encourage teachers to become visible by contacting us (which you can do via the book's website). We want to hear your stories about media literacy in your classroom and in the lives of your students. We want to hear how you have used media literacy education to create a culture of inquiry in your district.

In her acceptance of the 2006 Cable in the Classroom Leaders in Learning Award, acclaimed media literacy advocate Elizabeth Thoman likened the urgency of our need for media literacy education to the urgency of the nation's leap into the space race (and accompanying attention to science and math education) in the 1960s. We agree. Media literacy education is not only important to do but important to do *now*. If the nation has the will to make its citizenry media literate, hundreds of scholars and media literacy educators in schools across the country have the ways.

We look forward to the day when we can drop the word *media* from our work because everyone will automatically understand *literacy* to include inquiry and expression applied to all forms of media. We aren't there yet, but the roads we need to get there are under construction. In the meantime, media literacy education will remain fluid, which makes it ever challenging, often uncomfortable, and always incredibly exciting.

Appendices

Appendix A

Excerpts From Core Principles of Media Literacy Education in the United States

(November 2007)

*The purpose of media literacy education is to help individuals of all ages
develop the habits of inquiry and skills of expression that they need
to be critical thinkers, effective communicators, and active
citizens in today's world.*

This document was developed by the following past and present AMLA board members: Lynda Bergsma, David Considine, Sherri Hope Culver, Renee Hobbs, Amy Jensen, Faith Rogow, Elana Yonah Rosen, Cyndy Scheibe, Sharon Sellers-Clark, and Elizabeth Thoman.

For the complete document, see the book's website.

1. Media literacy education requires active inquiry and critical thinking about the messages we receive and create.

Implications for Practice

1.1 The process of effective media analysis is based on the following concepts:

   1.1.a All media messages are "constructed."

   1.1.b Each medium has different characteristics, strengths, and a unique "language" of construction.

   1.1.c Media messages are produced for particular purposes.

   1.1.d All media messages contain embedded values and points of view.

Note: Throughout this document, "MLE" will be used as an abbreviation for *media literacy education.*

1.1.e People use their individual skills, beliefs, and experiences to construct their own meanings from media messages.

1.1.f Media and media messages can influence beliefs, attitudes, values, behaviors, and the democratic process.

1.2 MLE teaches students to ask the specific types of questions that will allow them to gain a deeper or more sophisticated understanding of media messages.

The accompanying appendix—*Key Questions to Ask When Analyzing Media Messages*—provides a model of such questions. Because instructional practices must be modified appropriately for learners of different ages and in different settings, the process of critical questioning and the specific wording of questions may vary. Some questions may not apply to every media message, and questions will often have more than one answer. As with all critical questioning processes, the end goal is to enable students to regularly ask the questions themselves.

1.3 MLE emphasizes strong sense critical thinking, i.e., asking questions about *all* media messages, not just those with which we may disagree.

1.4 MLE trains students to use document-based evidence and well-reasoned arguments to support their conclusions.

1.5 MLE is not about replacing students' perspectives with someone else's (your own, a teacher's, a media critic's, an expert's, etc.). Sharing a critique of media without also sharing the skills that students need to critically analyze media for themselves is not sound MLE practice. This includes presenting media literacy videos, films, books, or other curriculum materials as a substitute for teaching critical inquiry skills.

1.6 MLE teachers do not train students to ask IF there is a bias in a particular message (since all media messages are biased), but rather, WHAT the substance, source, and significance of a bias might be.

1.7 For MLE teachers, fostering critical thinking is routine. MLE calls for institutional structures to support their efforts by actively encouraging critical thinking in all classrooms.

1.8 Simply using media in the classroom does not constitute MLE.

2. Media literacy education expands the concept of literacy (i.e., reading and writing) to include all forms of media.

Implications for Practice

2.1 Like print literacy, which requires both reading and writing, MLE encompasses both analysis and expression.

2.2 MLE enables students to express their own ideas through multiple forms of media (e.g., traditional print, electronic, digital, user-generated, and wireless) and helps students make connections between comprehension and inference-making in print, visual, and audio media.

2.3 MLE takes place in a variety of settings, including, but not limited to: schools, afterschool programs, online, universities and colleges, religious institutions, and the home.

2.4 MLE should be taught across the preK–12 curriculum. It can be integrated into nearly any subject area.

2.5 MLE welcomes the use of a broad range of media "texts," including popular media.

2.6 MLE recognizes that evolving media forms, societal changes, and institutional structures require ever new instructional approaches and practices.

2.7 Effective MLE requires classrooms to be equipped with the tools to both analyze and produce media.

2.8 MLE intersects with other literacies, i.e., is distinct from but shares many goals and techniques with print, visual, technology, information, and other literacies.

2.9 As a literacy, MLE may have political consequences, but it is not a political movement; it is an educational discipline.

2.10 While MLE may result in students wanting to change or reform media, MLE itself is not focused on changing *media,* but rather on changing *educational practice* and increasing students' knowledge and skills.

3. Media literacy education builds and reinforces skills for learners of all ages. Like print literacy, those skills necessitate integrated, interactive, and repeated practice.

Implications for Practice

3.1 Media literacy is not a "have it or not" competency, but rather an ever evolving continuum of skills, knowledge, attitudes, and actions.

3.2 The requirements of MLE cannot be addressed by a single event, class, day, or even week-long intervention. Rather, MLE teachers seek to provide students with numerous and diverse opportunities to practice and develop skills of analysis and expression.

3.3 MLE engages students with varied learning styles.

3.4 MLE is most effective when used with co-learning pedagogies, in which teachers learn from students and students learn from teachers and from classmates.

3.5 MLE builds skills that encourage healthy lifestyles and decision making; it is not about inoculating people against presumed or actual harmful media effects.

3.6 MLE teaches media management in a way that helps students learn to make informed decisions about time spent using media and which media they choose to use.

3.7 Making decisions for other people about media access or content is not MLE.

4. Media literacy education develops informed, reflective, and engaged participants essential for a democratic society.

Implications for Practice

4.1 MLE promotes student interest in news and current events as a dimension of citizenship, and can enhance student understanding of First Amendment rights and responsibilities.

4.2 MLE is designed to create citizens who are skeptical, not cynical.

4.3 MLE gives students the skills they need to take responsibility for their own media use.

4.4 MLE invites and respects diverse points of view.

4.5 MLE explores representations, misrepresentations, and lack of representation of cultures and countries in the global community.

4.6 MLE values independently produced media.

4.7 MLE trains students to examine how media structures (e.g., ownership, distribution, etc.) influence the ways that people make meaning of media messages.

4.8 MLE recognizes that *HOW* we teach matters as much as *WHAT* we teach. Classrooms should be places where student input is respected, valued, and acted upon.

4.9 MLE is not partisan.

4.10 MLE is not a substitute for government regulation of media, nor is government regulation a substitute for MLE.

4.11 Censorship or other efforts aimed at keeping selected media beyond the access of selected audiences do not achieve the skill-building goals of MLE.

4.12 MLE is not a substitute for media meeting their responsibility to serve the public interest. At the same time it is not about media bashing, i.e., simplistic, rhetorical, or over-generalized attacks on some types of media or media industries as a whole.

5. Media literacy education recognizes that media are a part of culture and function as agents of socialization.

Implications for Practice

5.1 MLE integrates media texts that present diverse voices, perspectives, and communities.

5.2 MLE includes opportunities to examine alternative media and international perspectives.

5.3 MLE addresses topics like violence, gender, sexuality, racism, stereotyping, and other issues of representation.

5.4 MLE shares with media owners, producers, and members of the creative community responsibility for facilitating mutual understanding of the effects of media on individuals and on society.

5.5 MLE does not start from a premise that media are inconsequential or that media are a problem.

5.6 MLE does not excuse media makers from their responsibility as members of the community to make a positive contribution and avoid doing harm.

6. Media literacy education affirms that people use their individual skills, beliefs, and experiences to construct their own meanings from media messages.

Implications for Practice

6.1 MLE is not about teaching students what to think; it is about teaching them how they can arrive at informed choices that are most consistent with their own values.

6.2 MLE helps students become aware of and reflect on the meaning that they make of media messages, including how the meaning they make relates to their own values.

6.3 MLE is not about revealing to students the "true" or "correct" or "hidden" meaning of media messages, nor is it about identifying which media messages are "good" and which ones are "bad." In MLE, media analysis is an exploration of riches, rather than "right" readings.

6.4 MLE recognizes that students' interpretations of media texts may differ from the teacher's interpretation without being wrong.

6.5 MLE recognizes and welcomes the different media experiences of individuals of varying ages.

6.6 MLE uses group discussion and analysis of media messages to help students understand and appreciate different perspectives and points of view.

6.7 MLE facilitates growth, understanding, and appreciation through an examination of tastes, choices, and preferences.

Source: National Association for Media Literacy Education.

Appendix B

Designing Media Literacy Lessons: A Checklist

A lesson, activity, curriculum, or initiative is likely to meet the goals of media literacy education if it

- ❏ goes beyond merely using media to teach and instead uses media to help students acquire new or improved critical thinking skills.

- ❏ teaches students to ask their own questions about media rather than just responding to questions that the teacher asks.

- ❏ teaches students to ask questions of *all* media (not just about the things that they find suspicious or objectionable and not just of electronic or digital media but also of printed media like books).

- ❏ teaches students to ask questions when they are *making*, as well as using, media.

- ❏ encourages students to use multiple means of expression (image, sound, and word) and helps them determine which ones will best achieve their goal(s).

- ❏ encourages students to seek multiple sources of information and helps them learn how to determine which sources are most appropriate or reliable for any given task.

- ❏ respects that students interpret media through the lens of their own experiences, so different people might interpret a media document or message in different ways (e.g., a student might disagree with a teacher without being wrong).

- ❏ requires students to justify opinions or interpretations with specific, document-based evidence.

- ❏ does not *replace* the investigative process with declarations about what a teacher or a cultural critic believes to be true.

- ❏ seeks rich readings of texts, rather than asking students to arrive at a predetermined "true" or "correct" meaning.

❑ incorporates into analysis (including semiotic or aesthetic analysis) an examination of how media structures (e.g., ownership, sponsorship, or distribution) influence how students make meaning of media messages.

❑ focuses on a media document's significance (including who benefits and who is disadvantaged) or what students might learn from it, rather than trying to determine whether a particular piece of media is "good" or "bad."

❑ includes media representing diverse points of view (e.g., does not reduce complex debates to only two sides and/or actively seeks alternative media sources).

❑ helps students move through anger and cynicism to skepticism, reflection, and action.

❑ provides for assessment of media literacy skills, as well as outcomes related to other subject area content or skills.

Source: © Faith Rogow, Creative Commons Attribution—No Derivative Works 3.0 United States License.

References

Abercrombie, M. L. J. (1960). *The anatomy of judgment: An investigation into the processes of perception and reasoning.* London, UK: Hutchinson.

American Federation of Teachers. (n.d.). *Teaching online safety to students.* http://www.aft.org/yourwork/tools4teachers/studentsafety.cfm

Anderson, L., Krathwohl, D., Airasian, P., & Cruikshank, K. (2001). *A taxonomy for learning, teaching, and assessing: A revision of Bloom's* Taxonomy of Educational Objectives. New York, NY: Allyn & Bacon.

Aufderheide, P. (1993). *Media literacy: A report of the National Leadership Conference on Media Literacy,* Queenstown, MD, December 7–9, 1992. Queenstown, MD: Aspen Institute. Retrieved from http://eric.ed.gov/PDFS/ED365294.pdf

Austin, E. W., Pinkleton, B. E., Hust, S. J. T., & Cohen, M. (2005). Evaluation of American Legacy Foundation/Washington State Department of Health media literacy pilot study. *Health Communication, 18*(1), 75–95.

Bagdikian, B. H. (2004). *The new media monopoly.* Boston, MA: Beacon Press.

Bahrami, B., Lavie, N., & Rees, G. (2007). Attentional load modulates responses of human primary visual cortex to invisible stimuli. *Current Biology, 17*(6), 509–513. doi: 10.1016/j.cub.2007.01.070

Baldwin, J. (1998). A talk to teachers. In Morrison, T. (Ed.), *James Baldwin: Collected essays* (pp. 678–686). New York, NY: Library of America.

Bazalgette, C. (Ed.). (1989). *Primary media education: A curriculum statement.* London, UK: British Film Institute.

Beach, R. (2007). *Teachingmedialiteracy.com: A web-linked guide to resources and activities.* New York, NY: Teachers College Press.

Bergsma, L., Peters, J., & Free, H. (2006, November). *Media wise families: Evaluation of a media literacy-based health promotion intervention.* Presentation at the American Public Health Association Annual Conference, Boston, MA. Video available at http://apha.confex.com/apha/134am/techprogram/paper_140822.htm

Best, J. (2008). *Stat-spotting: A field guide to identifying dubious data.* Berkeley: University of California Press.

Birkett, T. (1994). *Truax* (O. Lundgren, Illustrator). Memphis, TN: Wood Flooring Manufacturers Association.

Bloom, B. S. (1956). *Taxonomy of educational objectives: Handbook I. Cognitive domain.* New York, NY: McKay.

Booth, D., Lewis, K., Powrie, S., & Reeves, D. (1998). *Media sense* (3 vols.). Toronto, Canada: MeadowBrook Press.

Brean, H. (1958, March). "Hidden sell" technique is almost here: New subliminal gimmicks now offer blood, skulls and popcorn to movie fans. *Life,* March 31, 1958, 102.

Britzman, D. (2003). *Practice makes practice: A critical study of learning to teach* (Rev. ed.). Albany: State University of New York Press.

Brown, P. U. (2005). The "shadow curriculum." In G. Schwarz & P. U. Brown (Eds.), *Media literacy: Transforming curriculum and teaching* (pp. 119–139). Chicago, IL: National Society for the Study of Education.

Browne, M. N., & Keeley, S. M. (2010). *Asking the right questions: A guide to critical thinking* (9th ed.). Upper Saddle River, NJ: Prentice Hall.

Buckingham, D. (2003). *Media education: Literacy, learning, and contemporary culture.* Cambridge, UK: Polity Press.

Byrne, S. (2009). Media literacy interventions: What makes them boom or boomerang? *Communication Education, 58*(1), 1–14. doi:10.1080/03634520802226444

Caine, G., Caine, R. N., & Crowell, S. (1999). *MindShifts: A brain-compatible process for professional development and the renewal of education* (2nd ed.). Tucson, AZ: Zephyr Press.

Carr, D. (2010, May 16). Taylor Momsen did not write this headline. *New York Times.* Retrieved from http://www.nytimes.com/2010/05/17/business/media/17carr.html

Chakroff, J. L., & Nathanson, A. I. (2008). Parent and school interventions: Mediation and media literacy. In S. Calvert & B. J. Wilson (Eds.), *The handbook of children, media, and development* (pp. 552–576). Malden, MA: Wiley-Blackwell.

Christel, M. T., & Sullivan, S. (Eds.). (2007). *Lesson plans for creating media-rich classrooms.* Urbana, IL: National Council of Teachers of English.

Christel, M. T., & Sullivan, S. (Eds.). (2010). *Lesson plans for developing digital literacies.* Urbana, IL: National Council of Teachers of English.

Common Core State Standards Initiative. (2010a). *English language arts standards.* Retrieved from http://www.corestandards.org/the-standards/english-language-arts-standards

Common Core State Standards Initiative. (2010b). *Standards for mathematical practice.* Retrieved from http://www.corestandards.org/the-standards/mathematics/introduction/standards-for-mathematical-practice/

Condry, J. C. (1989). *The psychology of television.* Hillsdale, NJ: Lawrence Erlbaum.

Considine, D. M., & Haley, G. E. (1999). *Visual messages: Integrating imagery into instruction* (2nd ed.). Englewood, CO: Teacher Ideas Press.

Cooper, P. J., & Morreale, S. P. (Eds.). (2003). *Creating competent communicators: Activities for teaching speaking, listening, and media literacy in Grades 7–12.* Scottsdale, AZ: Holcomb Hathaway.

CSMEE (Center for Science, Mathematics, and Engineering Education). (1996). *National science standards.* Washington, DC: National Academies Press.

Damian, B. (2005). Rated 5 for five-year-olds. *Young Children, 60*(2), 50–53.

Danielson, C. (2010). Evaluations that help teachers learn. *Educational Leadership, 68*(4), 35–39.

De Abreu, B. S. (2007). *Teaching media literacy: A how-to-do-it manual and CD-ROM.* New York, NY: Neal-Schuman.

Delpit, L. (1995). *Other people's children: Cultural conflict in the classroom.* New York, NY: The New Press.

DeRoche, E. F. (2003, January 29). Read all about it: The case for newspapers in the classroom. *Education Week,* pp. 34, 36.

Dorr, A., Graves, S. B., & Phelps, E. (1980). Television literacy for young children. *Journal of Communication, 30*(3), 71–83.

Dretzin Goodman, R. D., & Maggio, J. (Directors). (2008). *Frontline: Growing up online* [Documentary]. USA: PBS.

Facing the Future. (2006). *Engaging students through global issues: Activity-based lessons and action projects.* Seattle, WA: Facing the Future: People and the Planet.

Feuerstein, M. (2007). *Media literacy in support of critical thinking.* Paper presented at the National Media Education Conference Research Summit, Saint Louis, MO. Retrieved from http://www.hiceducation.org/edu_proceedings/Mira%20Feuerstein1.pdf

Firestone, C. M. (1993). Foreword. In P. Aufderheide, *Media literacy: A report of the National Conference on Media Literacy* (pp. v–vii). Retrieved from http://www.eric.ed.gov/PDFS/ED365294.pdf

Fore, W. F. (1987, Summer/Fall). Escape from Gilligan's Island: Is make believe more real than real life? *Media & Values* (40–41). Retrieved from http://www.medialit.org/reading-room/escape-gilligans-island

Freire, P. (1973). *Education for critical consciousness.* New York, NY: Seabury Press.

Freire, P., & Macedo, D., (1987). *Literacy: Reading the word and the world.* South Hadley, MA: Bergin & Garvey.

Frey, N., Fisher, D., & Everlove, S. (2009). *Productive group work: How to engage students, build teamwork, and promote understanding.* Alexandria, VA: ASCD.

Fried, J. (2007). Higher education's new playbook: Learning reconsidered. *About Campus, 12*(1), 2–7. doi:10.1002/abc.197

Gee, J. P. (2003). *What video games have to teach us about learning and literacy.* New York, NY: Palgrave Macmillan.

Geisel, T. S. [Dr. Seuss]. (1971). *The Lorax.* New York: Random House.

Gilovich, T. (1991). *How we know what isn't so: The fallibility of human reason in everyday life.* New York, NY: Free Press.

Goodman, S. (2003). *Teaching youth media: A critical guide to literacy, video production, and social change.* New York, NY: Teachers College Press.

Greenfield, P., Bruzzone, L., Koyamatsu, K., Satuloff, W., Nixon, K., Brodie, M., & Kingsdale, D. (1987). What is rock music doing to the minds of our youth? A first experimental look at the effects of rock music lyrics and music videos. *Journal of Early Adolescence, 7*(3), 315–329. doi:10.1177/0272431687073007

Hagood, M. C., Alvermann, D. E., & Heron-Hruby, A. (2010). *Bring it to class: Unpacking pop culture in literacy learning.* New York, NY: Teachers College Press.

Hart, A. (Ed.). (1998). *Teaching the media: International perspectives.* Mahwah, NJ: Erlbaum.

Herrington, A., Hodgson, K., & Moran, C. (Eds.). (2009). *Teaching the new writing: Technology, change, and assessment in the 21st-century classroom.* New York, NY, and Berkeley, CA: Teachers College Press and National Writing Project.

Hobbs, R. (1998). The seven great debates in the media literacy movement. *Journal of Communication, 48*(1), 16–32. doi:10.1111/j.1460-2466.1998.tb02734.x

Hobbs, R. (2007). *Reading the media: Media literacy in high school English.* New York, NY: Teachers College Press.

Hobbs, R. (2010a). *Copyright clarity: How fair use supports digital learning.* Thousand Oaks, CA: Corwin.

Hobbs, R. (2010b). *Digital and media literacy: A plan of action; A white paper on the digital and media literacy recommendations of the Knight Commission on the Information Needs of Communities in a Democracy.* Washington, DC: The Aspen Institute. Retrieved from http://www.knightcomm.org/wp-content/uploads/2010/12/Digital_and_Media_Literacy_A_Plan_of_Action.pdf

Hobbs, R., & Frost, R. (2003). Measuring the acquisition of media-literacy skills. *Reading Research Quarterly, 38*(3), 330–355. doi:10.1598/RRQ.38.3.2

ISTE (International Society for Technology in Education). (2007). *National educational technology standards for students (NETS).* Retrieved from http://www.iste.org/standards/nets-for-students/nets-student-standards-2007.aspx

Jackson, B., & Jamieson, K. H. (2007). *unSpun: Finding facts in a world of [disinformation].* New York, NY: Random House.

Jackson, R. R. (2009). *Never work harder than your students & other principles of great teaching.* Alexandria, VA: ASCD.

Jacobs, H. H. (Ed.). (2010). *Curriculum 21: Essential education for a changing world.* Alexandria, VA: ASCD.

Jarman, R., & McClune, B. (2007). *Developing scientific literacy: Using news media in the classroom.* Maidenhead, UK: McGraw-Hill/Open University Press.

Jenkins, H., Clinton, K., Purushotma, R., Robison, A. J., & Weigel, M. (2006). *Confronting the challenges of participatory culture: Media education for the 21st century.* Retrieved from http://www.macfound.org/

Kellner, D. (1995). Preface. In McLaren, P., Hammer, R., Sholle, D., & Reilly, S. S. (Eds.), *Rethinking media literacy: A critical pedagogy of representation* (pp. xiii–xvii). New York, NY: Peter Lang.

Key, W. B. (1973). *Subliminal seduction: Ad media's manipulation of a not so innocent America.* Englewood Cliffs, NJ: Prentice Hall.

Kingdom Hearts II [Computer game software]. (2006). El Segundo, CA: Square Enix.

Kist, W. (2010). *The socially networked classroom: Teaching in the new media age*. Thousand Oaks, CA: Corwin.

Klein, N. (1999). *No logo*. New York, NY: Picador USA.

Knight Commission on the Information Needs of Communities in a Democracy. (2009). *Informing communities: Sustaining democracy in the digital age*. Washington, DC: Aspen Institute. Retrieved from http://www.knightcomm.org/wp-content/uploads/2010/02/Informing_Communities_Sustaining_Democracy_in_the_Digital_Age.pdf

Kress, G. R., & van Leeuwen, T. (1996). *Reading images: The grammar of visual design*. New York, NY: Routledge.

Langer, E. (1989). *Mindfulness*. Reading, MA: DaCapo Press.

Lindaman, D., & Ward, K. R. (2004). *History lessons: How textbooks from around the world portray U.S. history*. New York, NY: New Press.

Loewen, J. W. (1995). *Lies my teacher told me: Everything your American history textbook got wrong*. New York, NY: New Press.

Maness, K. (2004). Teaching media-savvy students about the popular media. *English Journal, 93*(3), 46–51.

Marsoli, L. A. (1998). *Disney's Mulan classic storybook*. Burbank, CA: Mouse Works Books.

Masterman, L. (1985). *Teaching the media*. New York, NY: Routledge.

Mayfield, K. (2003, January 28). Not your father's encyclopedia. *Wired*. Retrieved from http://www.wired.com/culture/lifestyle/news/2003/01/57364

McCannon, B. (2009). Media literacy/media education: Solution to big media? In V. C. Strasburger, B. J Wilson, & A. B. Jordan (Eds.), *Children, adolescents and the media* (2nd ed.) (pp. 519–570). Thousand Oaks, CA: Sage.

McLuhan, M., & Fiore, Q. (1967). *The medium is the massage: An inventory of effects*. San Francisco, CA: HardWired.

McMahon, B. (2003, June 27). *Relevance and rigour in media education*. Keynote presentation given at the National Media Education Conference, Baltimore, MD. Retrieved from http://www.eric.ed.gov/PDFS/ED478768.pdf

McManus, J. H. (2009). *Detecting bull: How to identify bias and junk journalism in print, broadcast and on the wild web*. Sunnyvale, CA: Unvarnished Press.

Moll, L. C. (1990). Introduction. In L. C. Moll (Ed.), *Vygotsky and education: Instructional implications and applications of sociohistorical psychology* (pp. 1–27). New York, NY: Cambridge University Press.

NAMLE (National Association for Media Literacy Education). (2007). *MEAL: Media education arts and literacy curriculum*. PDFs available at http://namle.net/2007/03/10/meal-media-education-arts-and-literacy/

Nash, J. M. (1996, May 20). Unraveling the mysteries of twisters. *Time*. Retrieved from http://www.time.com/time/magazine/article/0,9171,984562-1,00.html.

National Council for the Social Studies. (2009). *NCSS position statement on media literacy*. Retrieved from http://www.socialstudies.org/positions/medialiteracy/

Nieto, S. (2009). *The light in their eyes: Creating multicultural learning communities* (10th anniversary ed.). New York, NY: Teachers College Press.

November, A. (n.d.). *Teaching Zack to think*. http://novemberlearning.com/resources/archive-of-articles/teaching-zack-to-think/

Ogle, D. M. (1986). K-W-L: A teaching model that develops active reading of expository text. *Reading Teacher, 39*(6), 564–570. doi:10.1598/RT.39.6.11

Ontario Ministry of Education. (1989). *Media literacy resource guide, intermediate and senior divisions*. Toronto, Canada: Ministry of Education.

Opitz, M. F. (with Davis-Duerr, J.). (2010). *Literacy lessons to help kids get fit & healthy*. New York, NY: Scholastic.

Packard, V. (1957). *The hidden persuaders*. New York, NY: McKay.

Parker, J. K. (2010). *Teaching tech-savvy kids: Bringing digital media into the classroom, Grades 5–12.* Thousand Oaks, CA: Corwin.

Pena-Perez, J. (2000). *Participation, interaction, and meaning construction in a university-level course using a computer bulletin board as a supplement to regular class discussions: A case study.* Unpublished doctoral dissertation, Cornell University, Ithaca, NY.

Pew Research Center for People and the Press. (2004). *Cable and internet loom large in fragmented political news universe.* Retrieved from http://people-press.org/2004/01/11/cable-and-internet-loom-large-in-fragmented-political-news-universe/

Pew Research Center for People and the Press. (2008). *Internet now major source of campaign news.* Retrieved from http://pewresearch.org/pubs/1017/internet-now-major-source-of-campaign-news

Pink, D. H. (2005) *A whole new mind: Why right-brainers will rule the future.* New York, NY: Riverhead Books.

Pombo, M., & Bruce, D. (2007). Media, teens, and identity: Critical reading and composing in a video production and media education classroom. In A. Nowak, S. Abel, & K. Ross (Eds.), *Rethinking media education: Critical pedagogy and identity politics* (pp. 149–166). Cresskill, NJ: Hampton Press.

Potter, W. J. (2005). *Media literacy* (3rd ed.). Thousand Oaks, CA: Sage.

Pozner, J. L. (2010). *Reality bites back: The troubling truth about guilty pleasure TV.* Berkeley, CA: Seal Press.

Pratkanis, A. R., & Aronson, E. (2001). *Age of propaganda: The everyday use and abuse of persuasion* (Rev. ed.). New York, NY: Henry Holt.

Prensky, M. (2006). *"Don't bother me mom—I'm learning!" How computer and video games are preparing your kids for twenty-first century success and how you can help!* Saint Paul, MN: Paragon House.

Primack, B. A., Gold, M. A., Land, S. R., & Fine, M. J. (2006). Association of cigarette smoking and media literacy about smoking among adolescents. *Journal of Adolescent Health, 39,* 465–472. Retrieved from http://www.primack.net/professional/articles/2006jah.pdf

Quin, R. (1998). Media in Western Australia. In A. Hart (Ed.), *Teaching the media: International perspectives* (pp.107–126). Mahwah, NJ: Erlbaum.

Quin, R., & McMahon, B. (1993). Monitoring standards in media studies: Problems and strategies. *Australian Journal of Education, 37*(2), 182–197.

Rogow, F. (2011). Inquiring minds want to know: Media literacy education for young children. *Library Media Connection, 29*(4), 11–13.

Rother, I. L. (2008). *The struggle for literacy.* Calgary, Canada: Detselig Enterprises.

Ruscio, J. (2006). *Critical thinking in psychology: Separating sense from nonsense.* Belmont, CA: Thomson/Wadsworth.

Salomon, G. (1983). The differential investment of mental effort in learning from different sources. *Educational Psychologist, 18*(1), 42–50.

Scriven, M., & Paul, R. (1987). *Critical thinking as defined by the National Council for Excellence in Critical Thinking.* Presentation at the Eighth Annual International Conference on Critical Thinking and Education Reform, Sonoma State University, Rhonert Park, CA. Retrieved from http://www.criticalthinking.org/page.cfm?PageID=766&CategoryID=51

Semali, L. M. (1999). Critical viewing as response to intermediality: Implications for media literacy. In L. M. Semali & A. W. Pailliotet (Eds.), *Intermediality: The teachers' handbook of critical media literacy* (pp. 183–205). Boulder, CO: Westview Press.

Semali, L. M., & Pailliotet, A. W. (Eds.). (1999). *Intermediality: The teachers' handbook of critical media literacy.* Boulder, CO: Westview Press.

Sensoy, Ö., & Marshall, E. (2009). Save the Muslim girl. *Rethinking Schools, 24*(2), 14–19. Retrieved from http://www.rethinkingschools.org/archive/24_02/24_02_muslim.shtml

Share, J. (2009). *Media literacy is elementary: Teaching youth to critically read and create media.* New York, NY: Peter Lang.

Silverblatt, A. (2008). *Media literacy: Keys to interpreting media messages* (3rd ed.). Westport, CT: Praeger.

Slapin, B. (with Esposito, A., Ill.). (1994). *Basic skills: Caucasian Americans workbook.* Berkeley, CA: Oyate.

Smith, R. A. (2002). *Challenging your preconceptions: Thinking critically about psychology* (2nd ed.). Belmont, CA: Wadsworth/Thomson Learning.

Sperry, C. (1991). Democratic school governance: The tenth principle. *Democracy & Education, 5*(3), 35–37.

Sperry, C. (2006a, Winter). The search for truth: Teaching media literacy, core content, and essential skills for a healthy democracy. *Threshold,* 8–11. Retrieved from http://www.ithaca.edu/looksharp/SearchForTruth.pdf

Sperry, C. (2006b). Seeking truth in the social studies classroom: Media literacy, critical thinking and teaching about the Middle East. *Social Education, 70*(6), 37–43.

Sperry, C. (2010). The epistemological equation: Integrating media analysis into the core curriculum. *Journal of Media Literacy Education, 1*(2), 89–98. Retrieved from http://www.ithaca.edu/looksharp/PDF_Files/Epistemological_Equation.pdf

Spradley, J. P., & Rynkiewich, M. A. (Eds.). (1975). *The Nacirema: Readings on American culture.* Boston: Little Brown.

Squire, K. (2011). *Video games and learning: Teaching and participatory culture in the digital age.* New York, NY: Teachers College Press.

Strahan, E. J., Spencer, S. J., & Zanna, M. P. (2002). Subliminal priming and persuasion: Striking while the iron is hot. *Journal of Experimental Social Psychology, 38*(6), 556–558. doi:10.1016/S0022-1031(02)00502-4

Temple University's Media Education Lab and American University Center for Social Media. (2008). *Y2008 code of best practices for fair use in media literacy education.* Washington, DC: Center for Social Media. Retrieved from http://mediaeducationlab.com/code-best-practices-fair-use-media-literacy-education/

Thoman, E., & Jolls, T. (2005a). *Literacy for the 21st century: An overview & orientation guide to media literacy education.* Santa Monica, CA: Center for Media Literacy. Retrieved from www.medialit.org/sites/default/files/mlk/01_MLKorientation.pdf

Thoman, E., & Jolls, T. (2005b). Media literacy education: Lessons from the Center for Media Literacy. In G. Schwarz & P. U. Brown (Eds.), *Media literacy: Transforming curriculum and teaching* (pp. 180–205). Malden, MA: Blackwell.

Thomas, D. H., Ballantine, B., & Ballantine, I. (1993). *The Native Americans: An illustrated history.* Atlanta: Turner Publishing.

Tienken, C. H., Goldberg, S., & DiRocco, D. (2009, Fall). Questioning the questions. *Kappa Delta Pi Record, 46,* 39–43. Retrieved from http://www.kdp.org/publications/pdf/record/fall09/RF09_Tienken.pdf

Tomlinson, C. A., & McTighe, J. (2006). *Integrating differentiated instruction & understanding by design: Connecting content and kids.* Alexandria, VA: ASCD.

Tyner, K. R. (1998). *Literacy in a digital world: Teaching and learning in the age of information.* Mahwah, NJ: Erlbaum.

Umphrey, J. (2009). Toward 21st century supports: An interview with Linda Darling-Hammond. *Principal Leadership, 10,* 18–21.

UNESCO. (2008). *Literacy: An evolving concept.* Retrieved from http://www.unesco.org/new/en/education/ (no longer available online).

US Department of Education, Office of Educational Technology. (2010). *National education technology plan.* Washington, DC: US Department of Education Office of Educational Technology. Retrieved from http://www.ed.gov/technology/netp-2010/

Vasquez, J. A., Comer, M. W., & Troutman, F. (2010). *Developing visual literacy in science, K–8.* Arlington, VA: NSTA Press.

Wan, G., & Cheng, H. (2004). *The media-savvy student: Teaching media literacy skills, Grades 2–6.* Chicago, IL: Zephyr Press.

Wassermann, S. (2009). *Teaching for thinking today: Theory, strategies, and activities for the K–8 classroom.* New York, NY: Teachers College Press.

Yalof, D., & Dautrich, K. (2005). *The future of the First Amendment* (commissioned by the John S. and James L. Knight Foundation). Retrieved from http://firstamendment.jideas.org/

Zhang, S. N. (1998). *The ballad of Mulan*. Union City, CA: Pan Asian.

Zinn, H. (1980). *A people's history of the United States: 1492—present.* New York, NY: Harper & Row.

OTHER SUGGESTED READINGS

The following sources, while not cited specifically in this text, deeply informed our work and deserve mention.

Buckingham, D. (1998). *Teaching popular culture: Beyond radical pedagogy.* London, UK: UCL Press.

Kubey, R. (Ed.). (1997). *Media literacy in the information age: Current perspectives.* New Brunswick, NJ: Transaction.

Pacatte, R., & Hailer, G. (2007). *Media mindfulness: Educating teens about faith and media.* Winona, MN: Saint Mary's Press.

Pungente, J., Duncan, B., & Anderson, N. (2005). The Canadian experience: Leading the way. In G. Schwarz & P. U. Brown (Eds.), *Media literacy: Transforming curriculum and teaching* (pp. 140–160). Malden, MA: Blackwell.

Thoman, E. (1999). Skills and strategies for media education. *Educational Leadership, 56*(5), 53–54.

Endnotes

PREFACE (p. xi–xii)

1. We are confident that many of the ideas in this book will be helpful to people doing media literacy education outside of the United States, but we do acknowledge our focus and our limitations, including the fact that our sources were restricted to those available in English and that much good media literacy education work is happening in non-English-speaking parts of the world.

INTRODUCTION (pp. 1–9)

1. Oldsmobile first introduced this phrase in a marketing campaign in the late 1980s, with "This is not your father's Oldsmobile." That phrase has since been applied to a range of innovations—including "Not Your Father's Encyclopedia," a 2003 article by Kendra Mayfield in *Wired* magazine about 2-year-old Wikipedia.

2. ISTE's NETS Standards identify six skill areas that substantially overlap with the goals of media literacy education: 1) Creativity and Innovation; 2) Communication and Collaboration; 3) Research and Information Fluency; 4) Critical Thinking, Problem Solving, and Decision Making; 5) Digital Citizenship; and 6) Technology Operations and Concepts. Details about these areas are available at http://iste.org/standards/nets-for-students/.

3. The National Association for Media Literacy Education (NAMLE), a national membership organization, was founded in 2001 as the Alliance for a Media Literate America. It convenes a biennial conference on media literacy education and sponsors the online *Journal of Media Literacy Education* (see http://namle.net).

4. In an interview in *Principal Leadership* (Umphrey, 2009), Stanford professor of education Linda Darling-Hammond defined these skills as the ability to think critically; problem solve; identify, synthesize, and analyze information; develop resources and use them in novel situations; work collaboratively with others; frame a problem; reflect on one's own learning; improve one's work without always having to rely on someone else to manage the work; and learn new things on one's own (be self-guided and independent). Our approach to media literacy education addresses every one of these skills.

5. For an extended examination of why self-reflection is important to teachers, read the revised edition of Deborah Britzman's *Practice Makes Practice: A Critical Study of Learning to Teach* (2003).

CHAPTER 1 (pp. 11–17)

1. Thanks to Elizabeth Thoman and Renee Hobbs for this idea. For an example of how to use it with students, see the "Media & Activity Diaries" lesson plan in Chapter 7.

2.   We recognize that electronic books are now available via tablet devices, but in our experience, when people speak about "books," they mean hard copies of printed texts and not things they read on a screen.

3.   See, for example, www.tvturnoff.org or www.limitv.org. Some efforts to limit TV time have been sponsored by companies that sell electronic locks, timers, and similar tools that parents can use to block or monitor television usage. Ironically, some local Newspapers in Education initiatives and bookstores have partnered with media turnoff advocates in the (mistaken) hope that families who decrease screen time will turn to reading as an alternative (e.g., 2009 efforts by Barnes & Noble or the *Syracuse Post Standard*). However, there is no evidence that reducing screen time turns reluctant readers into fans of books or newspapers.

4.   We are not arguing against the value of exercises that involve refraining from media use for short periods in order to increase students' awareness of the media in their lives (e.g., see the "Media & Activity Diaries" lesson in Chapter 7). However, when such activities are premised on the predetermined goal of reducing or eliminating screen time, convincing children that media are harmful, or inducing guilt about media use, they undermine efforts to help students develop critical autonomy because they don't leave room for students to decide for themselves how to act on their new insights. Also, because they do not build skills, awareness activities by themselves never constitute adequate media literacy training.

Nor are we arguing against parents making decisions about how much media time is appropriate for their families. On the contrary, we believe responsible parents should create rules around media use for their children. However, parental media management strategies, like media turnoff initiatives, do not provide children with "habits of inquiry" or "skills of expression," and teachers are not parents. So, in the case of media literacy education, what might be quite appropriate at home does not translate into sound classroom practice.

5.   For a good example of a media literacy activity using maps, see Project Look Sharp's *Media Construction of the Middle East* Curriculum Kit, Unit 2, Lesson 6. For world map comparisons that illustrate how maps reflect the purposes of the people who produced them and the values prevalent during the time periods in which they were produced, see the Peters Projection Map that was created in 1974 to more accurately reflect the relative sizes of various nations and continents (www.petersmap.com), the McArthur Universal Corrective Map of the World that was developed in 1979 by an Australian who was weary of being depicted as being "down under" (www.odt.org/pictureembed.htm), an 1873 Mercator map that projects the United States at the center of the world and divides Asia so that half is on the far left and half is on the far right (http://davidrumsey.com/luna/servlet/detail/RUMSEY~8~1~28407~1120833:Map-of-the-World-on-the-Mercator-pr/), or a sixteenth-century European map that depicts Jerusalem as the center of the world (http://maps.library.yale.edu/images/public/11_1581_world.jp2).

6.   This focus on content appears to contradict what many people commonly understand to be Marshall McLuhan's assertion that "the medium is the message." McLuhan's book title, which is actually *The Medium Is the Massage* (McLuhan & Fiore, 1967), is believed to reflect his views on how media influence our perceptions and societies—or perhaps it is a pun on the "mass age" of new technologies. There is no question that messages are affected by their delivery systems (whether we are talking about interpersonal or mass communication), but that does not mean that the message itself is not important. Media literacy incorporates this evaluation of delivery systems into the analysis of media messages through critical questions about Authorship, Purpose, Techniques, and Context in which the message was shared.

7.   To explore further the use and influence of logos and branding, we recommend Naomi Klein's *No Logo* (1999).

8.   This set of concepts owes its origin to the eight Key Concepts outlined in the Ontario Ministry of Education's *Media Literacy Resource Guide* (1989). However, we disagree with some of that document's very broad proclamations, (e.g., "Media construct reality," and "Media have commercial implications."). Media are certainly part of our reality and some media have commercial implications, but our literacy-based approach and the interactivity afforded by media technologies that did not exist in 1989 lead us to take a less deterministic approach.

9.   This version of Key Concepts about the nature of media is excerpted from *NAMLE's Core Principles of Media Literacy Education in the United States* (see Appendix A). It is specifically designed to support an inquiry-based approach to media literacy education.

10. For a good example of media construction, search the Internet for "Dove Evolution." This short film, which depicts the transformation of an ordinary young woman into a supermodel, was created in 2006 as part of Dove brand's "Campaign for Real Beauty." In sharing this with students, engage them in a discussion of why Unilever (the maker of Dove products) would create the film. In addition to promoting a cause it believes in, what are the other possible benefits to the company? Would other makeup and skin care products be able to claim the same benefits? Why is Dove soap in a position to speak on behalf of "natural" beauty? For an extended classroom discussion, you might also check out some of the parodies of the ad at http://www.youtube.com/results?search_query=dove+evolution+parody&aq=0. (One ends with the provocative tag line "Thank God our perception of real life is distorted. Nobody wants to look at ugly people.").

11. Other popular versions of this Key Concept, such as the one developed by the Center for Media Literacy in its Media Lit Kit (http://medialit.org/cml-medialit-kit/), use more specific wording that emphasizes power and commercial interests, such as "Most media messages are constructed to gain profit and/or power." We have not adopted this wording primarily because it focuses only on one set of purposes, leaving out so many others (including education). Moreover, in the world of user-generated content, it is often not true; for example, most people crafting a Facebook page or creating a video for YouTube are not seeking profit, and while they may be seeking to influence others, their purpose is not "power" in the conventional sense. Also, it does not accurately describe (and therefore marginalizes) a great deal of independent media and media art.

Furthermore, such a strong emphasis on only one purpose may lead students to stop analyzing media messages after they have identified only the profit or power motives or to assume that only those motives are important. In contrast, a deep reading of media messages recognizes that profit and power motives, where they are present, often coexist with a variety of other purposes. Students who fail to acknowledge this complexity are much more likely to slip from skepticism into cynicism.

It *is* important, of course, to address the very significant roles of profit and power that are often related to media messages. Effective inquiry-based teaching best addresses these through the *Key Questions to ask when Analyzing Media Messages* (see page 39). Teachers should ask questions in the categories of Purpose and Economics (which address profit) and should also ask the Impact questions about benefits and harm (which address power relations).

12. Interpretations of or responses to media messages may occur consciously or unconsciously, but except for innate or reflexive responses (e.g., fight or flight), even unconscious interpretations and responses (e.g., feeling nostalgic without consciously realizing that you heard a song that reminded you of your past) reflect a person's prior experiences and beliefs. One of the goals of media literacy is to help students become more consciously aware of their responses to and interpretations of media messages.

13. Media literacy shares the recognition of the impact of individual differences with advocates for differentiated instruction and with brain-based educators; all recognize that every brain is uniquely organized and that variation in experience, purpose, and perspective lead individuals to "create unique maps of the world"(Caine, Caine, & Crowell, 1999, p. 215).

CHAPTER 2 (pp. 19—34)

1. Aside from a few scholars who focus more on communication theory than education (e.g., Potter, 2005), most people involved with media literacy use a three- or four-element version of this definition of the term. Here are a few examples:

"Media literacy is defined as the ability to access, understand, critically evaluate and create media content" (European Commission, 2007: retrieved from http://europa.eu/legislation_summaries/information_society/strategies/l24112_en.htm).

"We have defined media literacy as: 'the ability to use, understand and create communications'" (Ofcom [UK communications regulator]: http://stakeholders.ofcom.org.uk/market-data-research/media-literacy/about/whatis/).

"It is the ability of a citizen to access, analyze, and produce information for specific outcomes" (Charles Firestone's foreword to the 1992 Aspen Institute "National Leadership Conference on Media Literacy" report, retrieved from www.eric.ed.gov/PDFS/ED365294.pdf).

2. See, for example, Considine & Haley (1999, p. xvii); Tyner (1998, p. 119); Wan & Cheng (2004, pp. 1–2).

3. We use eight elements for several reasons. First, we want to avoid assumptions about what words mean that may not translate across national boundaries or disciplines. So, for example, some people assume that *analysis* includes *understanding* and *evaluation*, while others use *evaluation* also to mean *analysis* and *understanding*. In other instances, as with Ofcom's definition, it is not clear whether *understanding* implies *analysis* or whether this government agency intends to stay away from the controversies that come along with analysis. To avoid confusion, we break out the various terms.

Second, we list *understanding* separately because, although in upper grade levels analysis and evaluation naturally integrate understanding, this is not always the case in early childhood, early elementary, or limited English proficiency settings. As the field creates benchmarks and curriculum sequencing for younger children, *understanding* will be a step that is sometimes important to distinguish from other goals.

We add *reflection* to the list because it is essential to metacognition and the development of the self-motivated, lifelong learning that is required for the autonomous exercise of habits of inquiry. It is the element that requires students to take responsibility for their own learning, choices, and actions.

We also add *participation*, which has not traditionally appeared in the definition but has been suggested by advocates for new media literacies as being essential to navigate the interactivity that media technologies now enable. Some practitioners might see participation as included as part of *creation* or *access*, but as with other elements of the definition, we list *participation* separately to avoid confusion.

Finally, we add *act* in order to emphasize the importance of applying these skills to one's daily life and to make visible what is already the reality in the field. Nearly all North American media literacy organizations and many others across the globe explicitly support the position that media literacy should lead to active engagement in the community and the world.

4. Examples would include the Action Coalition for Media Education (ACME; http://acme-coalition.org) or the Media Literacy Project (http://medialiteracyproject.org). For an example of a government agency addressing advertising issues, see Admongo at www.admongo.gov, an online game created by the Federal Trade Commission. The Canadian group Adbusters (www.adbusters.org), which spoofs ads, is another popular resource for educators interested in this thread.

5. There are dozens of organizations and individuals who address media literacy for parents. One useful starting place is PBS Parents's "Children and Media" at www.pbs.org/parents/childrenandmedia/.

6. For more on a faith-based approach to media literacy, see Sr. Rose Pacatte's blog at http://sisterrose.wordpress.com/ or the articles on the Center for Media Literacy's "Media Literacy in Faith Communities" at http://medialit.org/reading-room/media-literacy-faith-communities/.

7. One good place to keep up with pop culture resources for classroom use is Ryan Goble's Making Curriculum Pop at http://mcpopmb.ning.com.

 8. A more detailed exploration of these threads is available on the book's website.

9. References to critical autonomy as a significant goal of media literacy are so common that it would take considerable space to list them all. A cursory sample of works including such references would include Considine & Haley (1999), Hart (1998), Kellner (1995), Masterman (1985), Semali and Pailliotet (1999), Share (2009), and Tyner (1998).

10. See, for example, Hart (1998).

11. A useful tool that summarizes this taxonomy of educational objectives is Michael Luhan's "Critical Thinking Wheel," available at www.mentoringminds.com.

12. See also "Critical Thinking: Where to Begin" at http://criticalthinking.org/starting/index.cfm for elements and standards along with a huge set of resources for teachers and students at different grade levels (K–12) and for educators in other contexts (e.g., homeschoolers).

13. For those who want to explore critical thinking more deeply, we recommend http://criticalthinking.org, Browne & Keeley (2010), and the first three chapters of Smith (2002). Don't be dissuaded by the subtitle of Smith's work, *Thinking Critically About Psychology*; Smith's content applies well beyond the field of psychology.

14. For a very good, single-source summary of new media literacies, see Jenkins, Clinton, Purushotma, Robison, and Weigel (2006), available as a free download from www.macfound.org.

15. One of the most important pieces of scholarship applying a literacy framework to media literacy is Tyner (1998).

16. Those who want to explore semiotics more deeply might want to read Kress and van Leeuwen (1996).

17. For an example of a fusion of mass communications with media literacy, see Silverblatt (2008) and Potter (2005).

18. Though this quote is often attributed to Sigmund Freud, it is not clear that he ever said those words. Researching the origin of the quote and the origin of the widespread belief that it is from Freud would make an excellent media literacy exercise.

19. See, for example, David Buckingham's discussion in *Media Education* (2003, pp. 36–38). Some scholars have argued that the term *literacy* is specifically tied to printed words (*lit* being from the Greek for "letter"). They conclude that the term's etymology cannot rightly be applied to images. While we acknowledge the word's origin, words often change in meaning over time, and expanding our understanding of the existing word to include nontext media makes more sense than attempting to invent a new word that encompasses text, image, and audio.

20. For another example of differing cross-cultural interpretations, see "Follow-up to the de Soto Decoding" in Chapter 4.

21. For color versions of the images shown and described in this section, see the companion website.

22. For another exercise demonstrating the power of media to create shared meaning, look at the "Branding Alphabet" created by artist Heidi Cody, in which every letter is taken from corporate logos (http://illegal-art.org/print/index.html#alphabet/). You may want to invite students to create their own "brand alphabets" by clipping letters from products they use. This can be an especially revealing exercise for students who are learning English and who may know the product by a different name (and who therefore may include different letters from the logo).

23. For a more in-depth look at the integration of visual literacy into science teaching, see the National Science Teachers Association's *Developing Visual Literacy in Science, K–8* by Vasquez, Comer, and Troutman (2010).

24. Dozens of books and websites provide lists of media production terms. An illustrated glossary of cinematic terms is available at www.filmsite.org/filmterms20.html. Several media literacy texts also include production vocabulary, including Beach's (2007) web-linked book *Teachingmedialiteracy.com*. For video games, the website for the PBS program *The Video Game Revolution* is helpful (www.pbs.org/kcts/videogamerevolution/inside/how/index.html), as is the work of James Gee or Kurt Squire (see, for example, Gee, 2003; Squire, 2011).

25. For other useful terms, see Pratkanis and Aronson (2001).

CHAPTER 3 (pp. 35–61)

1. See for example David Buckingham (2003, p. 4) or Art Silverblatt (2008). The latter writes that a principal goal of his detailed guide to the ways that media messages are constructed "is to provide students with the tools to develop a healthy independence from the pervasive influence of the media" (p. xi). We are not questioning the quality of Silverblatt's book, which we have used and recommended; rather we are arguing that by itself, the mastery of media deconstruction typically emphasized in a communications approach to media literacy will not result in students who exercise "healthy independence" or media literacy goals such as reflection or participation.

2. The usage of the term *citizen* here is not about specific legal declarations of rights bestowed on individuals by nation-states but, rather, about participation in the civic life of one's communities (e.g., school, neighborhood, team, religious congregation, etc.), irrespective of nationality.

3. In 1998, Renee Hobbs wrote an article entitled "The Seven Great Debates in the Media Literacy Movement," which included disputes over whether or not production was an essential component of media literacy. Today, in a world replete with user-generated content, debates over whether media literacy needs to include production are no longer relevant.

4. See for example, the questions included in the Key Concepts of Media Literacy on the website of Canada's Association for Media Literacy at http://aml.ca/whatis/.

5. Mergers, acquisitions, and spinoffs keep the exact number of corporate media owners in flux. People who are interested in an overview of ownership issues will want to read journalist Ben Bagdikian's seminal book, *The New Media Monopoly* (2004). To find current ownership information, visit www.freepress.net/ownership/chart/main/.

6. For example, because it is included in daily news reports, it seems normal to accept without thinking the performance of the Dow Jones Industrial Average (DJIA) as a barometer for the nation's economic health. But stock values often increase when companies lay off workers, so the DJIA is only a valid indicator of economic well-being for a select segment of the population, not for everyone. By choosing to report the DJIA rather than, say, a measure of how many family incomes rose above the poverty line today, agenda setters normalize a particular worldview about what constitutes the nation's economic success and marginalize potentially competing views.

7. Appreciation is an important part of media literacy, but by itself it is not adequate. So, for example, in a media literacy approach, the standard elementary school book report question "What did you like?" would ask for evidence and become "What did you like and why?" The question could also be deepened into an exercise in perspective taking by asking: "Why might someone else want to read this book?" If a teacher and librarian work together to create a computer comment forum (like Amazon.com's comments on books) in which students post their reviews, now you have taken a simple lesson with limited value and integrated digital literacy, increased language usage (because students are answering more complex questions), writing for an audience (which tends to improve performance), and an opportunity to read other students' comments in a way that can initiate productive and interesting classroom discussion about why readers agree or disagree about certain books.

8. For additional arguments questioning the utility of critical literacy for media literacy education, see Buckingham (2003, pp. 108–109).

9. Rather than narrow the possibilities, media literacy analysis would examine context and recognize that people wield power in varying degrees. Those who lack power in one situation may have it in another (e.g., a leader may fight on behalf of oppressed people against an abusive government only to adopt oppressive policies after winning power, or an American man may enjoy the privileges of being white and wealthy but still be disadvantaged by systemic discrimination that makes him vulnerable to violence or to being fired just for being gay). In such cases, privilege is not an all-or-nothing circumstance.

10. This relates to Mark Prensky's (2006) concept of students as "digital natives" and teachers as "digital immigrants" who struggle with the language and culture of new digital technologies. This insight is intriguing but paints a dichotomy that is probably too general.

11. Because what teachers actually do with students is as important as the content they share with students, NAMLE's *Core Principles for Media Literacy Education in the United States* (Appendix A) follows each Core Principle with a list of "Implications for Practice." This section will frequently cite from those lists.

12. For educators and students interested in further investigation and analysis of reality TV, see RealityBitesBackBook.com, the website for Jennifer Pozner's (2010) book, *Reality Bites Back: The Troubling Truth About Guilty Pleasure TV.*

13. For current media statistics related to children's media use, for younger children see the Kaiser Family Foundation (http://kff.org), and for adolescents see Pew Research Center's Internet and American Life Project (http://pewinternet.org).

14. Our favorite source for questions to ask about statistics is Joel Best (2008) *Stat-Spotting: A Field Guide to Identifying Dubious Data.*

15. For more information on cyberbullying, a good place to start is On Guard Online, a website run by the Federal Trade Commission (http://onguardonline.gov). Among other things, it points out that "the best tool you have to help avoid risks online is your brain" (see http://onguardonline.gov/topics/net-cetera-heads-up-introduction.aspx).

CHAPTER 4 (pp. 63–99)

1. For examples of using a wide range of different forms of media documents, see Project Look Sharp's online curriculum kits *Media Construction of Presidential Campaigns (1800–2008)* and *Media Construction of the Middle East.*

2. Also available is a booklet entitled *Code of Best Practices for Fair Use in Media Literacy Education*, which was developed by Temple University's Media Education Lab and American University's Center for Social Media (2008). The Lab's website has the full text of the booklet accompanied by case studies and suggestions for teaching about copyright and fair use (see http://mediaeducationlab.com/code-best-practices-fair-use-media-literacy-education/).

3. A good source for examples of questions that relate to specific curriculum areas is Chapter 7 in Beach (2007). For questions related to science (and news), see Appendices 2, 3, and 7 in Jarman and McClune (2007).

4. For resources related to girls and body image, seewww.about-face.org or www.thebodyposi tive.org. Girls Inc. and the Girl Scouts also have media literacy projects related to body image.

5. There are dozens of resources that we could recommend for antibias education strategies. Good starting places include the National Association for Multicultural Education (http://nameorg .org)and the Teaching Tolerance project of the Southern Poverty Law Center (www.tolerance.org). Books and articles by Lisa Delpit and Sonia Nieto are also helpful (see, e.g., Delpit, 1995; Nieto, 2009), as is any curriculum developed by Facing History and Ourselves (www.facinghistory.org).

6. We recognize that the US Department of Agriculture has recently replaced "my food pyramid" with "my plate" (www.choosemyplate.gov), which does not list sugars and fats as food groups but instead lumps them together in a category labeled "empty calories." We have based this example on the Project Look Sharp health kit lessons, which have been used by many early elementary teachers. The research assessing the effectiveness of those lessons shows that young children need a concrete way to think about and discuss nutritional issues like "fat" and "sugar." Given our experience delivering lessons to students, and feedback from teachers in response to efforts to incorporate My Plate into these lessons, we have retained sugars and fats as categories that are important for children to understand and identify as present in the foods that are adver- tised to them. We note that some fats are actually necessary for a healthy diet (for both children and adults). We also think it is unlikely that young children will understand the abstract concept of "empty calories," so it is not included in this lesson. But the decoding example illustrated here is not meant to be an exact script to follow, and teachers might well want to adapt it to incorpo- rate My Plate concepts and language.

CHAPTER 5 (pp. 101–119)

1. For additional sources on using the Super Bowl as part of a media literacy lesson, see the Media Literacy Clearinghouse (at http://frankwbaker.com/super_bowl/).

2. To understand the difference that attention makes, imagine skimming a magazine in a waiting room versus reading a magazine article with the intention of recounting its details to a friend or your students. You are likely to learn (and remember) much more of the content from the latter than the former, a result confirmed by psychologist Gavriel Salomon's research on attention (e.g., Salomon, 1983).

3. The K-W-L approach, which is widely used in elementary education, was first developed by Donna Ogle (1986).

4. For a specific example of ways to use media content as part of an assessment, see the "Twister" lesson in Chapter 7.

5. For an introduction to interpreting the various parts of a URL, see http://november- learning.com/resources/information-literacy-resources/iv-how-to-read-a-web-address/.

6. For quick summaries of search engines applicable to education, see Kathy Schrock's web- site (http://school.discoveryeducation.com/schrockguide/).Also, try searching for "meta search engines" on the American Library Association website (http://ala.org) or "search engines" on http://media-awareness.ca.

7. There are a number of good resources for discussing this with students, including http:// novemberlearning.com and www.ithaca.edu/looksharp/?action=webresources. See also the les- son plan "Fact or Fiction" in Chapter 7.

8. See, for example, Alan November's (n.d.) article "Teaching Zack to Think" at http:// novemberlearning.com/resources/archive-of-articles/teaching-zack-to-think/. It describes his experience as a social studies teacher when one of his students wrote a paper on why the Holocaust

never occurred, citing as his primary source an *.edu* website. Science teachers may prefer to make the same point about the unreliability of URL suffixes with the purposeful hoax site http://dhmo .org, which makes a case for banning the "dangerous" substance "dihydrogen monoxide" (water).

9. The target audience for this site is students (evidence: "Attention Students," "Rap lyrics," "Download flyers to pass out at your school"). Elements that lend credibility include "Civil Rights Library," "Suggested Books," "Historical Writings," and "Watch the new Martin Luther King Educational Video."Elements that are questionable include the content of the *Newsweek* quote on the left, "Why the King Holiday Should be Repealed," "Black Invention Myths," "Jews & Civil Rights," and the overall poor quality layout and graphics on the site.

10. Other strategies for determining website authorship include looking for an "about" section for organizational histories, board members, funding sources, and the like; finding out who links to the site by typing "link:<*the site's URL*>" to the search window at www.altavista.com; or trying a "who is" search under the Web Address tab at www.networksolutions.com.

11. The story of Stormfront president Don Black's effective use of the Internet to boost Stormfront membership is told chillingly in the video *Hate.com* (produced by the Southern Poverty Law Center, 2000), including an interview with Black in which he unabashedly describes his goals in targeting children and adolescents with the http://martinlutherking.org website.

12. For additional analysis strategies, see materials created by Ithaca City School District technology specialist Roger Sevilla, available at www.projectlooksharp.org under Other Resources.

13. Teachers looking for a less controversial site to practice with might prefer to have students analyze the hoax site designed for classroom use, http://zapatopi.net/treeoctopus/, which exhorts visitors to "Save the Endangered Pacific Northwest Tree Octopus from Extinction!"

14. A set of headlines that you can use with secondary students to discuss agenda-setting issues is available on the book's website. It is designed to help students examine which stories would be likely to get the most coverage and why.

15. There have been numerous reports of fictional TV characters receiving wedding presents and condolence cards when the character gets married or dies. A story by William F. Fore (1987) in the Center for Media Literacy's *Media & Values* magazine said that in the first week after the TV show *Gilligan's Island* premiered, the US Coast Guard was inundated with requests to rescue these people stranded on an island.

16. One source for teaching about VNRs and news sourcing is a video called *Toxic Sludge Is Good for You: The Public Relations Industry Unspun* (2003), available through the Media Education Foundation (mediaed.org).

17. The 2004 Pew Research Center report "Cable and Internet Loom Large in Fragmented Political News Universe" found, for example, that more than 20 percent of 18- to 29-year-olds cited comedy and late-night talk shows as sources from which they regularly learned about campaign news. By 2008, the Pew Research Center reported this had dropped to about 10 percent, replaced by Facebook and other social-networking sites.

18. Another helpful site is Dan Gilmor's http://mediactive.com.

19. Similarly, for videos that help students gain awareness about the structures of documentaries, see Scott Barrie's *In Search of the Edge* (1990), which "proves" that the world is flat, or the BBC's 1957 April Fool's Day spoof *The Spaghetti Harvest* (available at http://news.bbc.co.uk/ onthisday/hi/dates/stories/april/1/newsid_2819000/2819261.stm).

20. For a good exploration of this issue, see the video *Is Seeing Believing?* (1997). Produced by the Newseum, it includes a discussion of photo manipulation and other techniques that have been used to create controversial magazine covers, such as *National Geographic*'s altering of the pyramids and *Time*'s darkening of O.J. Simpson's skin.

21. For a good source on journalistic terms such as these, see Silverblatt (2008).

CHAPTER 6 (pp. 121–139)

1. This book by Song Nan Zhang is frequently included in middle elementary reading lists (e.g., see a lesson plan for third grade at http://greatsource.com/iwrite/pdf/TraitFocus_G3_2.pdf). Other versions of the Mulan story that could be used for this type of comparison include the

original poem "Ode of Mulan" (see http://chinapage.com/mulan.html for an English translation), the Disney storybook (Marsoli, 1998), or the video game Kingdom Hearts II (2006).

2. For an example see the media chronology lesson in Project Look Sharp's *Media Constructions of Martin Luther King, Jr.* kit.

3. This idea was suggested by Betsy Damian (2005).

4. For example, Considine and Haley (1999) suggest using the first five minutes of the film *A Beautiful Mind* (2001), which is perfect for this activity.

5. Both of these volumes are edited by Mary T. Christel and Scott Sullivan, with individual lessons written by classroom teachers. Each lesson includes a description of the context and school where the lesson has been taught, the rationale and objectives, necessary materials and preactivity steps, description of the activity, and suggestions for assessment. *Media-Rich Classrooms* includes a CD of handouts and materials, along with corresponding Internet links; *Digital Literacies* employs a companion website (similar to the one for this book), where teachers can access the relevant print and audiovisual materials and post their own experiences and suggestions.

6. This quote has been attributed to various authors, including Alex Haley. An earlier use of that phrase was by George Orwell, in an essay in the London *Tribune* on February 4, 1944 (see http://orwelltoday.com/orwellwarwritten.shtml). Tracking down the different ways this sentiment has been expressed would make a terrific media literacy project.

7. For students with limited drawing skills, there are many online resources that can facilitate this process: www.readwritethink.org/files/resources/interactive/comic/ (for younger students); www.funnytimes.com/playground (for older students, especially for political commentary); www.makebeliefscomix.com (which, despite its suffix, is an educational site and has the benefit of creating in several languages in addition to English).

8. See Wan and Cheng (2004) for a full description of such lessons.

9. Good web sources for descriptions and examples of counter-ads include the people who popularized the technique, Adbusters Media Foundation (http://adbusters.org), as well as the Media Literacy Project (http://medialiteracyproject.org), the Media Literacy Clearinghouse (http://frankwbaker.com) and The Badvertising Institute (http://badvertising.org).

10. Some examples of this appear on the companion website.

CHAPTER 7 (pp. 141–188)

1. Other excellent sources that incorporate both media literacy approaches and inquiry-driven pedagogies related to media content and production in curriculum-specific ways include *Creating Competent Communicators: Activities for Teaching Speaking, Listening, and Media Literacy* (two volumes, one for K–6 classrooms and one for Grades 7–12) edited by Cooper and Morreale (2003); *Media Sense* (three volumes for Grades 4–6) by Booth, Lewis, Powrie, and Reeves (1998); and *Bring It to Class: Unpacking Pop Culture in Literacy Learning*, edited by Hagood, Alvermann, and Heron-Hruby (2010).

2. Another example of a book with excellent curriculum-specific and inquiry-based lesson plans that could be easily tweaked (and strengthened) by adding media literacy questions is *Teaching the New Writing: Technology, Change, and Assessment in the 21st-Century Classroom*, edited by Herrington, Hodgson, and Moran (2009).

3. For example, the Media Literacy Project (http://medialiteracyproject.org) does a great job of providing interesting ads for analysis and even asks many of the same questions posed in this book, but it rarely includes more than perfunctory probes for evidence, and the "correct answers" are pretty much predetermined. Jessica Parker's *Teaching Tech-Savvy Kids: Bringing Digital Media Into the Classroom, Grades 5–12* (2010), Belinha De Abreu's *Teaching Media Literacy* (2007), and many of the lessons in Wan and Cheng's *The Media-Savvy Student: Teaching Media Literacy Skills, Grades 2–6* (2004) represent creative approaches to media literacy, just not quite the inquiry-based approach we would look for in lesson design.

Chapter Seven, Lesson Plan #3 (pp. 157–165)

4. For a more detailed look at why human beings are often led to believe things that aren't true, even when the flaws in the argument are obvious, see Tom Gilovich's *How We Know What Isn't So* (1991) and Jackson and Jamieson's *unSpun* (2007).

Chapter Seven, Lesson Plan #4 (pp. 166–170)

5. Thanks to science teacher Allison Murphy from the Windsor (New York) Central School District for this idea.

Chapter Seven, Lesson Plan #5 (pp. 171–176)

6. This idea originally came from Renee Hobbs (Temple University), who created it in collaboration with teachers in Billerica, Massachusetts.

Chapter Seven, Lesson Plan #6 (pp. 177–182)

7. According to Bryan Crandall, transactive writing is "writing with real-world purposes to real-world audiences . . . from the perspective of an informed writer to a less-informed reader, functional writing intended to present information" (Herrington, Hodgson, & Moran, 2009, p. 110).

8. Emily Brown was a senior journalism major who was doing an internship with Project Look Sharp in 2004 when we asked her to "cover" our annual conference, creating two different versions of newspaper articles about it—one making it look great, one making it look awful—without lying. At the final plenary session, we gave each participant a copy of the two versions of the article. It was eye-opening—and a little disconcerting to those of us running the conference—how effectively Emily could use things like word choices and selective use and placement of quotes to create positive or negative impressions about the conference without saying anything that was factually untrue. We have continued to use "the Emily Brown lesson" in our courses and workshops ever since, although eventually we changed the names of the organization, location, and individuals in the articles to make them more generic. Emily graduated from Ithaca College in 2005 and later went on to earn a master's degree in Library and Informational Studies with Teacher Certification at the University of Rhode Island. She is currently an elementary school librarian and hosts an active blog commenting on news, educational research, and other media reports.

9. A great source describing biased reportorial techniques can be found in the chapter on journalism in Silverblatt's *Media Literacy: Keys to Interpreting Media Messages* (2008, pp. 242–247).

Chapter Seven, Lesson Plan #7 (pp. 183–188)

10. Chris Sperry has been doing the Middle East Debates with his tenth-grade students at the Lehman Alternative Community School in Ithaca, New York, for more than twenty years as part of their authentic assessment and final performance in his global studies course. Articles documenting the success of the Middle East Debates have appeared in *Democracy & Education* (1991), *Social Education* (2006b), and the *Journal of Media Literacy Education* (2010).

11. See OxFeed (http://oxfeed.pbworks.com/w/page/4483925/Facing-History-and-Ourselves) for Chris Sperry's online news feed.

CHAPTER 8 (pp. 189–200)

1. The British Film Institute has also been a pioneer in the fashioning of developmentally appropriate media literacy. See *Using Film in Schools: A Practical Guide* (2010), retrieved from http://bfi.org.uk/education/teaching/using_film_in_schools.pdf.

2. Sources for additional stories are listed on the book's website.

3. Research on media literacy education is found in communications, psychology, and education journals, including the *Journal of Media Literacy Education* (http://jmle.org).

CHAPTER 9 (pp. 201–206)

1. The elementary school teachers who participated in this project were Laurie Rubin (Cayuga Heights), Millicent Clarke-Maynard (Beverly J. Martin), and Karen Griffen (Enfield) in the Ithaca City School District in upstate New York.

2. There is a large and convincing body of anecdotal evidence that media literacy education succeeds at engaging students, including those who previously have been uninterested or quiet; see specific sources listed on the book's website.

Index

CORWIN

A SAGE Company

The Corwin logo—a raven striding across an open book—represents the union of courage and learning. Corwin is committed to improving education for all learners by publishing books and other professional development resources for those serving the field of PreK–12 education. By providing practical, hands-on materials, Corwin continues to carry out the promise of its motto: **"Helping Educators Do Their Work Better."**